AND A BOTTLE OF RUM

A History of the New World in Ten Cocktails

Wayne Curtis

THREE RIVERS PRESS

NEW YORK

For my mother and father

Copyright © 2006, 2007 by Wayne Curtis

Published in the United States by Three Rivers Press, an imprint of the
Crown Publishing Group, a division of Random House, Inc., New York.
www.crownpublishing.com

THREE RIVERS PRESS and the Tugboat design are registered trademarks of
Random House, Inc.

Originally published in hardcover in slightly different form in the United States
by Crown Publishers, an imprint of the Crown Publishing Group, a division
of Random House, Inc., New York, in 2006.

Library of Congress Cataloging-in-Publication Data

Curtis, Wayne, 1957–
    And a bottle of rum: a history of the New World in ten cocktails/Wayne Curtis.—
1st ed.
    Includes bibliographical references.
  1. North America—History. 2. Caribbean Area—History. 3. Rum—North
America—History. 4. Rum—Caribbean Area—History. I. Title.
    E46.C87 206
    394.1'3—dc22   2006004992

ISBN 978-0-307-33862-4

Printed in the United States of America

Design by Lauren Dong

10 9 8 7 6 5 4 3 2 1

First Paperback Edition

[*Contents*]

AND A BOTTLE OF RUM

Introduction

[MOLASSES]

*How beverage alcohol is produced, distributed,
consumed, and regulated . . . offers a key to the nature
of a society and how it changes over time.*

—JACK S. BLOCKER JR.,
JOURNAL OF URBAN HISTORY, 2003

*Rum makes a fine hot drink, a fine cold drink, and is not
so bad from the neck of a bottle.*

—*FORTUNE* MAGAZINE, 1933

I'M STANDING IN FRONT of the City Tavern Restaurant in
Philadelphia's Old City. It's an austerely classical building, with
tall stone steps rising from the sidewalk to a recessed door. At
the top of the steps stands a young man with his hands behind his
back. He has a sallow complexion and wears a short blue jacket with
meringuelike ruffles about the neck. He has the air of a sentry, of
someone with whom I must negotiate in order to get past the door.

People in period dress always unsettle me. I dread the moment
they make eye contact, then snap into historic character and start
speaking with a surplus of enunciatory gusto about an esteemed

gentleman you've perhaps heard of by the name of Thomas Jefferson or some such thing. I understand some people enjoy this palaver. I am not one of them.

The tavern is a faithful reconstruction of the old tavern on the same spot, built from the ground up by the National Park Service in 1976. When the original tavern opened in 1773, it was arguably the finest in all the colonies and quickly became a social hub for the city and, in turn, for a young nation. Colonial representatives to the Continental Congress lodged and ate here during their deliberations, and through the tavern's doors passed such illustrious Americans as Thomas Jefferson, George Washington, Paul Revere, and John Adams, the last of whom called this "the most genteel tavern in America."

They arrived here seeking to craft a new nation. I have come seeking an old drink.

Rum is the history of America in a glass. It was invented by New World colonists for New World colonists. In the early colonies, it was a vital part of the economic and cultural life of the cities and villages alike, and it soon became an actor in the political life. Hoping to briefly visit that lost world, I ascend the steps of the tavern.

At the doorway Mr. Ruffles happily spares me ye olde time banter. He escorts me through the Subscription Room, where a melancholy woman in a mobcap plays something funereal on the harpsichord. Just beyond is the tavern, which is dusky and furnished with several nicely worn tables and benches. I am shown a seat in a corner, and handed a menu of rustic colonial fare, which includes West Indies pepperpot soup, prime rib with a Yorkshire pancake, and turkey potpie.

The food sounds appealing if a little severe, but I'm only interested in ordering a rum shrub, a popular colonial-era drink. The unusual name comes from the Arabic word for drink, *shrab.* Colonists would chop up fruit or berries (or a strong spice like ginger), boil the pieces in vinegar, then let it steep for a day. The concoction then would be boiled again with sugar, resulting in a dense, intensely flavorful syrup that could preserve the pleasing bite of the fruit into winter and beyond.

A little shrub added to a glass of water would make it come alive with taste and glimmer with a light pastel hue, and the concoction could be further enlivened with rum or brandy, and often was. Vinegar-based cocktails may not be the trend of the moment, but I am told by my ponytailed waiter, Chris, who was not at risk of lapsing into any un-provoked hilarity, that they accounted for 60 percent of the wine and spirit sales at the City Tavern. Chris further informs me that shrub was once a popular drink because it provided vitamin C throughout the year. Never mind that vitamin C wasn't actually identified until the 1920s. I nod my head gravely and order up a shrub.

The barkeep is housed in a sort of wooden cage in a corner, like a war criminal waiting to testify at a tribunal. He sets to work on my drink, but I can't see much. Other waiters lean on the counter in front of him and chat about "deuces" and "four-tops," which strikes my ear as pleasingly colonial. My shrub readied at last, Chris brings it over and sets it down. Pale pink and effervescent, the drink looks refreshing, and at the first sip I'm pleased to discover that not the slightest hint of vinegar comes through. It's tart and sprightly, like a dilute fruit punch, and has the thirst-cutting precision of a gin and tonic.

This is no doubt an enjoyable introduction to rum's early history. Yet I despair slightly, for I am getting no closer to finding colonial rum. The rum in this shrub is Captain Morgan, which, despite the colonial name, tastes nothing like its ancestor. From a marketing point of view, this is probably not a bad thing. The old-fashioned rum Jefferson and Adams ordered would have been cloying, greasy, nasty-smelling stuff. Colonial rum, made with a crude pot still and seat-of-the-pants technology, would have been laden with impurities, and could have been whiffed a block away. This rum shrub had been gentrified, making the past more potable.

Nor was there much choice in rum drinks. Shrub was it. An actual eighteenth-century tavern would have had a small riot of rum concoctions, along with a taverner conversant with them. Rum was by far the most popular spirit of the era, and often the only spirit sold. Guests could have ordered up a mimbo, a sling, a bombo, a syllabub, a punch, a calibogus, a flip, a bellowstop, a sampson, or a stonewall. Colonial tavern keepers were every bit as imaginative as today's $12-a-cocktail bartender and would have added molasses and dried pumpkin and coarse sugar and water and a bit of citrus and whatever else was at hand to give the drink some depth—and, more to the point, to mask the rum's taste. Few ingredients were off limits in pursuit of this goal.

To drink a rum shrub made with Captain Morgan was to linger in comfort at a safe distance from the past. Learning about rum at the City Tavern, it turns out, was like learning about the habits of wild bears at Walt Disney World's Country Bear Jamboree.

My journey would take longer than I thought.

A SHORT WHILE later I walk two blocks north for a wholly different rum experience. Cuba Libre is a trendy two-story restaurant and rum bar that opened in late 2000. This Friday evening it's packed with well-manicured professionals in suits, and I wedge myself sidewise to get through the downstairs crowd to the overflow bar on the mezzanine. The interior was created by a company called Dynamic Imagineering, which themed the place to convince customers that they were dining in a courtyard of Old Havana. It's all tile work and stucco, wrought-iron balconies and heavy wooden doors. Diners sit under palm trees that flutter gently under rattan ceiling fans; the songs of Ibrahim Ferrer float above the din. A huge photomural on one wall depicts a vintage American car with bulbous fenders.

Cuba Libre is one of a handful of destination rum bars that have blossomed around the nation. They're cropping up in the wake of martini bars and single-malt Scotch bars, small meccas of rum where the spirit is treated with unaccustomed deference. Much of the output of the West Indies and the Spanish Main is arrayed high and wide behind the bar, like heads on a trophy hunter's wall: rums from Haiti, Barbados, Puerto Rico, the U.S. Virgin Islands, Guyana, Jamaica, Mexico, Guatemala, and Colombia. Drinkers here select from sixty-two different varieties, priced up to $44 per shot. The drink menu is a spiralbound minitextbook that includes a brief course on the history of rum and a list of the rum drinks on offer, which include the Cuba libre, the daiquiri, the dark and stormy, the caipirinha (a sort of rough Brazilian daiquiri), and two variations on the mojito: regular and watermelon.

The mojito emerged from nowhere and by the late 1990s it was suddenly everywhere. In 2004, the town of Richland, New Jersey, the home of a large mint farm, renamed itself Mojito for a few weeks as part of a publicity stunt funded by Bacardi. Bacardi chose Mojito as a town name, according to a marketing executive, because the drink out-Googled "appletini" by a margin of fifteen to one.

The mojito's popularity isn't solely due to marketing stunts. It happens to be a superb drink with a fine pedigree. It's uncommonly refreshing—it's basically a tall daiquiri with the addition of mint and club soda. (It's also been called a Cuban mint julep.) It's not all that difficult to make. It combines strata of sweet and tart, lightly complicated with mint. It is summer in a glass.

"All of our specialty cocktails are authentic," boasts the Cuba Libre menu, and that's not far off the mark. The staff seems to take the same sort of pains crafting an authentic mojito as the design firm had in making an ersatz Cuba. The restaurant scouts produce markets for just the right kind of herba buena (spearmint is better than peppermint), and purchased an old sugarcane press to make its own guarapo—fresh sugarcane juice—to sweeten the drink. Two employees work nearly full-time to just support the local demand for mojitos—they clean and stem the mint, squeeze fresh limes, and crush the sugarcane daily. (Guarapo goes sour quickly and can't be stockpiled for future use.)

That workers are toiling so hard for authenticity amid a wholly artificial environment, meant to evoke another time and another place, causes my heart to skip a beat in admiration of the utter complexity of American life.

Here is how history is invented and then reinvented, a mill in which simple products of the earth are forged into lasting symbols.

RUM'S GENIUS HAS always been its keen ability to make something from nothing. It begins with molasses, a by-product of sugar making that had virtually no value at the outset of the sugar industry. Rum has persistently been among the cheapest of liquors and thus often associated with the gutter. But through the alchemy of cocktail culture, it has turned into gold in recent years. Rum is reinvented every generation or two by different clans, ranging from poor immigrants who flocked from England to the West Indies, to Victorians enamored of pirates, to prohibitionists and abolitionists, right down to our modern marketing gurus, who tailor it day by day to capture the fickle attentions of consumers attracted to bright glimmerings of every passing fad.

I won't make the argument here, which has been made for so many everyday items in recent books, that rum was the item "that changed the world." It certainly put its hand on the tiller of America's past now and again, but the value in examining it minutely lies elsewhere. A rum bottle serves better as a prism through which to see how America changed and developed from the arrival of the first European settlers to the present day. Rum didn't necessarily change history, but history certainly changed rum, and if you but look you can see all of us reflected in each variation.

Refracted through a bottle of rum, the world looks different: for instance, how the islands were once the central gateway to the colonial world, and the great mass of land that's now the United States was by and large the uninteresting backyard. Through that bottle you can see how pirates and the colonial slave trade and the domination of the Europeans over the native Americans actually happened, and how these episodes later became part of a national mythology.

To track rum to its source—back through the mojito craze, the Trader Vic interregnum, the Prohibition era, the grim slave epoch, the age of the pirates, and the first European settlement of North America—is to run to ground the story of America.

Rum, it turns out, is the most protean of American spirits. Like any liquid, it can change its form to fit its vessel. But unlike most liquids, it can also change its whole character. Rum disproves the tired bromide put forth by F. Scott Fitzgerald that there are no second acts in American life. In fact, American life is made up of nothing but second acts, and rum sets a fine example.

Bourbon fanciers, who often claim for their tipple the title of "America's spirit," drink one of the most regulated spirits known. To be labeled bourbon, it has to be made with a certain percentage of corn and aged in a certain kind of barrel. But excessive regulation is not the spirit of America. Unrestricted experimentation is. Rum embodies America's laissez-faire attitude: It is whatever it wants to be. There have never been strict guidelines for making it. There's no international oversight board, and its taste and production varies widely, leaving the market to sort out favorites. If sugarcane or its by-products are involved in the distillation process, you can call it rum. Rum is the melting pot of spirits—the only liquor available in clear, amber, or black variations.

Over the course of four centuries, rum has transformed itself from swill to swanky, and moved from the gutter to the great room. It began as the drink of the common man, the booze to guzzle when you turned up only lint and a few coins in your pockets. Through the wiles and persistence of its makers, rum has followed an upward trajectory and is now the drink of all classes. It's the great American story: the ne'er-do-well who overcame the unfortunate circumstances of its birth to be accepted in the more rarified world of the gentry.

Rum is a survivor. Its story is classically American in that it's a tale of a rise, a fall, and a comeback. Rum emerged out of the confusion of a freshly settled land, and its production became one of the dominant industries of the new economy. And then it all but disappeared, as if the knowledge of its manufacture had lapsed, not returning with any force for more than a century. And when it did, rum dusted itself off and, as it is wont to do, went looking for a party.

Rum has always had a distinctly American swagger. It is untutored and proud of it, raffish, often unkempt, and a little bit out of control. The history of rum tends toward the ignoble, many times pleasingly so. "Rum's early history is one long rap sheet," wrote Hugh G. Foster in 1962. This is especially true when compared to snooty old gin and its dull marriage to the martini, or upstart vodka, for which quality is regularly confused with marketing. And whiskey is still fighting its tired, ancient battles—Scotch versus Irish, Canadian versus bourbon—like feudal lords grappling for control of empty moors. Rum is always willing to try something new and sort out the consequences later. As the bon vivant James Beard put it in 1956, "Of all the spirits in your home, rum is the most romantic."

Rum, in short, has been one of those rare objects in which America has invested its own image. Like moonglow, the life of America is reflected back in each incarnation of rum.

IN THIS BOOK, I've chosen to tell the story of rum through ten drinks. Each era of North American progress has had its own rum drink, ranging from the harsh kill-devil of the earliest colonial days to the pleasantly sophisticated mojito of today. In each chapter, I'll look at the political, economic, and cultural environment that allowed each drink to arise. More generally, this book strives to answer three broad questions about rum: How did it grow to become the most important spirit in the New World in the eighteenth century? How did it come to be eclipsed by other drinks in the nineteenth century? And how did it manage to find its way back?

For this book, I immersed myself in rum for more than three years—not quite literally, but not far from it. I've consumed it in quantities that were of grave concern to friends and family, traveled great distances to sample it, mixed it with things that were probably not meant to be mixed and, in general, tested the forbearance of a patient wife. I recall awakening on more than one morning to a dull and distant sort of pain, then finding in my pockets unintelligible notes in what appeared to be my own handwriting—"Tolstoy/war and peace, window scene rum" was one.

Then, of course, there was the parade of unsolicited testimony from those who heard of my project—invariably involving a teenage indiscretion, a bottle of inexpensive rum (often Bacardi), and a special intimacy with shrubberies. These tales were almost always followed by a solemn vow never to touch rum again. It is impressive how many people have actually maintained that vow. When I tell folks who have not touched rum for many years that this spirit has now become a drink of connoisseurs, their eyebrows arch and they inquire after it with a genuine solicitousness, as if hearing of an old high school classmate with whom they haven't been in touch since that unfortunate episode after the senior prom.

Among those who inspired me to start on this journey in search of rum was, of all people, Henry David Thoreau. He lived through the spirit's most vigorous repression, when the great temperance movement was hell-bent on driving the demon rum not just out of the temple, but out of the home, the countryside, and the nation. In *Walden,* Thoreau wrote of a village near his New England home that was "famous for the pranks of a demon not distinctly named in old mythology, who has acted a prominent and astounding part in our New

England life." This demon, he continued, "deserves, as much as any mythological character, to have his biography written one day."

I sense a wistfulness in his tone. He understood something important was going undocumented. With this book, I hope to begin to document the raucous life and times of rum. And along the way, I hope to tell a story about ourselves.

[RUM]

RUM shall be the spirit obtained only by *alcoholic fermentation* and *distillation* of the MOLASSES, SYRUPS, or CANE SUGAR of sugar cane juice. Production must be carried out in such a way that the product has the *aroma* and *flavour* derived from the NATURAL VOLATILE ELEMENTS contained in the above materials or formed during the fermentation or distillation process of the named materials.

[RUM, AS DEFINED BY JAMAICA AND BARBADOS, 1937]

Chapter 1

[Kill-devil]

*The people have a very generous fashion that if one come
to a house to inquire the way to any place, they will make
him drink, and if the traveler does deny to stay to drink
they take it very unkindly of him.*

—Henry Whistler on Barbados customs, 1655

Rum—a spirit distilled from the juice of a sugarcane plant or
its by-products—was first invented in the early seventeenth
century on the British island colony of Barbados.

Or not. In which case it may have been invented on the Spanish
islands of Hispaniola or Cuba (where it would have been called *agua-
diente*, or "burning water"), or by Portuguese colonists on the coast
of Brazil (where it would later be called *cachaça*). Or possibly it was
first distilled by the French on one of their Caribbean island strong-
holds (where the poorer grades of rum were known as *tafia*). On the
other hand, it may have been first concocted in the 1400s somewhere
in Europe by secretive alchemists searching for the elixir of life and
feeding through their retorts whatever fermentable matter they could
get their hands on. Or just maybe it was invented even earlier by an
anonymous chemist tinkering near the cane fields of coastal India.

The thing is, no one really knows when rum first appeared. If you want to know about the history of sugar, overflowing archives provide enough information to lead to mental obesity. But for rum, it's a starvation diet. The West Indian island of Barbados has long claimed that first Barbadians invented rum, and it's telling that no historians have roused themselves to seriously dispute this point. Some, like rum expert Edward Hamilton, have argued that rum was first produced commercially in the Portuguese or Spanish colonies, probably in Brazil, and he has been rooting around for customs documents or ship manifests to back this up. He hasn't found anything yet. (And he guesses he may never: Rum exports from the colonies were prohibited by Spain and Portugal, which meant any rum produced was smuggled and undocumented. And even if it had been documented, the ports of the West Indies were laid waste by attackers with numbing regularity, so the archives of the earliest days are often nonexistent.)

This much at least is known about rum: Sometime around the middle of the seventeenth century, an outbreak of rum occurred almost everywhere the Dutch, Spanish, French, and English were engaged in their New World errand-running. The British sea captain John Josselyn wrote of a dinner held on a ship off the coast of present-day Maine in September 1639, at which another captain toasted him with a pint of rum. Laws controlling the sale of rum abruptly cropped up in different colonies, as a warden in pursuit of a persistent truant—in Bermuda in 1653, in Connecticut in 1654, in Massachusetts in 1657.

Then, sometime shortly before 1650, rum surfaced at an extravagant feast held at the Barbados estate of James Drax, the most important planter on Great Britain's most important island colony. For anyone curious about the cultural history of rum—or who wants to learn about the ancestry of that bottle of West Indian rum in the back of their liquor cabinet—I'd argue that this is as fine a place to begin the story as any.

BARBADOS IS PEAR-SHAPED and just twenty-one miles long by four-teen miles wide—or about one-seventh the size of Rhode Island. On a map of the Caribbean, Barbados lies far to the east, like a wayward child refusing to stand in line with the rest of the Lesser Antilles, which sweep in a great arc from Puerto Rico to Trinidad. Adventurers from Portugal and Spain landed here in the sixteenth century, but finding no precious metals to mine nor Indians to enslave, they lin-gered only long enough to name the island "Los Barbados," after the "bearded" fig trees. Barbados lay unmolested until 1625, when a British sailing ship stopped off while heading home from Brazil. The captain claimed the island for the British throne and reported on its pleasing qualities to Sir William Courteen, the ship's owner. Cour-teen hastened to cobble together a syndicate, then dispatched a ship with supplies to support several dozen colonists. On February 20, 1627, eighty colonists—plus ten slaves captured along the way—disembarked near present-day Holetown on the island's west coast.

The mandate given the first settlers by Courteen was not compli-cated: Go forth and produce. Specifically, produce for export such things as were in demand in England. The colonists tried growing cotton, indigo, and fustic wood, the latter a sort of tropical mulberry useful in making yellow dye. These crops did not produce great for-tunes. Taking a cue from the colony at Virginia, which had been set-tled two decades earlier, the islanders planted tobacco, which was then the most profitable agricultural staple in the colonies. But a glut in London soon undercut prices, and Barbados tobacco was ham-pered by another problem: It was "so earthy and worthless," wrote one seventeenth-century island visitor, that it provided "little or no return from England." A 1628 shipment was described as "foul, full of stalks, and evil colored." Even the islanders wouldn't smoke it.

And then came sugar.

The species *Saccharum officinarum* ("sugar of the apothecaries"), a freakishly tall and sharp-edged grass, had first appeared around 4000 B.C. in Asia, most likely in Papua New Guinea, where primitive agriculturists had selected the sweetest canes for further breeding. These plants migrated eastward with traders, to India and on to the Mediterranean. In 325 B.C. a general under Alexander the Great came upon sugarcane for the first time and described it with wonder as a plant that "brings forth honey without the help of bees."

Sugar soon became an essential crop in the colonial Atlantic islands off Africa, including Madeira, the Canary Islands, and the Azores. It made the leap to the New World with Christopher Columbus, whose father-in-law was a Madeira sugar planter. On the explorer's second trip across the Atlantic in 1493, he brought live sugarcane seedlings and oversaw their planting on Hispaniola. The sugar grew fabulously, and colonists were quick to establish plantations over the next two decades in Mexico, Cuba, Jamaica, and Puerto Rico. The Portuguese, demonstrating a flair for running complex businesses in difficult environments far from home, planted cane aggressively on the damp Brazilian coast and brought in sugar presses and copper boiling vats from home. The number of sugar refineries in Brazil grew from 5 in 1550 to 350 less than a century later. With great quantities of sugar now being produced in the New World, the price fell, and many of the sugar producers of the Mediterranean and the Atlantic islands were ruined. The New World sugar era was dawning.

Barbados made the most of it. In England, the demand for sugar soared as it quickly evolved from a luxury for aristocrats to a staple for the masses. It was in great demand for making sweets, masking the taste of rancid meat, and sweetening new beverages, including coffee (which arrived in Britain in 1650), chocolate (1657), and tea (1660). Between 1660 and 1700, the per capita consumption of sugar in England quadrupled, and then it doubled again in the next quarter century. The value of sugar shipped to England and Wales was worth twice that of tobacco by the end of the seventeenth century.

With reports filtering home of great fortunes being made, thousands of British colonists boarded ships for the West Indies. The well-off paid for their outbound trips and brought enough cash to acquire some acreage and build a sugar works or two. Those unable to afford the £6 trip traded passage and board by signing on as indentured servants, typically committing to seven years of labor on a plantation, after which they would be freed and given a small parcel of land. A third group washed ashore on the islands: thieves and petty criminals, who were exiled from England to the West Indies much as later undesirables would be shipped off to Australia. Slaves from Africa, too, were beginning to arrive in great numbers against their will, imported by the sugar planters to work the expanding fields. The population of Barbados swelled from just 80 in 1627 to more than 75,000 by 1650.

JAMES DRAX—LATER Sir James Drax—arrived on Barbados in 1627 among the first wave of settlers. He began by planting tobacco, then switched to sugarcane. He quickly amassed an estate of 850 acres, which yielded a torrent of cash. Drax was the first to build island windmills, which were expensive but more efficient and productive than cattle-powered mills. His wealth grew, and he had plenty of company. "It is seldom seen that the ingenious or the industrious fail of raising their fortunes in any part of the Indies," wrote one planter to an acquaintance in England. Another noted in 1655 that Barbados was "one of the richest spots of ground in the world," adding that the gentry there "live far better than ours do in England."

In England, architects had been flirting with a hybrid style for British manor houses, mixing elements of Gothic and classic. The results were often eye-catching, although not always in a good way. The planters commissioned dozens of similarly grand homes of coral stone smoothed with plaster. Drax's great house was three stories and featured a carved mastic archway near a grand staircase, the whole pile capped with angular gables and studded with corner finials. Such homes were notably ill-suited for the tropical weather, and many were, oddly, built with fireplaces. One visitor marveled that the planters, who spent afternoons indoors drinking spirits and smoking pipes, did not spontaneously combust.

Just as the houses were ill-designed for the stifling heat, so, too, were colonial island fashions. Merchant ships laden with current London styles would arrive with jackets and gowns unsuitable for the oppressive tropics. Yet the fashionable were undaunted. "One may see men loaded and half melting under a ponderous coat and waist-coat," noted an early visitor to Jamaica, another thriving British colony, "richly bedaubed with gold lace or embroidery on a hot day, scarcely able to bear them."

Through happy circumstance, these planters inhabited one of those rare junctures of time and place when money seemingly tumbled out of the sky. Sugar was king, the source of instant fortunes, taking on the role that railroads, oil, and the Internet would later play in North America. In the mid-seventeenth century, Barbados was the wealthiest colony in the budding British empire, as well as its most populous. The free white men of the islands had a net worth several times that of even the most industrious colonists on the North American mainland. Barbados produced more sugar and employed more shippers than all the other British West Indian islands put together. The island's moment was to last for decades; as late as 1715, the value of exports from Barbados exceeded not only that of the other islands, but of all the other British North American colonies (island and mainland) combined. The city of Bridgetown in the seventeenth century was bigger and more prosperous than Manhattan.

The wealth that flowed back to England was immense. A writer in 1708 likened Barbados to a massive gold or silver mine being excavated for the benefit of the homeland and claimed that trade with the island supported sixty thousand people in England. The other British islands, like St. Christopher, Nevis, Jamaica, and Antigua, also contributed to the fortunes flowing back across the Atlantic, and the planters and their agents saw little that couldn't be improved with gilding. In one well-known encounter, King George III and his prime minister were riding near Weymouth, England, when they were all but forced off the road by an extravagant carriage accompanied by a great many outriders in flamboyant clothing. The king was informed that the procession was that of a sugar planter from Jamaica. "Sugar, sugar, hey? All *that* sugar!" said the king. "How are the duties, hey, Pitt, how are the duties?"

One of those attracted to Barbados was Richard Ligon, who arrived under circumstances not wholly of his own choosing. A British royalist who had lost his business during the convulsions of the English rebellion, Ligon set off for the island in June 1647 with five acquaintances. The group acquired and managed a sugar estate, and Ligon remained on the island until 1650. His account is not only the chief source of information about early island life, but an enchanting chronicle, in large part because Ligon never lost his capacity to marvel in the face of great hardships. Barbados was in the throes of a yellow fever epidemic when he arrived, with the disease (by one accounting) killing six thousand inhabitants. Ligon, who nearly died of the fever three times himself, wrote that "the living were hardly able to bury the dead."

Yet Ligon was endlessly enthusiastic about the island's charms, including the incomparable taste of pineapple juice ("certainly the Nectar which the Gods drunk") and the succulence of the feral pigs descended from swine abandoned by early Portuguese mariners ("the sweetest flesh . . . and the loveliest to look on in a dish, either boyl'd, roasted, or bak'd"). Given his persistent good cheer, it's all the more striking that Ligon wrote *A True and Exact History of the Island of Barbadoes* (1657) while confined to an English debtor's prison, into which he was tossed upon his return from the West Indies. (Ligon's experience shows that not every colonist came home burdened with fortune.)

Historian Lowell Ragatz has written that new arrivals on the island were often astounded by the "gastronomic feats" performed at plantation feasts. "In violation of all rules of dietetics, huge quantities of heavy food and drink were disposed of," Ragatz wrote.

Indeed, Drax hosted one such feast, where the offerings might have intimidated Falstaff. Ligon was there, and he reported that it began with a first course of fourteen beef dishes, featuring a cow especially fattened in a private pasture of abundant forage. Its breast, rump, and cheeks were variously roasted, boiled, and baked. The legs and head went into a spiced stew, and the tongue and tripe were made into a meat pie seasoned with currants and finely minced sweet herbs.

Then came the second course. It included a leg of pork and boiled chicken and shoulder of mutton and a young goat, its belly filled with a pudding. There was veal loin dressed with oranges, lemons, and limes, and a suckling pig served in a sauce of claret, sage, nutmeg, and brains. (The pig was "the fattest, whitest, and sweetest in the world," Ligon wrote.) Then came three turkeys and two capons and two hens (served with their own eggs) and four ducklings and three rabbits and eight turtledoves and, for good measure, Spanish bacon. And oysters and caviar and olives and a potato pudding and a piquant relish made of fish eggs. Sweets—which at the time were typically served alongside the main courses and not as a separate dessert—included custards and creams, cheesecakes, puffs, melons, pears, custard apples, breads served with banana preserves, pancakes rolled with fruits, tansy pudding, watermelon, and that esteemed local delicacy, the pineapple.

As for drink, there were all sorts of imported beverages, including claret, white wine, Rhenish wine, sherry, sack, Canary wines, and "all Spirits that come from England." And Ligon noted another drink set out on the table, one with an odd name. It was a fiery spirit he called "kill-devil."

ALCOHOL IS CREATED when a microscopic fungus called yeast attacks sugar and rearranges it into alcohol and carbon dioxide. So crushed grapes left alone turn to wine, and apple cider left untended turns hard. Fermentation will slow and eventually cease when a batch reaches between 6 and 12 percent alcohol by volume, the level at which yeast loses its appetite for sugar. To make a product with an alcoholic content higher than about 12 percent, technology and human ingenuity are required.

Distillation had been mentioned in passing by Aristotle and Pliny the Elder, and by A.D. 800 enterprising Egyptians were experimenting with crude distillation, although they appeared to be more interested in making perfumes than drink. The converting of wine into its more potent cousin, brandy (a corruption of the Dutch *brandewijn*, or "burned wine"), was not taken up with gusto until after the early alchemists appeared. They were not particularly interested in inebriation. They were more interested in not dying. Alchemists experimented with basic stills in search of a potion that would extend human life, preferably forever. When they put meat and vegetables into the sharp-smelling liquid that emerged from those stills, they noted a small miracle: The food would not rot. Alcohol was the "quintessence"—*quinta essentia* in Latin, literally a fifth element, one that was neither fire, water, earth, nor air. It was like water, yet it burned, and left unattended it would turn quickly into vapor. It was mysterious and magical. No doubt it held the key to unlock the secret of everlasting life. Alchemists concluded, not unreasonably, that they were onto something vital.

"We call it *aqua vitae*, and this name is remarkably suitable, since it is really a water of immortality," wrote Arnauld de Villeneuve, a thirteenth-century professor in France. "It prolongs life, clears away ill-humors, revives the heart, and maintains youth." In France, the spirit was called *eau de vie;* in Scandinavia, *aquavit.*

The art of beverage distillation is generally credited to an Italian known as the "Master of Salerno," who regarded his experiments as important enough to record his results in a secret code. Brandy was initially the most common distillate, and word of its health-giving properties crossed the continent. A slug of brandy every morning was believed to ward off illness. A spoonful of brandy poured into the mouth of a dying person, it was also thought, would allow that person to utter a final word or two before taking his last breath.

The first whiskey—or "whisky," as the British prefer—may have appeared as early as the twelfth century, distilled from a coarse beer made of fermented grains mixed with malted barley—that is, barley that had been partially germinated and dried. Whiskey was most likely first produced in Ireland ("whiskey" is a corruption of *usque-baugh,* the Gaelic term for *aqua vitae*), although the first documented records don't surface until 1494 in Scotland. By the thirteenth century the frequent consumption of spirits had spread widely enough that laws had to be passed in central Europe to curb unruly *schnappssteufeln* ("schnapps fiends"), and the first known taxes on liquor were imposed. During the Black Death of 1348 and later plagues, alcohol was frequently (if ineffectively) prescribed as a cure, and strong drink marched in the wake of wholesale death from the cities into the smaller towns of Europe.

Early distillation methods were rudimentary at best. One seventeenth-century text offered a simple brandy recipe for northern climates: Store Canary wine in "warm horse dung" for four months, then set it outdoors in the frigid air of winter for another month. Remove the congealed "phlegm" (or slushy ice) and enjoy what's left: the "true spirit of wine." (This method would yield a drink of about 25 percent alcohol, if the ice were removed gingerly.)

A more practical way to make brandy was to heat the fermented low-alcohol mash in a sealed kettle with a single pipe for an outlet, from which the steam could be captured and condensed. Since alcohol is not only slower to freeze but faster to boil than water (about 173 degrees Fahrenheit compared to 212 degrees Fahrenheit for water), what first emerged from the condenser contained mostly alcohol, along with trace impurities that lent the spirit a distinctive taste.

Distillation concentrates and intensifies the subtle tastes found in the original low-alcohol product. Brandy has thus been called the distilled essence of wine, and whiskey the distilled essence of beer.

And rum? It is, as we shall see, the distilled essence of fermented industrial waste.

A SUCCESSFUL SUGAR planter needed many skills. He had to be a knowledgeable farmer and an efficient factory manager. He had to discipline slaves strictly to keep them in order, but not so harshly that they rebelled. He needed to know how to deal with agricultural diseases that blighted the cane and the human diseases that afflicted slaves and servants. He needed to know how to deal with the mechanics of the sugar works, as well as the mechanics of international politics to ensure a reliable overseas market. And he needed to be uncommonly knowledgeable about rats. Even when under control, rats often destroyed 5 percent of a sugar crop through incessant gnawing. The rats were wily, defeating even the most clever efforts to eradicate them, which included extensive use of poisons, ferrets, trained dogs, and slave children delegated to the task of clubbing them. In one rat roundup on a single West Indian sugar estate, some thirty-nine thousand rats were killed in a six-month period.

There remained one other issue the planter had to master: what to do with the waste generated in the sugaring process.

Sugar wastes were considerable. A mass of useless scummings would be skimmed off the boiling cauldrons during the cane juice reduction. Once cane juice was boiled down to a nearly crystallized syrup, it was cooled and cured. The curing process involved storing the crystallizing sugar in clay pots with holes in their bases, which allowed the waste matter bound up between the sugar crystals to ooze out. What emerged was molasses—a dark, sticky, caramelized liquid that resisted crystallization or further refining. The amount produced during the curing process varied widely, but a frequently cited ratio was one pound of molasses for every two pounds of marketable sugar.

With the more refined sugars, that amount might rise to as much as three pounds of molasses for every four of sugar.

In the mid-seventeenth century, molasses was a nuisance: It was too bulky to ship economically, and there was no demand for it anyway. Some could be mixed with grain and fodder to feed the cows and pigs, and some could be fed to slaves to supplement their meager diets. Molasses could be mixed with lime (or eggshells), water, and horsehair to make a crude but serviceable mortar. Molasses was also blended with various nostrums and injected into the urethras of both men and women as a cure for syphilis. But more often, it was simply discarded. One traveler noted of molasses produced on sugar plantations in the French West Indies that it is "never esteemed more than Dung; for they used to throw it all away." In the 1680s, the French were said to be discarding a half-million gallons of molasses each year. As late as 1665, molasses accounted for less than 1 percent of exports from Barbados. Molasses was industrial waste, an effluent best gotten rid of by dumping it into the ocean.

But somewhere someone figured something out: The scummings and the molasses contained enough residual sugar to attract the attention of yeast. "As the use of the still was then known," wrote Samuel Morewood in *An Essay on . . . Inebriating Liquors . . .* (1824), "it may be conjectured, that not long after this period the distillation of rum suggested itself, as the only means to compensate the planter for loss incurred in disposing of the scumming and molasses . . ."

Exactly where the distillation of rum first "suggested itself" is unknown. Medieval alchemists, busy with their search for an elixir of life, no doubt concocted a proto-rum from sugarcane juice or molasses. But since sugar was a scarce luxury at the time, it made little sense to continue to use sugar or molasses to manufacture spirits when more abundant and cheaper grapes and grain were available. If the alchemists invented rum, they just as quickly forgot it.

In the sixteenth and seventeenth centuries, both extensive sugar cultivation and the knowledge of distillation made their way through the New World tropics, like seeds scattered across fertile land. At some point, the two came together and germinated, producing rum. No one yet knows where the first dram of New World rum dripped out of a still.

Yet an argument may be made for Barbados's cultural paternity. The first documented appearances of both the words *kill-devil* and *rum* surfaced in Barbados. In 1652, a visitor to the island observed that "the chief fuddling they make in the island is Rumbullion, alias Kill-Divil, and this is made of sugar canes . . ." A 1658 deed for the sale of the Three Houses Plantation included in the sale "four large mastrick cisterns for liquor for rum," which is the first known official appearance of the word *rum* on any of the islands. (Laws governing liquor had previously been passed by the Barbadian assembly, but these referred only to "this country's spirits.")

Barbados can also claim to be home to the oldest-known continuously produced rum—from the Mount Gay distillery. A sugar plantation has existed at the northern tip of the island since the earliest years of settlement, on land where the Mount Gay currently distills rum from both modern column stills and old-fashioned pot stills. Records suggest that a still house was producing rum here as early as 1663, but the first solid evidence dates to February 20, 1703. On this date, a deed listed equipment transferred in a sale to include "two stone windmills . . . one boiling house with seven coppers, one curing house and one still house." (In comparison, the oldest continuously operating Scotch distillery is believed to date to the 1780s, and the oldest registered whiskey distillery in the United States to the 1860s.)

The island's immense sugar profits allowed planters to make extensive investments in up-to-date technology and production methods. By reducing operating costs through the building of windmills, planters could reap even more profit from sugar and then invest their gains in still houses that would wring out even more cash from the sugar fields. A still house was expensive; each cost about the same as constructing and outfitting a sugar-boiling house. But the money from rum paid for the investment and more. The economist Adam Smith wrote in *The Wealth of Nations* (1776) that "a sugar planter expects that the rum and molasses would defray the whole expense of his cultivation"—the substantial sugar sales were almost entirely profit. Smith likened the situation to a farmer covering his cultivation costs through the sale of chaff and straw. Where you'd find a boiling house for sugar, a still house was probably not far away. A well-managed sugar estate of four hundred acres might have four stills in operation; smaller estates might have one or two.

HERE'S HOW AN early rum distiller would turn industrial waste into cash. He began by mixing in a large cistern a liquid mess composed of three ingredients: the blackish scum that rose to the surface during the sugar-boiling process; the dregs remaining in the still after a previous batch (called lees or dunder); and water used to clean out the sugar-boiling pots between batches. This mixture—called wash—was then left to stand in the tropical heat. Since it was contaminated with yeasty bits of stalks and dirt, the stew would begin to ferment and bubble. Once the first bubbles appeared, the distiller would feed the fermentation by mixing in six gallons of molasses for every one hundred gallons of wash. (These ratios were prescribed by the planter Samuel Martin, who wrote that the "judicious distiller" could profitably tinker with these measures.)

The wash would ferment for anywhere from several days to a week. The temperature of the wash had to be closely monitored, since fermentation would slow or cease if it grew too hot or too cold; windows in the still house were opened and closed to regulate the air temperature. Martin recommended that when the wash rose to near "blood-heat," pails of cold water be added to cool the fermentation's fever.

If the fermentation was cool and sluggish, pails of hot water could be added, or "a little hot, clean, sea-sand" to bring up the temperature.

Distillers could add lemons, tamarinds, or tartar if the wash was not acidic enough. If it was *too* acidic, live coals or "new-made Wood ashes" could help. George Smith, the author of *The Nature of Fermentation Explained* . . . (1729) also noted, "the same effect will be produc'd by an Onion dipped in strong Mustard; or a Ball made of quick Lime, Wheat Flower, and the White of an Egg beat up into a Paste." Carcasses of dead animals or dung could be tossed in the vats to kick-start a batch that resisted fermentation. On Jamaica, according to an account by John Taylor, other substances were added to the wash, but for other reasons: "Perhaps the overseer will empty his camberpot into it . . . to keep the Negroes from Drincking it."

When the wash temperature fell and the bubbling stopped after a few days, the mildly alcoholic brew was ready for distillation. The wash was conveyed to the still via taps placed several inches from the bottom of the fermenting cisterns, a technique to leave the sediment behind. ("If the sediment passes into the still," wrote Samuel Martin, "it will not only give the spirit extracted, a fetid smell and taste, but incrust the bottom of the still, and corrode the copper.") A low and even fire was applied to the main vat of the pot still, and the steam generated would rise and progress through a bit of copper tubing called a worm. The worm had to be constantly cooled to get the steam to condense. If a stream flowing with cool water could be diverted around it, all the better. If not, as was the case on water-scarce Barbados, the steam-warmed water had to be refreshed with water cooled in the yard, a chore performed by slaves with pails or, later, by wind-powered pumps.

The spirit that came out of that first distillation could be drunk as is or run through the still a second or even third time. Barbadians preferred the "spirit of the first extraction" and usually had their rum casked after just one pass, resulting in "a cooler spirit, more palatable and wholesome," according to Martin. The island of Jamaica, which would overtake Barbados in rum production in the nineteenth century, produced a double-distilled rum, which was as strong as it was harsh. Martin noted that the Jamaican approach "seems more profitable for the London-market, because the buyers there approve of a fiery spirit which will bear most adulteration." The higher-alcohol Jamaican rum contained more benders per cask, and thus was more efficient to ship overseas than single-distilled rum.

PRODUCTION IS ONLY half a market; consumption makes up the other half. And in this the early residents of Barbados admirably filled a need. Planters could expand their estates, confident that the drinkers of Barbados would purchase what rum they produced. By 1655, an estimated 900,000 gallons a year of kill-devil was being produced on Barbados. Yet virtually no export market existed. Small amounts were shipped abroad as early as 1638, but distillers hadn't yet established any major outlets. As late as 1698, a mere 207 gallons of rum were officially exported to England from Barbados. This figure is likely low, given smuggling to England and unrecorded sales to the crews of visiting ships. Even so, Barbadians drank something on the order of 10 gallons per person per year. That is a feat not to be underestimated.

Who made up this market? Ninety-four percent of those setting off for Barbados in 1635 from England were male, and most were young and poor. While the gentry did fabulously, the majority of islanders lived rough lives. In 1631, Henry Whistler described Barbados as "the dunghill whereon England doth cast forth its rubbish. Rogues and whores and such like people are those which are generally brought here. A rogue in England will hardly make a cheater here."

Disappointment among early settlers was as endemic as smallpox. Those who came with a little cash hoping to start a small plantation soon discovered that they were too late—the land had been snapped up by larger landowners—and their dreams went unrealized. Indentured servants likewise found that the English promises of upward mobility were overblown at best. The small plots granted to freed servants were of use only to scratch out enough vegetables for a subsistence diet. Few other jobs were available; landowners had made the discovery that slaves imported from Africa could perform the work of sugar- and rum-making more economically than hired workers. Although slaves initially cost twice as much as indentured servants, they needn't be freed in seven years and were less prone to tropical disease; and if slothfulness proved a problem, a whip could cure it.

For disheartened British settlers, quaffing rum provided relief from chronic disappointment. And those in need of a drink didn't need to look far. Captain Thomas Walduck in 1708 neatly summarized the development of the West Indies: "Upon all the new settlements the Spaniards make, the first thing they do is build a church, the first thing ye Dutch do upon a new colony is to build them a fort, but the first thing ye English do, be it in the most remote part of ye world, or amongst the most barbarous Indians, is to set up a tavern or drinking house."

Tippling houses, as they were generally known in the West Indies, emerged as a social and political issue as early as 1652 when the Barbadian assembly first licensed them. (At the time, Bridgetown had roughly one tippling house for every twenty residents.) In 1668, an act was passed "preventing the selling of brandy and rum in Tippling Houses near broad-paths and highways." The legislation noted that on the Sabbath day, "many lewd, loose, and idle people do usually resort to such tippling-houses." The early British settlers had a fondness for drinking that was unmatched by any other nation, with the possible exception of the Dutch. As the historian Alison Games writes, "inebriation was hardly limited to Barbados, although all visitors there seemed thoroughly impressed by the island residents' commitment to drink."

Sir Henry Colt, who arrived on Barbados in 1631, was one such visitor. He noted he had long been accustomed to downing two or three drams of spirits daily in his native England. But his new companions on Barbados, he said, soon had him up to thirty drams daily. Had he remained on the island, he reported, he would no doubt be downing sixty. "Such great drunkards" was how another Barbadian settler described his new companions in 1640, noting that they would scratch up enough cash to "buy their drink all though they goe naked." A traveler, Thomas Verney, wrote home that Barbadians were often so potted that they passed out where they stood, and in their be-nighted state were savaged by the tiny land crabs that plagued the is-land. "The people drink much of it," echoed Richard Ligon, "indeed, too much; for it often layes them asleep on the ground, and this is ac-counted a very unwholesome lodging."

The islander's commitment to drink seems all the more impres-sive given the likely quality of the product. We can never know what exactly it tasted like, but it was no doubt a coarse and uneven liquor, varying widely from plantation to plantation and batch to batch. It might be agreed that early rum was horrid, but each batch was horrid in its own way. The French priest Jean Baptiste Labat deemed kill-devil "rough and disagreeable," and an anonymous visitor to the West Indies in 1651 noted that kill-devil was "a hot, hellish, and terrible liquor." Richard Ligon wrote that it was "not very pleasant in taste." Indeed, no seventeenth-century account has surfaced that has any-thing nice to say about the taste of kill-devil.

No surprise, that. Distillers hadn't sorted out the variables, and the early technology didn't allow for any sort of precision in rum mak-ing. The quality of the cane, water, and fermentation would have played a secondary role in the quality of the output, and the taste would have been determined largely by the condition and oversight of the still. If the distiller were distracted for a few minutes, a batch could be irretrievably fouled. If the water cooling the worm were to evapo-rate, the rum would acquire "a burnt, disagreeable taste, not whole-some for those who drink it," wrote Martin. But it was probably sold anyway and drunk eagerly.

Stills needed to be thoroughly cleaned between batches, lest the next batch take on a singed taste. Some have pointed out that this was not necessarily bad. Drinkers had discovered that rum distilled in

Britain from imported molasses almost never tasted like rum from the West Indies. George Smith, in 1729, looked into this intriguing fact. He attributed part of the difference to the "newness and richness of the Molasses" used in the West Indies. But he put forth another theory: that the estate overseers and slaves who operated the island stills simply neglected to clean stills between batches, sometimes even for an entire distilling season. "As nothing is more viscous and adhesive than Molasses," Smith wrote, "it cannot be expected but that a great quantity of the grosser matter must adhere to the sides and bottom of the still, and consequently burn thereto." That slightly burned taste survived distillation, giving West Indian rum a caramelized flavor. Smith said that British distillers hoping to mimic the taste of imported rum "must not stand too much upon Niceties," and he suggested they might adopt the indolent island practices when it came time for cleaning.

Aging was another way of improving the taste of rum, but this was another nicety that few distillers would have bothered with. Colonists knew that leaving rum in a cask or barrel for months or, better yet, years would dull the burrs of new rum and give it a richer, smoother taste. Rum shipped abroad was always better when it arrived. "All rum is improved by time in wooden casks, by exhalation of ether and absorption of oil," explained Bryan Higgins in 1797. Later markets would demonstrate a preference for the aged spirit. New rum sold for seven shillings per gallon in the 1700s, whereas aged rum brought eighteen shillings. But early Barbados rum consumed on the island was almost certainly pure moonshine, raw and harsh.

And it was often toxic. Lead pipes were typically used in the early distillation process, which put the tippler at risk of a painful condition called "the dry gripes." In 1745, Thomas Cadwalader wrote an essay on the dry gripes and its treatments, and noted among the symptoms "excessive griping pains in the pit of the stomach and bowels, which are much distended with wind . . . at other times there is a sensation, as if the bowels were drawn together by ropes." In some cases, "the patient begins to break wind backwards, which is some times exceed-ing offensive." (It strains the imagination to think of times this would not be "exceeding offensive.") Other associated problems included paralysis of the limbs and, in dire cases, death. The supposed remedy was scarcely better than the dry gripes itself: A molasses enema was often prescribed.

All the same, rum drinking was just as often linked with good health as with illness. To drink to one's health was more than an idle phrase in the seventeenth century. Europeans who first explored the West Indian islands and the East Indian archipelagoes initially be-lieved that the constant heat would eventually be fatal to those of northern constitutions, and that one could only stand so much heat before dropping dead in one's tracks. Theories of health at the time posited that a proper balance needed to be maintained between the four humors—blood, yellow bile, phlegm, and black bile—and this balance was determined by the climate in which one was raised. Ven-turing someplace with a radically different climate would upset that. In the tropics, yellow bile would predominate and unwellness and death would ensue. William Vaughan, a British writer on medical subjects, stated definitively in 1612 that a European transplanted to the tropics would perish in five years. In 1626, he revised his figure upward to fifteen years, presumably based on fresh evidence that colonists were not, in fact, dying of the heat in wholesale quantities.

In his *A Natural History of Barbados* (1750), Rev. Griffith Hughes detours for five folio pages from his inventory of the island's flora and fauna to expound on his intricate theories regarding tropical heat and blood. His own belief was that well-being stemmed from "an equal Motion of the Fluids and the Resistance of the Solids." In hot cli-mates, he wrote, where sweating is constant, the blood loses its fluid-ity and becomes "more viscid, and Consequently the Circulation is more languid." Those with slow, turgid blood soon become less logi-cal, and "overlook those Rules of Method and Connexion, that are observed by Europeans of a cooler and more regular Fancy." By way of example, Hughes notes that southern Spaniards tended toward the "pensive, melancholy, and revengeful." Fortunately, an easy antidote could be had. Viscous blood could be "counterbalanced by the daily Use of a great Quantity of Diluters of every kind," which included a punch made with rum.

Richard Ligon also dabbled in theories on blood and heat, although he believed that the blood of colonists was not more viscid, but rather "thinner and paler than in our own Countreys." Happily for the colonists, the remedy was the same: "Strong drinks are very requisite, where so much heat is," Ligon wrote, "for the spirits being exhausted with much sweating, the inner parts are left cold and faint, and shall need comforting, and reviving."

RUM'S APPEAL TO the rougher classes is suggested by what the first drinkers named this spirit. "Kill-devil" was for much of the mid- and late seventeenth century the most common name for rum. It appeared not only in traveler's accounts, but in official bills of lading and other documents. It's a rather ambiguous name. Does it suggest that this spirit is potent enough to kill the devil? Or is it a product of the devil and thus lethal in its effect? Irish naturalist Hans Sloane appeared to back the latter; in 1707, after spending fifteen months in Jamaica, he wrote that "rum is well-called Kill-Devil, for perhaps no year passes without it having killed more than a thousand." The term migrated over time from the English to the Danish, who called it *kiel-dyvel,* and to the French, who pronounced it *guildive,* a term that lives on today in Haiti. The origins of the word *rum* are no less a mystery. Rum is a blunt, simple word, and admirably Anglo-Saxon. In an 1824 essay about the name's derivation, Samuel Morewood suggested it might be from British slang for "the best," as in having "a rum time." Morewood writes, "As spirits, extracted from molasses, could not well be ranked under the name whiskey, brandy, arrack, &c. it was called rum, to denote its excellence or superior quality." Given what was known about the taste of early rum, this is unlikely. Among those unconvinced by this argument was Morewood himself, who went on to suggest another possibility: that it was taken from the last syllable for the Latin word for sugar, *saccharum,* an explanation that is often heard today.

Other word detectives have mentioned the gypsy word *rum,* meaning "strong" or "potent." Tantalizingly, this variation of rum has been linked to rumbooze (or rambooze) and rumfustian, both popular British drinks of the mid-seventeenth century. Unfortunately, neither of these drinks is made with rum, but rather with eggs, ale, wine, sugar, and various spices.

The most likely derivation is that *rum* is a truncated version of *rumbullion* or *rumbustion.* Rumbullion and rumbustion both first surfaced in the English language around the same time as *rum,* and both were British slang for "tumult" or "uproar." This is a far more convincing explanation and brings to mind fractious islanders cracking one another over the head in rumbustious entanglements at island tippling houses. Nothing more need be said on the matter.

As product names go, modern marketing consultants would no doubt prefer *rum* over kill-devil—it's easier to rhyme, for starters, and has less unsavory associations. No matter what one called it, though, rum marked one of the more successful product introductions in history. It dominated life in the West Indian islands for several decades while the beverage and the colonists both gained their footing, but rum was soon ready to set sail. It had larger appointments to keep.

And so it began its voyage from the sugar islands to the larger world beyond. At the outset, it was more hitchhiker than paying passenger. Rum didn't have the luxury cachet of sugar. No one in Europe or the North American colonies was yet clamoring for the new and harsh liquor, for few had yet tried or even heard of it. But like a glass spilled across a tavern table, rum seeped slowly into the colonial world's small fissures, dribbling into large harbors and small coves alike. It found a particularly warm welcome in the northern colonies, where the colonists were starved for cheap diversion. A merchant captain in the mid-seventeenth century might load a cask or two aboard his vessel to buoy himself and his crew on their northward voyage. He would have shared the marvel of rum in distant ports as he chased trade and the winds. Colonists would ask the captain to bring back another cask or two when his ship next sailed from the Indies. Word of rum spread. Between 1650 and 1700, rum raised itself from an oddity of the islands to a respectable bulk cargo that was stored in increasing quantity in ships' holds alongside barrels of molasses, rough brown sugar, and indigo.

Rum still had to overcome many obstacles in finding a wider acceptance beyond the West Indies. It had to cross from the tropical islands to distant markets through unpoliced seas, and do this without attracting the attention of pirates, buccaneers, brigands, and others who took a keen interest in the colonies' burgeoning trade.

In this, as we shall see, rum was not terrifically successful.

[GROG]

Pour *two ounces* of RUM into an *eight-ounce* glass. Fill with WATER. Add a touch of fresh LIME juice or BROWN SUGAR to taste.

Chapter 2

[GROG]

Captain Morgan is a lot more than flavor. . . . It reflects an attitude. It's fun and adventurous. It has a real personality and an appealing proposition—good taste, good times, good fun.

—LAURA GOLDENBERG,
U.S. RUM CATEGORY MANAGER FOR SEAGRAM'S

CAPTAIN HENRY MORGAN was born in Wales in 1635, at the outset of the great British rush to the sugar islands. The son of a prosperous farmer, Morgan had no interest in harrows or furrows and instead went off to seek—in the words of a contemporary—"some other employ more suitable to his humour." The teenaged Morgan found himself at a Welsh port, where he boarded a ship bound for the West Indies. He eventually disembarked on Barbados, where accounts suggest he found employ as an indentured servant.

His career on the island was evidently short-lived. In 1655, a British fleet manned by some twenty-five hundred sailors and soldiers was dispatched across the Atlantic by Oliver Cromwell, with the aim of expanding the British presence in the islands. The fleet landed first at Barbados, where it took on some four thousand Barbadian colonists to supplement the fighting force. This included a number of indentured servants who were seized over the objections of the planters who had paid for their contracts. Morgan may have been among them; the historical record is sketchy. The fleet then sailed off with high purpose, intent on sacking the wealthy Spanish colony on Hispaniola. The attack did not go well; the British force was all but routed by the Spanish after blundering their assault on the city of Santo Domingo. The British fleet withdrew, and the commanders hastily came up with another plan: strike and capture the lightly defended Spanish settlement on Jamaica, near present-day Kingston.

Here, the British prevailed. The great force scattered the hapless and outnumbered Spanish into the hills and easily took control of the settlement, and thus of the thinly populated island. Although the attack lacked heroism, it marked two historical milestones: It was the first state-financed naval operation by the British in the West Indies. And Henry Morgan had his formal coming out.

Young Morgan rapidly proved himself something of a prodigy in the art of combat. He led raids on Dutch settlements as second in command during the Anglo-Dutch War of 1665 to 1667. Soon after, at the age of thirty-two, Morgan was named head of the Brethren of the Coast, a loosely organized group of privateers. Privateers, unlike pirates, had the official blessing of their government to attack ships flying the flags of the enemy. Privateers weren't paid by the government but got to keep a generous percentage of the spoils. The arrangement was a good deal for everyone except those attacked. England got an extended navy without putting up any hard cash, and the more rapacious privateers earned far more than a sailor could hope to see in the standing navy. The distinction between privateer and pirate was often vague, since months might elapse between the signing of a truce and word of the peace getting to a captain on a mission of plunder. Even if that word did come through, privateers had little incentive to cease their marauding, since other ships were where the gold was. "To the buccaneers a treaty of peace meant merely a change from public employment to private enterprise," as historians J. H. Parry and P. H. Sherlock put it.

Morgan was wildly successful in his engagements, being particularly drawn to Spanish ships and villages, since they were the richest. Since the early sixteenth century, the Spaniards had been wrenching gold from the mines of Mexico and Peru and carting it to well-defended ports to await the sailings of the Armada, which escorted the treasure back to Spain. Morgan built his reputation through ruthless and audacious attacks, including one on well-defended Puerto Príncipe (now Camagüey) in Cuba, and others on several Spanish villages along Lake Maracaibo in present-day Venezuela. Between 1655 and 1671, Morgan sacked a total of eighteen cities, four towns, and thirty-five villages, and captured more than $100 million worth of gold, silver, and trade goods.

Two episodes transformed Morgan from mortal to legend, and both took place in Panama. With its three stout fortresses, Portobelo on Panama's Caribbean coast was among the best defended towns in New Spain, bettered only by Havana and Cartagena. Morgan knew enough not to attack these forts directly, so in 1668 he quietly landed his force of 460 men on a stretch of undefended coast some distance away. The troops marched overland by night, and then struck at dawn, catching guards by surprise and quickly overwhelming most of the town's citadels.

Morgan's appearance in the streets of Portobelo that morning was a surprise, but his reputation for brutality had no doubt preceded him. Coastal residents generally found it to be unwise to withhold information about hidden riches if Captain Morgan knocked on their doors. Those who did would be stretched on the rack, or have flaming sticks tied between their fingers, or a cord twisted around their heads so tightly that their eyeballs popped like grapes from their skins. Other recalcitrants would be hoisted by their wrists with weights tied to neck and feet while being burned with flaming branches. In Maracaibo, an elderly Portuguese man had been ratted out (falsely) by a neighbor as being from a wealthy family. While demanding to know the location of his supposed fortune, Morgan's men suspended him from the ground by tying his thumbs and big toes to four stakes, then placed a two-hundred-pound rock on his belly and hammered at the cords with clubs, all the while burning him with palm leaves. And he was one of the *lucky* ones. Some had their feet burned off while still alive; others were said to be suspended by their testicles and battered with sticks until a violent anatomical separation ensued.

In Portobelo, Morgan did little to dull his reputation for ruthlessness. He forced priests and nuns to serve as shields when his men advanced on a fortress that still held out. He calculated that the Spaniards were too pious to fire on their own clerics. He calculated wrongly, and the priests and nuns fell. Morgan still managed to overtake the redoubt and punished the resisters by herding them into a room, packing explosives under the floor, and blowing them into the sky. His demands for a gold ransom to spare the rest of the town were eventually met, and he sailed for Jamaica with a half-million pieces of eight and some three hundred slaves.

Two years later, Morgan outdid himself by sacking the capital of Panama City on the distant Pacific Coast. He assembled nearly two thousand men and thirty-six ships, sailed to Panama's Caribbean coast, and then left his fleet behind for a long and grueling march through the jungle. The expedition seemed doomed at times; at one point the men had to boil their shoes to stave off their hunger. Morgan would eventually lay waste to Panama City after a fierce, two-hour battle—the task considerably simplified by the panicked mayor, who torched his own town as Morgan arrived. Morgan made off with four hundred thousand pieces of eight, yet his triumph was bittersweet: He narrowly missed seizing a Spanish ship with five million pieces that had fled into the open Pacific as Morgan's men appeared at the gates.

What we know about Morgan's exploits is chiefly due to a remarkable account published by a Dutchman who wrote under the name of Alexander Exquemelin. He spent eight years with the pirates in the Caribbean, a large part of that with Morgan. His 1678 book, *De Americaensche Zee-rovers,* was translated into English and published in 1684 as *Bucaniers of America,* and proved as enduring as it was popular. Although riddled with inaccuracies and exaggerations, Exquemelin's lavish account is considered the best source of information on Captain Morgan and the habits of pirates. The detail in Exquemelin's book is so rich and so lavish that it grieves me slightly to make one observation. At no time is rum ever mentioned.

TODAY, CAPTAIN MORGAN serves as something of a mascot to the rum industry, thanks to the continuing success of Captain Morgan rum, which accounts for about one-third of the billion-dollar premium rum market in the United States. It was introduced in 1945 on Jamaica, where the Seagram Company decided to market a high-end rum made by blending rums from other distillers. In the fall of 1949, Captain Morgan rum was imported for the first time to the United States amid great marketing hullabaloo; in New York, it was touted in newspaper ads with an illustration of a statuesque pirate wearing a malicious grin in front of the Manhattan skyline, as if about to set out in search of Wall Street bankers to hang by the testicles.

The brand caught on. In 1953, Seagram acquired its own rum distillery in Jamaica to supply the growing demand. Captain Morgan rum was then a light rum designed for mixing. ("Lighter, cleaner," boasted the first ads, "especially designed for the American taste.") When Americans drifted off in favor of even lighter white wine spritzers and light beer in the 1980s, Seagram set about tinkering with the brand, adding spices and flavorings and reinventing Captain Morgan as a spiced rum. Today, it's produced and sold by Diageo, the world's largest producer of liquor.

Although rum and pirates are like smoke and fire (you rarely find one without the other), the marriage was actually the product of the Victorian era (about which more later). The spectacular plunderings of the real Captain Henry Morgan would not have involved rum for a simple reason: It wasn't a common spirit in the Spanish colonies he raided. While the Spanish did have sugar plantations and a surplus of waste molasses, rum hadn't taken off as it had on the British islands, because Spanish winemakers and brandy distillers made sure that it didn't. Afraid of competition from cheap rum, they prevailed upon the Spanish crown to ban spirits exports from the islands. So when buccaneers sacked villages, they found Madeira and Canary wines and brandy in the cellars and storehouses, but little rum. Being pirates and not terribly picky, they were happy to guzzle it down.

After they sacked a village and tortured or sent its inhabitants into flight, Morgan's men broke into the storerooms and drank with gusto. Following the conquest of Portobelo, Exquemelin wrote, the men "fell to eating and drinking, after their usual manner—that is to say, committing in both these things all manner of debauchery and excess." The spectacle of drink and mayhem lasted two full weeks. Exquemelin conjectured that a Spanish contingent of "fifty courageous men" could have routed the besotted pirates, who numbered nearly ten times as many. The beleaguered Spanish mustered no such force.

During the long march to Panama City, "fifteen or sixteen jars of Peruvian wine" were uncovered in one village along the way. The men fell upon it "with rapacity" and consumed it without pause. No sooner was the wine emptied than the drinkers began vomiting copiously. Suspecting that the wine had been poisoned, the soldiers sat back moaning and awaited their grim fate. Remarkably, no one died. Exquemelin suspected that the reaction was from drinking too hastily on very empty stomachs.

As the planters of the sugar islands planted more cane and built more windmills to meet the clamor for sugar in Europe, they scrambled to find an outlet for their growing rum surplus. Rum was consumed eagerly and prolifically by islanders, but local consumption couldn't absorb all of it, nor did local imbibing provide useful hard currency to pay off overseas debts and expand trade. Moreover, sugar planters had devoted nearly every acre of arable land to sugarcane and produced virtually no food to feed themselves or their slaves. They were much in need of anything edible. So livestock and produce sailed south from the northern colonies, and rum, in turn, began to sail north. "Good Rume and Mallasces . . . is most vendable heare," wrote a Newport, Rhode Island, merchant to his Barbados agent in the 1660s.

Demand for rum grew steadily. By 1699, the British writer Edward Ward noted that "rum, alias Kill Devil, is as much ador'd by the American English. . . . This is held as the Comforter of their Souls, the Preserver of their Bodys, the Remover of their Cares, and Promoter of their Mirth; and is a Sovereign Remedy against the Grumbling of the Guts, a Kibe-heel [chilblains on the heel], or a Wounded Conscience, which are three Epidemical Distempers that afflict the Country."

By the early eighteenth century, the most popular West Indian destinations for northern colonial merchant ships were Antigua or Barbados, since rum was most easily obtained in trade there. In 1738, Philadelphia merchant Robert Ellis instructed the captain of the *Sarah and Elizabeth* to consider selling his cargo at St. Kitts if a good price could be had for his cargo, but added he would "rather yould dispose of it at Antigua for you'll be more likely to get rum there." More than 90 percent of rum exported from Barbados and Antigua headed to mainland North America; on other islands, rum exports to the northern colonies were often 100 percent, since no market had yet emerged in England or Europe. Export figures from 1726 to 1730 show that the most important rum exporter was Barbados, which shipped 680,269 gallons of rum to the northern colonies; this was followed by Antigua with 235,966 gallons, and St. Kitts and Montserrat, which together shipped about 14,000 gallons of rum. Benjamin Franklin, the publisher of the *Pennsylvania Gazette,* printed up 228 words and phrases that were slang for being drunk. These included "cock'd," "juicy," "fuzl'd," "stiff," "wamble crop'd," "crump-footed," "staggerish," and one other: "Been to Barbados."

The pirates, increasingly disappointed by the spoils of the waning Spanish empire, gradually moved north to harass British traders. When they found rum, they consumed it with gusto. After the pirate George Lowther captured a ship in 1722 en route from Barbados to Boston, he took pains to inventory his haul: five barrels of sugar, six slaves, a box of English goods, and thirteen hogsheads of good rum.

As the eighteenth century progressed, rum came to displace wine in accounts of pirate debauchery—and to be associated with disorder and mayhem on the seas.

"I soon found that any death was preferable to being linked with such a vile crew of miscreants," wrote Philip Ashton, a ship's captain captured by pirates in 1724. "Monstrous cursing and swearing, hideous blasphemies, and open defiance of Heaven" appalled him deeply, as did one other bad habit: "prodigious drinking."

Captain George Roberts of London was overtaken by the Boston pirate Ned Low. The psychopathic Low was precisely the person you would prefer not to meet on the high seas; he reportedly forced one captive to eat his own ears freshly sliced from his head and another to eat the fresh-plucked heart of a fellow sailor. Low evidently took a small liking to Roberts. Not only did he not force him to eat his own organs, he served him claret and a rum punch mixed up in a two-gallon silver bowl.

Roberts's account of the ordeal suggests an uncommon interest in rum on the part of his pirate captors. They passed their idle time boasting, then "drinking and carousing merrily, both before and after dinner, which they eat in a very disorderly manner, more like a kennel of hounds, than like men, snatching and catching the victuals from one another." At night, after Low had turned in, Roberts stayed up drinking with the other men to maintain their good favor. "We took a dram of rum," Roberts reported, "and enter'd into discourse with one another, on different subjects; for as a tavern or alehouse-keeper endeavors to promote his trade, by conforming to the humours of every customer, so was I forc'd to be pleasant with every one, and bear a bob with them in almost all their sorts of discourse, tho' never so contrary and disagreeable to my own inclinations; otherwise I should have fallen under an odium with them, and when once that happens to be the case with any poor man, the lord have mercy upon him, for then every rascally fellow will let loose his brutal fancy upon him . . . artificially raised by drinking, passion, & c." Low kept Roberts captive ten days before setting him adrift in a boat.

Pirate life wasn't all anarchy and the snatching of food. Pirates were often bound by charters they signed when they joined a crew— miniature constitutions that governed life aboard the ship and dictated the distribution of the spoils. Some of these even codified the rules of drinking. The charter of Bartholomew Roberts, better known as Black Bart, had a provision stating that each man "has equal title to the fresh provisions or strong liquores at any time seized, and may use them at pleasure unless a scarcity make it necessary for the food of all to vote a retrenchment." (Curiously, Roberts himself was a teetotaler, and his ship's charter also prohibited drinking below deck after eight o'clock in the evening. His sobriety may have helped his career; he captured some four hundred vessels and is generally regarded as one of the most successful of pirates.) During one string of attacks in the West Indies in 1720, Roberts and his crew captured so much liquor that an observer wrote that "it was esteemed a crime against Providence not to be continually drunk." Two of his crew members were noted to be particularly dissolute; Robert Devins was always in his cups and scarcely fit for any duty, as was reported at his trial after he was captured. And crewman Robert Johnson became so thoroughly incapacitated that at one point block and tackle had to be employed to remove him from the ship like a sack of yams.

THE DE FACTO capital of the British pirate world was Port Royal, Jamaica's chief port, situated across the harbor from present-day Kingston. After the British vanquished the Spanish in 1655, enterprising colonists established a makeshift town on a long sandspit at the mouth of the harbor. Jamaica would eventually become a sugar superpower, but the island economy was founded on trade, much of it illegal, with Port Royal serving as an entrepôt for contraband goods and treasure seized by privateers and pirates.

Port Royal made an especially appealing base for pirates since island governors were happy to turn a blind eye to their activities. The pirates were a useful nuisance. They brought in gold and silver to buoy the local economy—so much that the notion of establishing a British mint was considered in 1662—and served as an ad hoc naval defense force at no cost to the governor. With its abundance of captured gold, Jamaica was an inviting target for French or Spanish marauders. But a harbor teeming with heavily armed pirate ships manned by predatory seamen greatly reduced the odds of such an attack.

After his raids, Captain Morgan and his men would sail to Port Royal to whore and drink and spend their money. The more carelessly they could rid themselves of their gold, the happier they were. "Wine and Women drained their Wealth to such a Degree that in a little time some of them became reduced to Beggary," reported pirate chronicler Charles Leslie. "They have been known to spend 2 or 3000 Pieces of Eight in one Night; and one of them gave a Strumpet 500 to see her naked." Morgan "found many of his chief officers and soldiers reduced to their former state of indigence through their immoderate vices and debauchery." Then they would pester him to get up a new fleet for further raids, "thereby to get something to expend anew in wine and strumpets."

The port was ungoverned at the outset, and in short order became ungovernable. Literate visitors engaged in a sort of informal competition to best describe the sheer hellishness of the place. It was the "most wicked and sinful city in the world," wrote one British man of the cloth. Another English clergyman, eager to begin the Lord's work in reforming the city, instantly abandoned his hopes of salvation. "This town is the Sodom of the New World," he wrote, and "the majority of its population consists of pirates, cutthroats, whores, and some of the vilest persons in the whole of the world." He left aboard the same ship that brought him.

Edward Ward took the prize for the most colorful description, describing Port Royal as "the Dunghill of the Universe, the Refuse of the whole Creation, the Clippings of the Elements, a shapeless Pile of Rubbish confused'ly jumbl'd in to an Emblem of Chaos, neglected by Omnipotence when he form'd the World into its admirable Order. . . . The Receptacle of Vagabonds, the Sanctuary of Bankrupts, and a Close-Stool for the Purges of our Prisons. As Sickly as a Hospital, as Dangerous as the Plague, as Hot as Hell, and as Wicked as the Devil."

Port Royal had a density of taverns that made the tippling houses of Barbados appear woefully inadequate. Even discounting the unlicensed and undocumented rumshops—of which there were surely many—Port Royal had one legal tavern for every ten male residents. In one month—July 1661—the local council granted forty licenses for new taverns and punch houses. A governor of Jamaica noted that the Spanish often wondered why the British were always suffering from extravagant illness, "until they knew the strength of their drinks, but then wondered more that they were not all dead."

All sorts of liquor could be had in Port Royal. The reasonably well off drank Madeira wine, and the "servants and the inferior kind of people"—wrote one visitor in a letter in 1664—drank rum. Another visitor wrote that kill-devil was the "main drink sold in the taverns," but other popular pirate drinks included bumboo or bombo, a mix of rum, water, sugar, and a bit of nutmeg.

(Modern archaeology has done little to contradict the idea that Port Royal residents lived in a state of constant pottedness. In the early 1970s, the archaeologist Robert Marx excavated a portion of Port Royal now underwater. A thick mantle of silt covered everything, but he uncovered hundreds of "onion bottles," so called because they consisted of a round bulbous bottom attached to a long tapering neck and were traditionally used for putting up rum. Sadly, no potable rum was recovered.)

Port Royal offered sanctuary to Captain Morgan between his raids in the late seventeenth century, and in retirement it became his home. After he quit attacking the Spanish, he was lionized as a hero in England. Knighted, he returned to Jamaica as lieutenant governor and acquired a plantation in the nearby parish of St. Mary, eventually amassing twelve hundred acres. Now nostalgic for the Welsh countryside he was once eager to leave, Morgan named his estate after his old home, Llanrumney. He constructed a handsome house atop a hill, equipping it with stout stone walls and shutters thick enough to repel bullets. Morgan had acquired many enemies, and for them he was ready.

After giving up his post in 1682, Morgan mounted a vigorous defense of his sullied name. He sued two English publishing houses for libel when Exquemelin's account of his exploits was translated into English, collecting just £410 but winning the retractions he sought. One publisher, William Crooke, wrote that Morgan did not torture a fool on the rack, did not torture a rich Portuguese citizen, did not force a Negro to kill several prisoners, and did not engage in "the hanging up of any person by the testicles."

Most of all, retirement meant that Morgan could now frequent the rumshops more often, regaling all with tales of his past adventures. But soon his health declined, and even visits to the rumshops became too taxing for him. He was confined to his estate, where he spent his days drinking with the few friends who hadn't abandoned him. Each morning began with a bout of vomiting. His legs were so swollen that he couldn't walk. He was unable to urinate and often weak from diarrhea. The naturalist Hans Sloane described him as "lean, sallow-colored, his eyes a little yellowish and Belly jutting out or prominent." Captain Morgan's later life goes unmentioned in the marketing material for his namesake rum.

On August 25, 1688, Captain Henry Morgan died at age fifty-three. He was given a state funeral and a twenty-one-gun salute; a brief amnesty was declared in Port Royal to allow outlaws to surface and pay their final respects. Morgan was buried in the Port Royal cemetery.

Four years later, on the morning of June 7, 1692, the first of three fierce earthquakes hit Port Royal. In a matter of minutes, 90 percent of the city was destroyed, most of it gulped down by an unstable earth. Houses that once lined cobblestone lanes were suddenly below water as the ground opened up and swallowed whole city blocks. A tsunami followed, sweeping the ships into the rubble of the city. Washed up on the ruins like little arks, grounded ships served as sanctuaries in the coming weeks, until the port could begin to rebuild. About two thousand people were killed in the first moments after the quake; the fresh dead floated in the harbor with the old dead, as cemeteries opened and disgorged corpses. Captain Morgan's remains may have been among them. Just as his life began with mystery, so, too, it concluded.

PIRATE ACTIVITY IN the Atlantic peaked around 1720, when some fifteen hundred to two thousand pirates were estimated to be plying the waters between New England and the West Indies. Pirates were not viewed as colorful outlaws but a worrisome drag on the expanding commerce trade between the mainland colonies and the islands. Pirates went from the hunters to the hunted. Some sailed off to ransack ships in the Indian Ocean, with Madagascar the new Port Royal. Those who remained were hunted down by fleets commissioned by colonial governors, then hanged in mass executions.

Between 1716 and 1726, an estimated four hundred to six hundred Anglo-American pirates went to the gallows. In 1718, eight pirates "swang off" at one hanging in the Bahamas. In July 1723, twenty-six pirates were hanged in Newport, Rhode Island, on a single day. England passed a law that harshly punished even passing contact with pirates, making it a capital offense. Six turtle fishermen were hanged in 1720 when they had the misfortune of being caught sharing a rum punch with the pirate John Rackham.

Captured pirates ascending to the noose were offered a last chance to repent their wayward life, and some experienced gallows conversions. Before being executed in 1724, John Archer said that the "one wickedness that has led me as much as any, to all the rest, has been my brutish drunkenness. By strong drink I have been heated and hardened into the crimes that are now more bitter than death unto me." John Browne, hanged at Newport in 1723, instructed all youth to obey their parents, to "beware the abominable Sin of Uncleanliness," and, above all, "to not let yourselves be overcome with strong drink." (These deathbed entreaties have the whiff of the temperance movement about them, and one suspects the heavy hand of an editor.)

Others, no doubt a majority, failed to experience such conversions, demanding another dram of rum up until the moment the rope went taut. William Lewis, who was hanged in the Bahamas, bedecked himself in red ribbons for the occasion and "scorn'd to shew any Fear to dye but heartily desired Liquors enough to drink with his fellow sufferers . . . and with the Standers by." Captain William Kidd—who was either a pirate or privateer, depending on whom you believe— asserted his innocence until hanging day. Few reports of Kidd's execution fail to mention he was much inebriated as he was marched through teeming crowds to the gallows at the Execution Dock in London. Drunk, Kidd dropped through the hatch, whereupon the rope broke. Dazed and befuddled, he sprawled on the ground, then was marched up the steps again and fitted with a new rope. This time the rope held. When the twitching stopped, Kidd's corpse was taken down and hung along the Thames to be pecked at by crows, a warning to those considering a similar path.

The pirate most associated with rum was undoubtedly Edward Teach, better known as Blackbeard. A privateer during the War of the Spanish Succession (1701–1714), he turned pirate and harassed merchant ships plying the seas between Virginia and the Caribbean. Already tall and muscular, Blackbeard further cultivated his appearance to give fright. He had eyebrows like small shrubs, and in a time when beards weren't common, he let his grow and would braid it and tie it up with colorful ribbons, which he would "turn about his ears." As a final flourish, he would tuck slow-burning, smoky fuses made of hemp cord, saltpeter, and lime under his hat, and ignite them during battle, moving about in a wreath of acrid smoke, like an emissary from the underworld. In one eighteen-month period, he captured some twenty ships.

Blackbeard's fondness for rum was legendary. He and his crew would make stops on islands between harrying raids for feasting and indulging in massive quantities of drink. "Rum was never his master," wrote his biographer, Robert Lee. "He could handle it as no other man of his day, and he was never known to pass out from an excess." Among his cocktails was a potion of gunpowder mixed with rum, which he would ignite and swill while it flamed and popped.

Blackbeard's career ended, as pirate careers often did, with extravagant bloodshed. He had set himself up in November 1718 along the Outer Banks of North Carolina, using Ocracoke Island as a base for his ship, the *Adventure Galley*. Governor Alexander Spotswood of Virginia found the harassment of traders increasingly intolerable and sent out a pair of naval sloops, the *Pearl* and the *Lyme,* to put an end to it. On the evening of November 21, the two ships came upon the *Adventure Galley* at anchor with Blackbeard and about two dozen of his men aboard. The sloops dropped anchor as the sun set and prepared for a morning engagement.

Blackbeard and his men readied for battle the way they knew best: They drank heartily. Some days earlier, Blackbeard had written of a melancholy predicament in his ship's log: "Such a day, rum all out:—Our company somewhat sober:—A damned confusion among us!" He overheard talk of insurrection among his men, and at length, succeeded in sacking a ship with "a great deal of liquor on board, so kept the company hot, damned hot; then all things went well again."

At first, all went well on the morning of November 22. The dawn encounter began with missteps by the Virginia sloops, which ran aground on sandbars that Blackbeard knew to avoid. Freed after tossing ballast and water casks overboard, the government sloops resumed pursuit and caught up with the *Adventure Galley*.

Blackbeard fought with his accustomed vigor, firing volleys of shot and old iron from a cannon, which killed the captain of the *Lyme* and dismasted the ship. The crew of the *Pearl*, undaunted, closed in on Blackbeard. According to newspaper accounts, the pirate taunted the sloop as it neared, calling the crews "cowardly puppies," then hoisted aloft a drinking glass (of "liquor" in some accounts, "wine" in others) to Lieutenant Robert Maynard of the *Pearl*, yelling, "Damnation seize my Soul if I give you Quarter, or take any from you." Maynard hollered back that he expected no quarter, nor would he give any.

Blackbeard leaped aboard Maynard's ship with ten of his men, assuming that his volleys had decimated the crew. He was in for a surprise. All but two of Maynard's men were hiding beneath the decks with weapons readied; when they swarmed onto the deck, Blackbeard and his men found themselves outnumbered. They fought fiercely. Maynard's fingers were wounded by a slash from Blackbeard; his men swarmed to his aid. One of Maynard's men, a stout Scottish Highlander, landed a blow that sliced Blackbeard on the neck. At this, the pirate called out, "Well done, lad!" The Scotsman wasn't finished. According to the account in the *Boston News Letter*, the Highlander replied, "If it not be well done, I'll do it better." With that, he gave him a second blow, which cut off his head, "laying it flat on his shoulder." Blackbeard went down not only headless and lacerated with horrific gashes, but with five bullets in him.

Blackbeard's head was suspended from the bowsprit of the captured *Adventure Galley,* which Maynard sailed back to Williamsburg, Virginia. He turned over the head, the sloop, and the pirate's effects to his commander.

That wasn't the end of Blackbeard's head. After serving as an ornament suspended from a tall pole at the entrance to Hampton River, a grisly memo to would-be pirates, the head was taken down. The skull, it's been widely reported, was later adorned with silver plate and crafted into the base for a bowl from which rum punch was served at the Raleigh Tavern in Williamsburg. People still claim they know of people who knew of other people who once drank from it, but no one really knows what, at last, came of Blackbeard's head.

IF YOU COME across a pirate and he bellows for "grog," he is, in all likelihood, not a real pirate. Grog was invented well after the decline and fall of piracy, becoming an improbable symbol of order, rather than disorder, on the high seas. To understand how this happened, we must switch to the other side: the British navy ships that were the bane of pirates.

Rum was first officially doled out to British navy sailors in 1655, during the triumphant British assault on Jamaica. We do not know why, but we can surmise. Drinking water was exceedingly difficult to store on long ocean voyages, especially in the tropics: It would became algae-ridden and musty in its casks. Beer was a reasonable alternative: The modest alcohol content kept it from fouling, but the taste tended to go off, and sailors commonly groused about "stinking beer." French brandy and Spanish wines, especially rosolio and mistela, were popular. (Sailors took to calling the latter "Miss Taylor.") But these were difficult to provision with any consistency to ships stationed in the West Indies.

Then there was rum. This new spirit was increasingly abundant on the islands, especially in Antigua and Barbados, as more sugar planters imported stills to convert their waste molasses into a marketable commodity. Rum had the merit of remaining sweet almost indefinitely in a cask and improving in flavor over time as the wood of the cask tempered the harsher qualities of the sharp-edged distillate. It also had the advantage of being more potent than beer or wine and so required less room for storage than its lower-alcohol kin.

Another push to distribute rum aboard British navy ships came from the island planters, who envisioned the growing British navy as a lucrative market. By 1769, the Society of West India Merchants had organized themselves sufficiently to commission the writing and printing of three thousand copies of a booklet entitled *An Essay on Spirituous Liquors, with Regard to Their Effects on Health, in Which the Comparative Wholesomeness of Rum and Brandy Are Particularly Considered.* Rum, it should come as no surprise to hear, was found the more wholesome. A decade later, the naval provisioning office was officially authorized to contract for West Indian rum to replace brandy in ship stores. It was among the earliest, but by no means the last, instance of the sugar and rum industry organizing to ensure its economic good health. Island plantation owners could cooperate when need be, and they would do so most effectively in ensuring their own interests at the expense of the northern colonies in the run-up to the American Revolution.

An overly fertile imagination is not needed to understand the broader appeal of a midday dram of rum to the common seaman. The naval sailor was typically in his mid-twenties (the average age in the early eighteenth century was twenty-seven), and he was likely from a poor family, for the well-off tended not to embrace the great risks and endless unpleasantries of life at sea. The life of an eighteenth-century mariner could be appallingly bleak—stuck in cramped quarters with unhygienic men, many of whom no doubt suffered from ailments of the lower gastrointestinal tract. A sailor's private quarters consisted of just enough space below decks in which to sling a hammock, plus a small trunk in which to stash possessions. As Marcus Rediker has pointed out in his study of eighteenth-century seaman, life at sea was rarely a matter of man against nature. It was man against man aboard floating prisons. "Their isolation was communal," he wrote. "They could escape neither their loneliness nor each other."

Drink offered brief escape. The officers and crew would drink to relieve the tedium of shipboard life and to smooth over tensions. They drank to forget life between the decks, to warm up to their fellow crewmen, and to toast to the king, their wives, their mistresses. One seaman wrote in 1723 that he "never had any great fancy for fuddling," but tippled more "for the love of my company than for the drink." Also, rum was safe and relatively palatable, whereas the food on board was neither. "Good liquor to sailors," wrote Woodes Rogers, an English privateer and later governor of the Bahamas, "is preferable to clothing." In Tobias Smollett's novel *The Adventures of Roderick Random* (1748), rum was called "Necessity." Nothing rang better in a sailor's ear than the call to "splice the main brace"—the euphemism for doling out rum. This is attributed to the hard work needed to repair a parted main brace, or the stoutest of the running rigging, and seamen who accomplished the task were typically rewarded with a double ration of rum.

For a captain stationed in the West Indies in the early eighteenth century, balancing morale and discipline was made all the more difficult by the distribution of rum rations. Tipsy sailors were more likely to be injured—it's difficult enough to scramble about the rigging in a galloping swell or blustery wind when stone sober, never mind while drunk. And rum could inflame the passions and cause smoldering frictions between seamen to combust.

Rum-induced crises did not go unnoticed by Admiral Edward Vernon of the British Royal Navy. The admiral was well educated, much admired by his men, and possessed of an uncommon competence. (Lawrence Washington, George Washington's half brother, named his Virginia estate after him, and George kept the name Mount Vernon when he inherited the plantation.) Vernon served in the West Indies between 1698 and 1712, commanding a sixty-gun ship, and by 1739 had been elevated to vice admiral. That happened to be the year that England declared war on Spain—the so-called War of Jenkins' Ear—which was triggered when the master of a British merchant vessel had his ear cut off by a vengeful Spanish captain.

Vernon regarded rum as a competitor for his men's affections, noting that its charms often led to men permanently abandoning their posts. Vernon wrote in a letter to the Admiralty that some five hundred seamen had vanished from Jamaica "since being in my command; which I believe to have all been seduced out and gone home with the homeward bound trade, through the temptations of high wages and 30 gallons of rum, and being generally conveyed drunk onboard their ships from the punch houses where they are seduced."

Vernon assailed the "pernicious custom of the seamen drinking their allowance of rum in drams, and often at once." This resulted in "many fatal effects to their morals as well as their health, which are visibly impaired thereby." What's more, rum, quaffed straight, caused a "stupefying [of] their rational qualities, which makes them heedlessly slaves to every passion." Distributing copious amounts of potent rum, Vernon realized, was not a formula for building a navy that would dominate the maritime world.

The alcoholic content of early rum is unknown to us because it was unknown to those who consumed it. Not until 1816 was the Sikes hydrometer invented, which made it possible to measure the percentage of alcohol in liquor. Before that, alcohol content was determined by mixing the spirit with a few grains of gunpowder and then subjecting the concoction to the focused rays of the sun under a magnifier. If the gunpowder managed to ignite but the liquid didn't flare up, this was said to be "proof" of its proper alcoholic content.

What was Vernon to do? Eliminating the rum ration would likely give rise to mutinies or, at the least, a sullen crankiness among seamen who had learned to live from tot to tot. So Vernon fashioned an alternative strategy: He would dilute the rum.

In an order issued at Port Royal in 1740, Vernon called for rum served to naval crews to be "mixed with the proportion of a quart of water to every half pint of rum," resulting in a concoction that was one part rum to four parts water. To ensure that the effects on the men would be reduced, Vernon decreed that this diluted rum was to be served over two sessions daily, rather than at once, as had been the custom. Between ten in the morning and noon, the first tot was to be ladled out, and the second between four and six in the afternoon. Because the mixing of rum and water left itself open to shortchanging by dishonest pursers—and the general belief among seamen was that every purser was dishonest—Vernon's edict required that mixing occur on deck, "and in the presence of the Lieutenant of the Watch, who is to take particular care to see that the men are not defrauded in having their full allowance of rum." (The writer Edward Ward reserved a special wrath for the purser: "The worser Liquor he keeps, the more he brews his own Profit," Ward groused, and "he shall draw more Gain from wretched gripe-gut Stuff, in one Forenoon, than a Dozen Ale-wives from all their Taps, on a Day of Thanksgiving.")

The order for diluted rum was circulated throughout the fleet, and the new drink made its way from the West India station throughout the Royal Navy over the next two decades. By 1756, the daily distribution of watered rum was codified in the Admiralty's naval code.

The new, less-potent ration needed a name. It was no longer rum, and it no longer had the kick to be called kill-devil. An ingenious solution presented itself to some anonymous seaman. Vernon had a fondness for wearing a coat made of a material called "grogram," a woven fabric stiffened and weatherproofed with gum. Vernon's nickname among sailors was "Old Grogram," and so his new rum was dubbed "grog." The name stuck.

In grog, one also finds evidence of a proto-West Indian cocktail, an early precursor to the daiquiri and the mojito. Vernon's 1740 order to distribute grog rather than "neat" rum included a provision that allowed crewmen to exchange their salt and bread allotment for "sugar and limes to make [grog] more palatable to them." Although the order was likely issued with the sailor's palate, rather than his health, in mind, it had an unexpectedly tonic effect. Scurvy had been devastating sailors for years with bleeding gums, sore joints, loose teeth, and a slow healing of wounds, but it was still a great medical mystery. Rum was issued as a preventative, but later experiments, starting in 1747, identified the cause as a deficiency of ascorbic acid—found in citrus fruit, among other things. By 1753, the Scottish surgeon James Lind had proved that a regimen of juices from lemons, limes, or oranges would keep scurvy away. Two years later, the naval regulations called for a half-ounce of lemon or lime juice per day "to be mixed with grog or wine." English sailors became known as limeys. And so Vernon, by luck or instinct, was well ahead of the movement toward citrus.

Over time, the dispensing of grog became more fixed and cere-monial. The pseudonymous Jack Nastyface (a common nickname for a cook's assistant) wrote in 1805 that the time around noon was "the pleasantest . . . of the day," since that's when the "piper is called to play *Nancy Dawson* or some other lively tune, a well known signal that the grog is ready to be served out." The purser would haul to the open deck a premeasured portion, with each of the crew allotted one-half cup of rum per session. The mixing water would be tested to en-sure it wasn't salty. If it passed muster, the grog would be blended and promptly doled out, often to the cook, who would in turn distribute it to his messmates below decks. The ritual would be repeated in the late afternoon.

Even diluted, the grog ration was still equivalent to about five cocktails per day, assuming an ounce and a half of rum per cocktail. That's an agreeable amount by any standard. Perhaps too agreeable.

As the navy became more professional and the temperance movement gained a foothold, grog rations fell further into disfavor. In 1823, the ration was cut in half, and then halved again in 1850—effectively slashing the rum allotment by three-quarters in less than three decades. The nineteenth-century writer and sailor Richard Dana, author of *Two Years Before the Mast,* groused that cutting back rations was a curious way to promote the idea that "temperance is their friend," since it "takes from them what they always had, and gives them nothing in place." In fact, the navy did provide some compensatory reward, often greater rations of tea, cocoa, and meat, as well as a token increase in pay.

And there was other good news: As the quantity of rum diminished, its quality improved. The navy's longtime blender and supplier of rum, E D & F Man, decided to appeal to the more discerning tastes of officers, and British naval rum developed an almost cultish following among navy men. The exact blend codified by the Admiralty in 1810 was a highly guarded secret. (It was, broadly, a blend of heavy rums from Guyana and Trinidad, leavened with three lighter rums.)

The British custom of serving up daily tots persisted into the twentieth century, a feral habit that resisted eradication even as it fell out of favor with crewmen. By the 1950s, only about a third of a hundred thousand British sailors opted for their daily grog rations. As navy operations become more complex and computers and advanced weapons systems demanded more mental acuity than hauling tar buckets, questions surfaced about the wisdom of distributing rum to sailors on duty. The advent of the Breathalyzer didn't help: A British newspaper unsportingly pointed out that sailors could be legally drunk after consuming their allotted grog rations.

By 1970, it was hard to ignore the clamor to eliminate the Royal Navy's daily rum ration. The House of Commons debated the matter; the secretary of the navy, sensing a looming defeat, lobbied for just compensation. In lieu of rum rations, a lump sum of £2.7 million was donated to the Sailor's Fund, which paid for such things as excursions for sailors in foreign ports and improved equipment for discotheques on naval bases.

July 31, 1970, is known in British naval circles as Black Tot Day—that last day rum was officially rationed out to sailors. On British navy ships around the globe, sailors wore black armbands and attended mock funerals. Among the more elaborate affairs was a ceremony aboard the HMS *Fife,* a guided-missile destroyer then in port at Pearl Harbor in Hawaii. It was the closest ship to the international date line and thus the last in the Royal Navy to serve rum. The crewmen mustered on the top deck, tossed back their rations, and heaved their glasses overboard, along with the whole rum barrel. The historic moment was marked with a twenty-one-gun salute. And so ended a 325-year tradition.

Naval rum had a second, somewhat debased life. In 1980, the Admiralty Board voted to release the secret formula for the blend to Charles Tobias, an American entrepreneur who believed that it would find a ready market among retired sailors and a public intrigued by its lore. In exchange, Tobias pledged to pay ongoing royalties from rum sales into the Sailor's Fund. The rum was called Pusser's, slang for "purser." This heavy, flavorful spirit is still manufactured and sold throughout much of the world.

THERE IS ONE further matter to address. Where did the most famous rum-related phrase come from, and what does it mean? You know the one: "Yo-ho-ho and . . ." Well, if you don't know how it goes, flip to the cover of this book. The phrase goes back to at least August 1881, the month that a thirty-one-year-old writer settled in with his young family at a holiday cottage in Braemar, Scotland. His name was Robert Louis Stevenson, and his fame at the time had as much to do with his family—noted lighthouse keepers—as for anything he had written. One stormy, rain-lashed afternoon, Stevenson came upon his twelve-year-old stepson, Lloyd Osbourne, drawing a fanciful map of a make-believe island to pass the hours. Stevenson scribbled some place-names and wrote "Treasure Island" in an upper corner. The map seemed to call for more elaboration, so he set about composing a story to go with it, reading it aloud in the evenings over the following two weeks. The dull parts were edited out by Lloyd, who, like any sensible twelve-year-old, was interested only in untimely deaths, the discovery of duplicity, or both. Stevenson later described the process as "not writing, just drive along as the words come and the pen will scratch."

A houseguest suggested Stevenson send the story to *Young Folks,* a magazine for boys. The editor bought it for £30 and published it as a serial in the fall and winter of 1881 and 1882 under the pseudonym of Capt. George North. The tale didn't attract much attention until it was republished in book form in 1883 and became one of the best-selling books of all time.

Treasure Island shaped the public perception of pirates, and so did the American artist N. C. Wyeth, who illustrated a popular edition of it. In 1904, Stevenson's countryman, James Matthew Barrie, created Captain Hook in *Peter Pan.* Pirates would no longer be portrayed as murderous bandits who forced innocents to eat their own offal. They became figures of romance: one-legged scoundrels with foppish hats, squawking parrots, and hooks instead of hands. They became caricatures, and caricatures they would remain.

Rum didn't make its literary debut in *Treasure Island*—Robinson Crusoe discovered "three large runlets" of it on his fictional island in 1719. But Stevenson uses it as a motif. The pirate Billy Bones displays an abiding fondness for the stuff. ("I lived on rum," he tells the young protagonist, Jim. "It's been meat and drink, and man and wife, to me.") It's a predilection shared by other pirates, among them the unfortunate Captain Flint, who died on the gallows in Savannah bellowing for rum, not unlike Captain Kidd.

But the most defining appearance of rum is the nonsensical ditty first muttered by Billy Bones and repeated (and repeated) by the other pirates:

"Fifteen men on the dead man's chest
Yo-ho-ho, and a bottle of rum!
Drink and the Devil had done for the rest
Yo-ho-ho and a bottle of rum!"

It's a dark and odd little rhyme, evidently composed by the author—although some have speculated that it was based on a traditional sea chantey, now lost. Although it doesn't make much sense, it fired the public imagination, becoming the nineteenth-century equivalent of an Abba song, something that becomes lodged in one's brain quite against one's will. Ten years later, Young E. Allison, the American editor of a trade journal called the *Insurance Field,* stretched those lines out into a much longer narrative poem entitled "On Board the Derelict." A decade after that, Allison's poem became the basis of a Broadway play and anchored itself in the popular imagination. To this day if you say "yo-ho-ho" to any native English speaker, the odds are that they'll complete it.

Pirates and rum would never be separated again.

[FLIP]

Mix *one cup* BEER [a stout like Guinness works best], *two tablespoons* of MOLASSES, and *one ounce* Jamaican-style RUM into *mug* or *tankard*. Heat *loggerhead* to red hot in an open fire [a fireplace poker knocked clean of ashes will do], then thrust into drink. Keep loggerhead in place *until foaming and sputtering ceases*. Drink hot.

Chapter 3

[FLIP]

Have been genteely treated and am now going to be
drunk. This is the first time.　　[*November 30, 1775*]

All of us got most feloniously drunk.
　　　　　　　　　　　　　　[*January 6, 1776*]

Went to bed about two o'clock in the afternoon, stupidly
drunk.　　　　　　　　　[*January 7, 1776*]

Spent evening at the Tavern.... A confounded mad
frolic.　　　　　　　　[*February 19, 1776*]

Got most feloniously drunk. This is a bad preface to the
new volume of my diary.　　　[*October 1, 1776*]

A very mad frolic this evening. Set the house on fire
three times and broke Mr. Dream's leg... got drunk and
committed a number of foolish actions.
　　　　　　　　　　　　　[*November 19, 1776*]

—FROM THE JOURNALS OF
NICHOLAS CRESSWELL, A BRITISH TRAVELER
IN THE NORTH AMERICAN COLONIES

D R. ALEXANDER HAMILTON—not to be confused with Mr. Alexander Hamilton of the $10 bill—was faring poorly in late 1743. A Scottish physician who had left cosmopolitan Edinburgh for the more rustic colonial life of Annapolis, Maryland, Hamilton had been plagued by "fevers and bloody spitting" and "an Incessant cough," and had nearly died from consumption. But by early 1744, his health was on the rebound. To complete his cure, Hamilton prescribed for himself an outsized dose of fresh air. So off he went on a four-month, sixteen-hundred-mile journey through the northern colonies, traveling as far as the province of Maine (then part of Massachusetts) before heading home. He spent most of his time in the cultural citadels of Philadelphia, New York, and Boston, traveling between them by horse and boat, and laying over at taverns in smaller towns and along rural byways. Hamilton's detailed journals capture a colorful slice of mid-eighteenth-century tavern life.

Shortly after he set off, Hamilton wrote of arriving at a Maryland tavern called Treadway's, where he found a drinking club concluding its order of business. "Most of them had got upon their horses and were seated in an oblique situation," he wrote, "deviating much from a perpendicular to the horizontal plane, a posture quite necessary for keeping the center of gravity within its proper base for the support of the superstructure; hence we deduce the true physical reason why our heads overloaded with liquor become too ponderous for our heels. Their discourse was . . . an inarticulate sound like Rabelais' frozen words athawing, interlaced with hiccupings and belchings." The tavern's landlord offered some excuses for the rowdy behavior of his guests. "While he spoke thus," Hamilton continued, "our Bacchanalians, finding no more rum in play, rid off helter skelter as if the devil had possessed them, every man sitting his horse in a see-saw manner like a bunch of rags tyed upon the saddle."

Hamilton discovered on his tour what most colonists well knew: The British North American colonies had become a Republic of Rum. Starting about 1700, the colonial taste for home-brewed beer and hard cider began to fade and was displaced by an abiding thirst for stronger liquors. Rum turned up everywhere, in homes and doctor's offices, in clattering seaports and rough-edged inland villages. With its arrival came a fundamental shift in the colony's political, economic, and social alignments. If grog was an emblem of the triumph of order over disorder on the open seas, rum—especially in the form of a popular drink called "flip"—was a symbol of the new order displacing the old in the colonies.

THE FIRST PURITANS to settle the northern colonies brought not only a thirst for drink, but the drink itself. When the Pilgrims arrived in New England in 1620, beer was among their supplies. When they exhausted it, they started brewing it. It was a story repeated throughout the colonies, as settlers from England, Holland, France, Sweden, and Germany arrived with their Old World tastes intact. The beer favored in many northern colonies was typically 6 percent alcohol, heavy and dark, and probably tasted rather like modern-day stouts or porters. Enterprising colonists loath to sacrifice good grain made beer from Indian corn and pumpkin, sometimes flavoring it with birch or spruce bark.

Also found in the better colonial cabinets were imported wines, especially Madeira, which could be shipped directly from the Portuguese islands off the coast of Africa without roundabout routing or fraudulent paperwork. (Trade with most wine-producing nations was prohibited by the British Navigation Acts; an exception was made for the Atlantic islands.) The Madeira was not of the highest quality—it wasn't fortified to develop its distinctive flavor until later in the eighteenth century—but it was still a welcome luxury, and one that most of those who were eking out a life in the colonies could ill afford.

Hard cider was the most popular drink among the settlers, at least from the apple-growing regions of Virginia northward. It could be made with almost no effort or investment. A single tree could produce enough apples for five or six barrels of cider, and then a farmer needed only patience for it to ferment. Even without a still, cider could be made into higher-proof applejack in winter just by leaving it outdoors to freeze, then skimming off the watery slush. Hard cider was versatile: A mug served warm in winter chased away the chill, and in summer could be diluted and flavored with nutmeg. But cider was less than ideal: It caused gastric distress if consumed too early, and was vinegary if drunk too late. And as Israel Acrelius wrote in his 1753 history of Swedish settlements in North America, some colonists believed that cider "produces rust and verdigris, and frightens some from its use, by fear that it may have the same effect in the body."

Alcohol's appeal was enhanced by the colonists' deep-seated distrust of water. This apprehension had been imported from Europe, where crowded, contaminated cities made free-flowing water unfit to drink. The pristine lakes and tumbling rivers of the New World were regarded with a similarly dark suspicion—concerns not eased by stories of the first Virginia settlers in 1607. "They have nothing but bread of maize, with fish; nor do they drink anything but water," wrote one appalled visitor. As a result, "the majority [were] sick and badly treated." Once the long-suffering colonists in Virginia started to import alcoholic beverages, their health improved markedly. Water, it was thought, was suitable for hogs and cows, but for human consumption only in dire emergencies.

The leaders of the early colonies, including the famously dour Puritan elders, gave their stamp of approval to the drinking of fermented beverages, and regarded beer, cider, and wine, like sunshine and apples, as gifts to be revered. "Drink is in itself a creature of God," said minister Increase Mather in 1673, "and to be received with thankfulness."

And then came rum.

VARIOUS STRONG SPIRITS had arrived in the northern colonies before rum. When John Winthrop sailed aboard the Puritan ship *Arbella* in 1630, he groused that "a Common fault in our yonge people [is] that they gave themselves to drink hot waters very immoderately." (He failed to specify what those spirits were.) A crude whiskey made out of the leavings of fermented beer was distilled by a Dutchman near Manhattan as early as 1640. And primitive backyard stills, called "lembics," were not uncommon in the colonies; they were useful for making spirits out of fermented honey and pears and, in the southern colonies, from peaches.

But this petty dabbling in strong drink did little to prepare colonial society for the arrival of the vast merchant fleets trafficking with the sugar islands. Barrels of rum soon clattered through teeming colonial ports of Boston, Philadelphia, and Newport, shipped in from the West Indies in great wooden casks from which storekeepers and taverners could dispense smaller quantities by jug or mug. The cost of imported Barbados rum fell by about a third between 1673 and 1687 as the supply soared, then rose slightly before leveling off. In current dollars, a fifth of rum cost about $4 in 1700, or half the price of a bottle of inexpensive rum today. Cotton Mather, the son of Increase Mather, lamented that it took but "a penny or two" to get drunk on rum.

Almost overnight, rum found its way into nearly every aspect of colonial life. A colonist would toss back a dram in the morning to shake off the night chills and to launch the day in proper form. Steeplejacks would clamber down from their labors for dinner at midday and, in the words of Rev. Elijah Kellogg, "would partake of rum, salt-fish, and crackers." During the bleak northern winters, alcohol provided tinder to warm one's insides, and in the sweltering southern summers rum aided in perspiration and cooling. In the evenings, a dram of rum helped with digestion at supper, and afterward a few rounds of rum cemented the bonds of friendship at a local tavern. Rum was not just a diversion; it was nutritionally vital to colonists who labored to coax a meager sustenance out of a rocky, stump-filled landscape and cold seas. Alcohol has fewer calories per ounce than straight fat but about the same as butter. It's five times more caloric than lean meat, and has ten times the calories of whole milk. A bottle of rum squirreled away in a Grand Banks fishing dory provided the energy to haul nets and aided in choking down hardtack and salt cod. Farmers, timber cutters, coopers, and shipbuilders soon learned that a dram of rum made a long day shorter.

Rum was embraced in sickness and in health, and for better or worse. Rum was the first remedy when feeling punky and was taken liberally as a restorative. Leaves of the tansy plant were steeped in rum to create tansy bitters, which was a popular cure-all in colonial homes. Children were given rum to cure minor ailments, and rum was employed to soothe the chills and fevers from malaria in the southern colonies. A colonial diarist wrote that following an illness his doctor told him to drink "a little more Rum than I did before I was sick" and warned him that "being too abstemious" was likely the cause of his problems. Swedish traveler Peter Kalm noted that by 1750 rum had come to be considered far healthier among English North American colonists than spirits distilled from grain or wine: "In confirmation of this opinion they say that if you put a piece of fresh meat into rum and another into brandy, and leave them there for a few months, that in the rum will keep as it was, but that in the brandy will be eaten full of holes."

Rum was always on hand for emergencies. Published instructions for reviving victims of drowning in Massachusetts called for blowing tobacco smoke up the victim's rectum (machines were built specifically for this purpose) while bathing the victim's breast with hot rum. If rum failed to restore you to life, it would be served to those who attended your funeral, even if you were poorly off, since the purchase of spirits for a final send-off had priority over paying off your creditors.

Rum ingrained itself in the emerging civic culture of the colonies. A major public building project always meant drinking, and rum was doled out liberally to citizens who helped raise a barn or meetinghouse. It was also widely accepted as currency in cash-poor colonies, swapped for insurance premiums, for the construction of new buildings, and used to tip workers for services well done. Employers budgeted for rum and molasses; hires expected it both as payment and as a liquid enticement to remain on task. A 1645 law in Massachusetts sought to forbid colonists from paying workers with drink, but the decree was ignored. When the economist Adam Smith published *The Wealth of Nations* in 1776, he noted that ship carpenters earned "ten shillings and sixpence currency, with a pint of rum worth sixpence sterling." And the records show that in the mid-eighteenth century, Paul Revere's mother, recently widowed, paid her rent with a mix of cash, rum, and a silver thimble.

If shipments of rum overwhelmed the local market and contributed to a brief price drop, merchants could warehouse it; not only was it not perishable, but it also improved—and could be sold for more— with age. The larger peril was receiving a shipment of rum so bad that no one would take it. Certain islands developed reputations, some favorable and some not. Rums from Barbados, Antigua, Montserrat, and Grenada, and increasingly from Jamaica, were considered among the finest, and commanded higher prices in the colonial seaports. Rums from Tobago were regarded as reasonably palatable. Rums to be avoided included those from St. Vincent, Dominica, and Nevis, islands that were known to cheat their customers by shortchanging their fermentation tanks of molasses. (If a distiller used less than one gallon of molasses to make one gallon of rum, it was thought to result in a more wretched product.)

Merchants trusted their onboard masters sailing abroad to contract for the best quality rum, although fraud and bait-and-switch gambits were endemic. George Moore, an eighteenth-century trader on England's Isle of Man, larded his letters with references to being swindled. One batch was "deficient in every of the known qualities of Barbados rum." After a Scotsman sold him five thousand gallons of "good Barbados," Moore found that he ended up with "very bad, not merchantable Barbados rum." Poor-quality rum lingered in the shops and taverns and could be sold only for less than the merchant had paid for it.

RUM CAME, AND rum went, often alighting only briefly in Boston or Newport before being shipped to other coastal colonies. Among the more popular destinations were the British fishing villages that ringed the island of Newfoundland (where cold, damp fishermen eagerly swapped rum for dried cod) and the tobacco plantations of Virginia (whose owners were notorious for promising payments that would never be made). Rum also moved inland to the frontier and far from the thin coastal veneer of European colonial society. Some colonists packed rum to keep warm while hunting and trapping. But an increasing number discovered it more profitable to cart casks of rum to remote forts and trading posts, where it could be traded to great advantage with the Indians.

The first European settlers found much to fault in the appearance, manners, and morals of the natives they first encountered along North American shores. But what may have irked them most was their stubborn lack of interest in becoming consumers. The eastern woodland Indians simply didn't have vast needs—they made what they wore and hunted or grew what they ate.

The Indians were tremendously skillful hunters, able to amass great stocks of beaver and mink pelts that colonial traders coveted. Furs in the seventeenth century were, like sugar, a luxury item reserved for noblemen who sought to convey their lofty social status. Indians were at first willing to swap pelts for trifles like beads, glass, mirrors, woven blankets, combs, and kettles. But the thrill of gazing at one's neatly parted hair in a mirror evidently wore off quickly, and the demand for baubles dried up. Traders needed something else to exchange for furs, something easy to obtain that would create its own demand.

Rum would be the ticket.

Tribes in southwestern North America—parts of Mexico and what would become the southwestern United States—were passingly familiar with alcohol even before the great overland Spanish expeditions lumbered through with their brandy. Many knew how to brew a drink of fermented corn, which was used chiefly in ceremonies. The eastern Indians, on the other hand, had no tradition or truck with any sort of alcohol. Fiery rum, like wine and beer, was as bizarre as it was magical, and the first sip must have been as startling and powerful as hearing the first report of a rifle. New words had to be invented to describe it and the behavior it provoked.

At prevailing rates of exchange, a trader might be able to double his money by trading furs for blankets or cookware. Rum was far more profitable—it could be traded for at least four times what it cost. Even better margins could be had by watering it down—a keg could be diluted by one-third without raising a fuss. Traders so clamored for rum that for years it cost more in New York, a major base for fur traders heading up the Hudson, than it did in Boston or Philadelphia.

In the late seventeenth century, rum dribbled into the mountains and woodlands, but by early the next century it had swelled into a torrent. A glass of rum would open negotiations between traders and Indians as a sign of friendship and good faith, and it would close negotiations to seal the deal. Rum also was often consumed during the business at hand, if for no other reason than the Indians asked for it, and the traders—having dispensed with the friendship and good faith part of the transaction—preferred to barter with someone whose power of reasoning was compromised. (John Lederer, in his 1672 account of trade with the Indians, boasted that with liquor one could "dispose them to a humour of giving you ten times the value of your commodity.") Rum was also brought out for feasts and toasts: Indian traders were often happy to toast to King George, whomever he might be. An agent to the Choctaws estimated that liquor accounted for four-fifths of trade with the natives in 1770, and superintendent of Indian affairs in the southeast estimated in 1776 that ten thousand gallons of rum was moving in trade to the Indians *every month*. Most was exchanged for furs, but traders often held back a few bottles for buying sex with young "trading girls," the exact cost of which was negotiated with the tribal leader.

For their part, shrewder Indians tried to bargain for goods other than rum, but the colonial traders often proved adept at convincing them to settle for spirits. "When our people come from Hunting to the Town or Plantations and acquaint the traders & People that we want Powder and Shot & Clothing, they first give us a large cup of Rum," complained Aupaumut, a Mohican, to the governor of New York in 1722. As a result, "all the Beaver & Peltry we have hunted goes for drink, and we are left destitute either of Clothing or ammunition." In 1754, Governor Arthur Dobbs of North Carolina hosted eleven hundred Indians at a trading session, and provided them with meat and abundant liquor. "By repeated presents and liquor," the governor reported, the Cherokees were persuaded to relinquish their claims on lands toward the Mississippi to the British Crown.

Rum also served broader strategic purposes, underwriting the equivalent of a Great Wall that arced from northern New England down the Appalachian Mountains. The wall protected the British from the meddlesome French, who had settled along the St. Lawrence River in present-day Canada and moved freely on the west side of the Appalachian Mountains. By providing the Indians with rum, the British diverted them from allying with the French, who were proving increasingly deft in their incursions on British settlements. Without the free flow of rum, Indians might have turned to the French for brandy. Some historians have suggested that a general preference for the taste of rum over brandy actually kept some tribes from defecting to the French.

As a weapon, rum came up short in one major respect: It tore apart the Indian civilization it sought to recruit. In his history of South Carolina and Georgia (1779), Alexander Hewatt noted that the downfall of the impressive Indian nation was due to many colliding forces: capture and enslavement to the West Indies; smallpox infection; denying access to coastal lands and fertile soils; and warfare with other tribes after Europeans forced them to share ever-shrinking territory. "But of all the causes," Hewatt continued, "the introduction of spirituous liquors among them, for which they discovered an amazing fondness, has proved the most destructive."

Few of those who encountered eastern Indians in the colonial era failed to remark on the effect of alcohol. Intoxicated Indians were variously likened to "mad foaming bears, "many raging devils," and "a gang of devils that had broke loose from hell." Nicholas Cresswell wrote in his journal during travels in Ohio and Indiana in 1775 that the Indians he encountered were "inclined much to silence, except when in liquor which they are very fond of, and then they are very loquacious committing the greatest outrages upon each other." In the early 1770s, a British official visiting the Choctaws reported that he "saw nothing but Rum Drinking and Women Crying over the Dead bodies of their relations who have died by Rum."

What's likely the most quoted account of Indians and alcohol was written by Benjamin Franklin, who was among those negotiating a treaty with a large delegation in Pennsylvania. The Indians asked for rum during the negotiations; Franklin resisted, believing that they would become "very quarrelsome and disorderly" and derail the talks. But Franklin assured them after business was concluded, they'd have "plenty of rum." He was good to his word. As he recalled in his autobiography, they

> claim'd and receiv'd the rum; this was in the afternoon; they were near one hundred men, women, and children, and were lodg'd in temporary cabins, built in the form of a square, just without the town. In the evening, hearing a great noise among them, the commissioners walk'd out to see what was the matter. We found they had made a great bonfire in the middle of the square; they were all drunk, men and women, quarreling and fighting. Their dark-colour'd bodies, half naked, seen only by the gloomy light of the bonfire, running after and beating one another with firebrands, accompanied by their horrid yellings, form'd a scene the most resembling our ideas of hell that could well be imagin'd; there was no appeasing the tumult, and we retired to our lodging. At midnight a number of them came thundering at our door, demanding more rum, of which we took no notice.

Some colonists could not ignore the wrenching effect of rum on the tribes and tried to restrict the trade. This was less altruism than self-defense—colonists believed that rum-sodden Indians were more likely than sober Indians to attack settlements. In 1772, an agent to the tribes reported to his superintendent, "Unless there is a stop to sending Rum in such large quantities amongst the Indians no man will be safe among them."

The tribes themselves also pushed to ban the rum trade. "Rum," said Shawnee chief Benewisco in 1768, "is the thing that makes us

Indians poor & foolish." Another Shawnee chief wrote that the white people "come and bring rum into our towns, offer it to the Indians, and say, drink; this they will do until they become quite beside themselves and act as though they were out of their heads. . . . The white people [then] stand, point at them with their fingers, laugh at them and say to one another, see what great fools the Shawanose are. But who makes them so foolish, who is at fault?"

Efforts to curb the trade started early. Trading liquor with Indians was made illegal in Massachusetts in the 1630s, in New Hampshire in the 1640s, and in New Netherland in 1643. (The ban did not sit well with Dutch traders, who thought that "to prohibit all strong liquor to [the Indians] seems very hard and very Turkish. Rum doth as little hurt as the Frenchman's Brandie, and on the whole is much more wholesome.") Rhode Island banned the trade in 1654, Pennsylvania in the 1680s. South Carolina banned the sale of liquor to Indians on their own lands in 1691, and banned rum trade to all Indians in 1707, in an "Act Regulating the Indian Trade and Making it Safe to the Publick." Indians were also banned from taverns throughout the colonies.

Although they varied from colony to colony, the restrictions were dealt with in a uniform manner: They were revoked, watered down, or simply ignored. The interests of the merchants, traders, and settlers in the remote regions outweighed concerns about intoxicated rampages or the destruction of Indian culture.

"Little Turtle petitioned me to prohibit rum to be sold to his nation for a very good reason," wrote former president John Adams to a friend in 1811. "He said, I had lost three thousand of my Indian children in his nation in one year by it. Sermons, moral discourses, philanthropic dissertations, are all lost upon this subject. Nothing but making the commodity scarce and dear will have any effect." Adams was shrewd enough to know that steep prohibitory taxes on liquor would go nowhere, and critics "would say that I was a canting Puritan, a profound hypocrite, setting up standards of morality, economy, temperance, simplicity, and sobriety that I knew the age was incapable of." Rum continued to flow. And the eastern native cultures were weakened to the point of collapse, and then beyond.

RUM HAD A profound if less final impact on European colonial life. By the late eighteenth century (based on imprecise figures), the *average* American over fifteen years of age consumed slightly under six gallons of *absolute* alcohol each year—the equivalent of about seventy-five fifths of rum at 80 proof, or about five shots of rum per day. (Historian John McCusker more generously estimates consumption at about seven per day.) "If the ancients drank wine as our people drink rum and cider," wrote John Adams, "it is no wonder we hear of so many possessed with devils."

Tavern account books indicated a preference for rum over all other drinks. In 1728, a group of backcountry surveyors in North Carolina reported finding rum nearly every place they ventured and marveled that some settlers even used it in the cooking of bacon. One tavern keeper's books for 1774 in North Carolina showed that of 221 customers, some 165 had ordered rum by itself, and another 41 ordered drinks that contained rum. In Philadelphia, the sales at the One Tun tavern for five months in 1770 show that drinks made with rum, including toddy, grog, and punch, outsold beer and wine combined.

Rum's chief channel of distribution was the tavern. Taverns were an established part of the American landscape from the late seventeenth century through the nineteenth century, when hotel bars displaced them. Few villages were without a public house, where travelers and locals alike could find a meal, a bed, a dram of rum, a place by the fire in winter, and drinking companions year-round.

In 1656, Massachusetts made it mandatory for every town to have a licensed tavern. This ensured judges riding the circuit a place to sleep and dine. (In New York and Maryland, laws required that some of the rooms have "good feather beds," presumably to accommodate the magistrates.) Throughout the colonies, taverns could be found near virtually every courthouse, and court sessions in winter were often held inside the taverns, since they were nicely preheated. Taverns could always be found near ferry landings, where they provided a place to eat and drink while awaiting the ferryman.

Taverns occupied a motley array of buildings, ranging from establishments that were almost regal (like the Blue Anchor in Boston), to crude wooden shacks with swaybacked benches in the hinterlands of the Carolinas. Tavern account books suggest that an average tavern was a converted two- or three-story home that looked not unlike nearby private homes; not until after the American Revolution was it usual to construct a building specifically for drinking. They were typically run by men, but widows were often granted licenses to convert their homes to profit-making enterprises, in large part to keep them from burdening the town with requests for charity.

Almost every aspect of tavern keeping was subject to regulation. A taverner needed a license. The vessels in which drinks were served had to be branded with its actual capacity—a tradition still seen on glasses in British pubs but long since lost in the United States. Prices for drinks were set by local officials and had to be prominently displayed in a common room. In Pennsylvania, justices of the peace set "reasonable rates" four times each year, and these were proclaimed by the town crier and then posted on the courthouse door. Local jurisdictions could be even more restrictive. The liquor license granted by the Massachusetts Bay colony to one vendor noted he could "sell strongwater at retail only to his own fishermen." In South Carolina, tavern keepers were permitted to sell strong drink to seaman for just one hour out of any twenty-four.

Since prices were tightly regulated, ambitious tavern keepers striving to increase their income had to make their establishments more enticing than the one next door. Some hosted freak shows, with traveling curiosities paraded out for the astonishment of locals. In 1796, a "great curiosity" was paraded at "Mr. Buddy's" tavern in Philadelphia—"a man born entirely black" and who at age thirty-eight started to become white. ("His wool is coming off his hands, face, and arms, and long hair growing in place similar to that of white persons.") A two-foot-tall "satyr" was put on display in Philadelphia ("like a human being, observable to anyone with a shilling"). Exotic animals also made for popular diversions, and for a penny or two taverngoers might gape at moose, lions, cougars, polar bears, eight-legged and two-tailed cats, or a camel. ("It is impossible to describe the creature . . . ," read a newspaper advertisement for the latter. "A Curiosity never before seen, and very likely never again.") Drinking contests were not unknown. At the Red Lion in Philadelphia, a man named Thomas Apty bet other customers that he could suck down twelve pints of fortified cider in a half hour. He won, but failed to collect his winnings, as he promptly keeled over stone dead.

Another tavern attraction, traveling waxworks, became a small mania. Popular figures included the royal family, the bishop of New York, George Washington, and a mechanized figure of a madwoman named Moll who attempted to strike those who neared her. Perhaps most famous of the mechanized waxworks was one that depicted grisly scenes from the French Revolution. As described by one newspaper, after the waxen king lays his head on the guillotine, the blade drops, "the head falls into a basket, and the lips which are at first red, turn blue. The whole is performed to life by an invisible mechanism."

TAVERN KEEPERS HAD one other way to distinguish themselves. They concocted unique drinks that attracted a devoted following.

The Swedish clergyman Israel Acrelius arrived in the colonies in 1749 as provost of the Swedish congregations. He traveled widely and published his observations in 1759, after his return to Sweden. What he observed was drinking. He cataloged forty-five different drinks, noting them as carefully as a naturalist enumerating beetles. Of these, eighteen were made of rum.

The modern cocktail is often said to owe its lineage to the nineteenth century and Jerry Thomas, regarded as the nation's first notable bartender. (He wrote the first American bar guide.) While Thomas deserves to be recognized, his lionization gives short shrift to the remarkable creativity of the colonial tavern keeper, who had access to great amounts of rum, many interesting ingredients to employ as mixers, and vast amounts of time in which to experiment.

Rum was often consumed straight up, followed by a chaser of water. It could be diluted with three parts water to one of rum to make the grog familiar to seamen, and two parts water to one of rum to make a sling. With shavings from a sugarloaf, rum and water were transformed into mimbo, a drink that was especially popular in Pennsylvania. With molasses instead of sugar, it was called bombo, named for obscure reasons after English admiral John Benbow.

Tavern account books inventory casks of various flavorings. Lime juice was perhaps the most common, then as now, but there was also cinnamon water, clove water, and mint water, the last of which when mixed with rum was believed to strengthen one's stomach. (Mint had long been used in Europe to treat various maladies.) Rum with cherry juice was cherry bounce, and when mixed with bilberries (similar to blueberries) it was called a bilberry dram. Warmed rum flavored with juniper berries was served at funerals in some middle colonies.

Little was considered off limits in mixers. Rum with milk, sugar, and nutmeg was regarded as a refreshing summer drink, which Acrelius reported was "good for dysentery and loose bowels." Warm milk with rum and spices was syllabub. Sweetened vinegars, called beveridge, switchel, or shrub, date back to the Roman army and mixed with rum to good effect. Rum went well with hard cider; a warmed combination of the two was called a sampson. Rum mixed with a little molasses was a blackstrap.

Rum added to small beer made a drink called manatham. Spruce beer mixed with rum was a calibogus, a drink especially popular in Newfoundland and aboard ships. This could be further doctored by adding egg and sugar (to make an Egg Calli), or heated up (a King's

Calli). On Captain Cook's voyage around the world, the crew made a drink similar to spruce beer from ingredients harvested at the Cape of Good Hope. To this beer they mixed rum and sugar, and reported that it tasted "rather like champagne." They called it Kallebogus after the North American drink.

But perhaps the most famous early American rum drink was flip. The first references crop up around 1690, and by 1704 an almanac published this paean:

> *The days are short, the weather's cold*
> *By tavern fires tales are told.*
> *Some ask for dram when first come in.*
> *Others with flip and bounce begin.*

After two decades, flip's popularity bordered on a mania and would remain in demand for more than a century.

To make the drink, a tavern keeper started with a large earthenware pitcher or an oversized pewter mug. This would be filled about two-thirds with strong beer, to which was added some sort of sweetener—molasses, loaf sugar, dried pumpkin, or whatever else was at hand. Then came five ounces of rum, neither stirred nor shaken but mixed with a device called a loggerhead—a narrow piece of iron about three feet long with a slightly bulbous head the size of a small onion. It was originally created for heating tar or pitch, with the bulb buried in the glowing coals until it blazed red-hot, then quickly withdrawn and plunged into the pitch to make it pliable. The instrument served a similar heating function when plunged red-hot into a beer-rum-and-molasses concoction. The whole mess would foam and hiss and send up a mighty head. This alcoholic porridge was then decanted into smaller flip tumblers, which could hold as much as a gallon each, a measure that attested to the great thirst of the early settlers.

The searing loggerhead gave flip a bitter, slightly burned taste, which was much esteemed among the colonists. (This also distinguished it from the British variation of flip, which was made by heating the mixture in a saucepan, and which failed to develop a similar cult.) There were nearly as many variations of flip as there were taverns. It was sometimes made with cider rather than beer, and often a fresh egg would be added, in which case it was called bellowstop or battered flip. Several Massachussetts taverns, including Danforth's in Cambridge and Abbott's in Holden, were famous for their flip concoctions and became popular stage stops. The best-known flip, though, was made in Canton, Massachusetts, where the tavern keeper distinguished himself from the great mass of flip pretenders. He beat together a batch of cream, eggs, and sugar, which he would ladle into the pitcher with the other ingredients. Fans reported that this gave his flip a much vaunted creaminess.

The loggerhead was sometimes called a flip-dog or a hottle. Through repeated reheatings it sometimes broke and had to be repaired by a blacksmith. The cost of the repair, we know from one Massachusetts tavern ledger, was ten ounces of West Indian rum. A person who was slightly dim would be referred to as a loggerhead—like comparing someone's intellect today to a soap dish. ("I'm sure you never heard me say such a word to such a loggerhead as you," muttered Captain Kidd, the accused pirate, to a former shipmate who had testified against him.) Loggerheads made convenient weapons during tavern brawls, when men in their cups would grab the lethal instruments and whale away at one another, often with bloody results. While flip has wholly vanished from today's bar scene (and shouldn't be confused with a more modern drink called flip), the drink lingers in ghostly fashion each time someone speaks of adversaries being "at loggerheads."

"IT COMES ROLLING in, hogshead after hogshead!" groused Rev. Samuel Niles of Braintree, Massachusetts, in his 1761 screed against the rise of rum and the proliferation of taverns. His was only one voice among many—although it would not be until the next century that they would all coalesce into the more organized temperance movement. In the eighteenth century, these attacks reflected the more narrow concerns of the ministry. Rum, it seemed, was quietly reshaping colonial society, and it was the ministers who had the most to lose.

The rise of strong liquors in colonial America wasn't an isolated phenomenon. Across the Atlantic in England, French brandy was coming ashore in record amounts (liquor imports would peak in England in 1733). When it was banned after an outbreak of hostilities between the nations, gin from Holland filled the gap and launched an enduring craze, with the demand soon met by British distillers. Cheap gin rampaged through the poorest urban neighborhoods, and the besotted state of London's slums was captured most famously in the series of Gin Lane etchings by William Hogarth. Between 1729 and 1751, England struggled to stem the craze, passing a series of strict laws to limit gin sales and at last gaining some control over unbridled drinking.

Rum was the gin of the New World. But it was more than a quick ticket to a fast drunk. Rum's rise marked a rite of passage for the struggling colonists. Merely by drinking it, they effectively announced a change in their role on the global stage. They were no longer a people who made do with crude and rustic beverages concocted in their own kitchens. They could now pay for valued goods with the sweat of their labor. Rum not only appealed to the colonists' love of speedy inebriation, but also brought a measure of status and suggested the first steps toward cultural independence.

It also marked an increasing independence from the old order. While the "good creature" alcohol was a friend of the clergy in the form of beer, cider, and wine, it morphed into a formidable adversary when transformed into rum. The debauchery resulting from rum drinking in taverns was a challenge to the existing social order, perhaps nowhere as strikingly as in Puritan Massachusetts. By the early

1700s, ministers had already seen their stature begin to erode. Younger, native-born colonists were less mindful of the religious suppression that had prompted their elders to flee England and were more interested in bettering their own lives materially. They aspired not to the parsonage at the crossroads, but to the mansion near the docks. Merchants were building ostentatious homes that vastly outshone the humble houses of the ministry, and a growing number of ministers were forced to tend their own vegetable gardens in order to survive. They couldn't have afforded to enjoy rum in the taverns even if they had been so inclined.

Of course, few were so inclined. Rum was the enemy. Rum drinking, the ministers came to believe, led not only to a slackening of morals, but bred indolence and idleness, two afflictions that Puritans greeted as warmly as gout and consumption. "Idleness, the parent of every vice, has been introduced by the fatal and pernicious use of foreign spirits," fumed a Connecticut resident in a letter to a newspaper in 1769. "Not one extravagance, among the numerous follies we have been guilty of, has been more destructive to our interests than tavern haunting, and gratifying our appetites with intoxicating liquors." The harmless conviviality bred by beer, cider, and wine was supplanted by rum's more intractable sullenness and addiction. Rum was the snake in the garden.

The more devout led a campaign to encourage settlers to abandon rum and return to beer and cider. This, they hoped, would reverse the drift into dispiriting (if spirited) secularism and would roll back the clock to the allegedly more wholesome and industrious time of the forefathers. In the first book printed by Benjamin Franklin, in 1725, Francis Rawle complained that because of "the Depravity and Viciousness of our Palates and the so frequent use of Spirits, there has not been due Care in the Brewing of beer." He called for higher duties on imported liquor, and the elimination of all taxes on beer and cider, thereby encouraging a return to that imaginary period of pastoral grace.

Cities like Boston actively encouraged brewers and cider makers to offer an alternative to rum. But such measures were too late. The old order had been deposed. The tavern keepers, the de facto governors of the Republic of Rum, had no intention of relinquishing their power.

A taverngoer in the early eighteenth century had to endure a great many inconveniences—rancid meat, surly company, and (if overnighting) thin straw mattresses filled with biting insects. A more insidious hazard was getting caught up in endless rounds of toast making.

The practice of toasting the health of one's king, host, or mistress—or even a stranger who has just walked through the door—apparently dates back to Elizabethan England. The origins are murky, as is the case with many rituals associated with drinking. Toasts were so popular in the late seventeenth century in England that they provoked a backlash: Pamphlets were printed attacking the practice as sacrilegious. "How can any man drink another's health," asked one, quite sensibly, in 1682, and "by what new kind of transubstantiation can his health be converted into a glass of liquor?" The pamphlet went on to describe more than one hundred instances in which health drinkers suffered from the wrath of a put-upon God, including one group who toasted "in a strange manner" and soon after all died mysteriously.

Among the short-lived tavern regulations was one to outlaw toasts. But like the bans against rum sales to Indians, it was blithely ignored. A late-eighteenth-century French visitor to Philadelphia lamented the "absurd and truly barbarous practice, the first time you drink and at the beginning of dinner to call out successively to each individual, to let him know you drink his health." As a result, before the toast is concluded, the person with glass held aloft is "sometimes ready to die with thirst." Another traveler noted that dining room doors might be bolted to prevent guests from fleeing during toasts.

According to tavern historian Peter Thompson, toasts were an effort to draw all present into an agreeable fellowship, whether they
wanted to be drawn in or not. At its best, the practice knitted together
people from different classes into a comity of good cheer. At worst,
they actually sowed conflicts by prompting those who disagreed to
insult the others present by not raising a glass.

Whether taverngoers of different classes managed to bond, the
early taverns were relatively egalitarian. Since regulations prevented
raising prices to discourage riffraff, tavern owners sought to boost
their sales by encouraging any and all to drink. As the traveling physician Alexander Hamilton learned, there was no telling who you'd find
yourself sitting next to in a tavern. Congregationalists drank with An-
glicans, and blacksmiths with attorneys. (One group was notably ab-
sent: women. Those who were present were mostly travelers in search
of lodging.)

The tippling rooms at taverns tended to be cozy, with privacy at a
minimum. As such, the business of one was the business of all. Taverns were cramped places, often low-ceilinged, and smoky from pipes
and fireplace backdrafts. They became a place for the spread of pesti-
lence, like yellow fever, which swept through the colonies with deadly
regularity. But the taverns were also places in which new ideas were
fermented—ideas for a new republic, in which no person should be
subject to "taxation without representation."

Despite the nostalgic portraits of some historians, taverns weren't
all bonhomie and genteel discussion. They were more often a place of
constant low-grade conflict, where wildly clashing ideas ricocheted
around the room. Colonists learned when to keep quiet, when to speak
up, when to go along for the sake of consensus, and when to make a
stand and defend it—with loggerheads, if needed. The taverns, in
short, offered training in policy debate and the grooming of future
leaders. "Commerce and politics were so inextricably mingled that
rum and liberty were but different liquors from the same still," wrote
historian Frederick Bernays Wiener in 1930.

Into these mini maelstroms, aspiring politicians and budding rev-
olutionaries mingled, increasingly riled by the tone-deaf actions of the
British Crown. John Adams was a young lawyer in the coastal Massachusetts town of Braintree in the 1760s. He launched an early and
abortive crusade against taverns, of which there were a dozen in
Braintree. "Few things have deviated so far from the first design of
their institution, are so fruitful of destructive evils, or so needful of a
speedy regulation, as licensed houses," he groused, siding with ministers who wanted tighter reins on the rum sellers. But as Adams's
prominence grew, he came to realize that taverns were a habitat in
which those in search of influence could thrive. "You will find the
[tavern] full of people, drinking drams, phlip, toddy," Adams wrote. A
leader had to learn to "mix with the crowd in the tavern" and develop
his popularity by "agreeable assistance in the tittle-tattle of the hour."
Influence or elective office was not automatically granted those with
breeding, religion, education, or connections, but by entering into the
rummy world of the tavern and showing what stuff you were made of.
As the Hessian mercenary Baron Friedrich Adolph Riedesel noted,
"New Englanders all want to be politicians, and love, therefore, the
tavern and the grog bowl, behind the latter of which they transact
business, drinking from morning till night."

As conflict with Britain loomed, a new wave of tavern reformer
briefly appeared on the political landscape—those who wished to fan
the flames of armed rebellion against England but were fearful that
rum-addled colonists would be ill-prepared to stand up against King
George. They agitated vainly to shutter the taverns to ensure a sober
fighting force that was ready for resistance.

As it turned out, they had no cause to worry. Rum would prove to
be the spirit of '76.

[BOMBO]

In short glass, pour *two ounces* RUM
and *two ounces* fresh WATER. Add
one-half teaspoon MOLASSES. Dust
with NUTMEG.

Chapter 4

[MEDFORD RUM]

*I know not why we should blush to confess that molasses
were an essential ingredient in American independence.
Many great events have proceeded from much smaller
causes.*

—PRESIDENT JOHN ADAMS

PAUL REVERE WAS LATE. "He's always late," said Thomas
Convery. Convery was eating a Danish as he peered out on
the street from behind a curtain inside the Gaffey Funeral
Home in Medford, Massachusetts. It was Monday, April 21, Patriot's
Day, and the morning was sunny, windless, and sixty degrees. Some
dozen members of the Medford High School marching band in
mailbox-blue uniforms were playing "Louie, Louie" on the sidewalk
with more enthusiasm than expertise. The crowd numbered about
250. Parents in baseball caps and windbreakers held small video cam-
eras and instructed their kids to keep a respectful distance from the
yellow plastic tape, which held a space open in front of the funeral
home. Two or three cell phones rang out, followed by shouts to
friends: Paul Revere was crossing the bridge and in a few minutes
would gallop into town.

"Crowds are getting thinner every year," Convery said. "When I was in high school, the band had one hundred and one pieces. And we *always* celebrated Patriot's Day on April 19. Not two days after, but on the nineteenth. Now it's the twentieth, the twenty-first, when-ever." His voice trailed off, as if creeping Monday-ism was a sad and incurable disease. Convery, who was seventy-eight years old, likes tra-dition. He was wearing his VFW hat studded with a great many pins, and had written two forthrightly titled books of local history: *When I Was a Kid* and *I Remember When.* Convery is the one to talk to if you need to know anything about Medford As She Was.

I had called Convery a few weeks earlier to ask about the account in several history books that Paul Revere, partway into his famous midnight ride, had stopped at Isaac Hall's home and downed a dram or two of rum to fortify him on his mission to Lexington. H. F. Willkie, the brother of former presidential candidate Wendell Willkie, wrote that the rum Revere drank in Medford was strong enough to make "a rabbit bite a bulldog." In 1944, the fact-checkers of *The New Yorker* magazine signed off on a story that reported "Paul Revere had a stiff snort before starting on his midnight ride." Another account claimed that Revere lingered long enough for "several stirrup-cups of rich, tawny Old Medford Rum," which imparts an image of Revere making favorable comments to his host about the richly caramelized hues before mounting up and galloping off to the first battle of the American Revolution. These accounts notwithstanding, for someone as famously in a hurry as Paul Revere, it seemed an odd time for a so-cial drink. Was it true? Convery said I should come to Medford on Patriot's Day and see for myself.

At the former home of Captain Isaac Hall, where all traces of his residency had long since been hidden under the beige carpets and acoustic tile ceilings of funeral homes everywhere, I heard footsteps treading lightly upstairs. Convery pointed toward the ceiling with his half-eaten Danish. I walked to the top of the stairway. An elderly man stood by the window, wearing a white dressing gown and a white nightcap. From my perch on the landing, I could see his brown trousers and business shoes sticking out from underneath. He was peering out the window, awaiting his cue. This was Captain Isaac Hall. Like us, he was waiting for Paul Revere.

Revere's original visit, late on the night of April 18, 1775, was wholly by accident. Revere never intended to pass through Medford. On that much everyone agrees. He was one of two messengers on that fateful night dispatched from Boston to Lexington to warn of British regulars amassing outside the city, with the intention of confiscating colonial militia arms and seizing rebel troublemakers Sam Adams and John Hancock. The British soldiers were hoping for a surprise attack, so they planned to cross the Charles River by boat, then approach the town along a more lightly traveled route. This was the famous "two if by sea" route, with a signal sent by posting two lanterns high in Boston's North Church. Another messenger, William Dawes, was sent overland via the more heavily traveled main road. As a backup in the event Dawes was captured, Revere was dispatched across the Charles River, his oarlocks muffled with a petticoat so as not to attract the attention of sentries. Once across the river, Revere set off on a borrowed horse, galloping along a direct route from Charlestown toward Lexington.

Revere later recalled it was a "very pleasant" night, with a bright moon lighting the way. Not far outside of Charlestown, however, he stumbled upon a pair of redcoats on horseback. He quickly reversed course, the patrollers in pursuit. He outrode one; the other mired down in a muddy swale as he sought to cut off Revere's retreat. Revere then struck out on an alternate route, beating a northward arc through the village of Medford. When he arrived, accounts concur, he rapped on the door of Captain Hall, the head of the Medford minutemen. As soon as he left, Hall sent instructions to set off the calls to muster. Supporters fired guns, beat drums, and rang bells.

Did Revere really down a dram of rum while at Isaac Hall's to stiffen his resolve for the long ride? "Yes, he had a bit of the grog," Convery told me with conviction. The evidence? Convery thought for a moment, then noted that he himself had played Captain Isaac Hall some years back, and had personally served Revere a shot of rum. "It was like paint thinner," he said. "It made you ride to the nearest toilet." A shot of rum had always been a local tradition for the reenactment—sometimes more than a shot. "When I was a kid," he said, "I remember Paul getting a leg up, then going right over the top of the horse. But it's usually softer stuff today."

How about historical evidence? Convery eyed me askance, as if I were more than a little simpleminded. "It was the only drink they had!" he said, throwing up his hands. "If you're going to stop by the house of the distiller, you're going to get rum. They're not going to give you a Pepsi-Cola."

The sound of sirens filled the front hall of the funeral home. Police on motorcycles arrived first, followed by a green pickup truck pulling a horse trailer. Then Paul Revere came into view, his tri-cornered hat bobbing up and down above the crowd. Revere, played by a reenactor named Matthew Johnson, had left Boston earlier that morning, and he had a loud, clarion call that carried over the sirens and the rising applause and hoots of the crowd. "The regulars are out! Captain, the regulars are out!" he hollered up to the second-floor window as he reined to a halt in front of Isaac Hall's house. Captain Hall hit his cue precisely, and stuck his head out the window. "Come on in," he hollered out, then thudded down the steps.

Revere walked in, huffing and a bit flushed. "A little warm out there," he said. He was followed by several city councilmen, the mayor, and a U.S. congressman. The group stood awkwardly in a semicircle around the pile of doughnuts and pastries on a folding table, nobody saying or eating much. "Doughnut for the ride, Paul?" someone asked. Paul eyed the pile, then demurred.

"Do you want something to drink?" Convery asked. Paul nodded, and said, "I might take a water." He went to the cooler, uncapped a bottle of Poland Spring, and guzzled it down. "Do you want anything else?" Convery asked, expectantly.

"No, thanks," Revere said. Then he unfastened his cape and went off to find a toilet.

QUESTIONS PERSIST ABOUT Revere's ride, but this is known for sure: Isaac Hall made rum—a lot of it. He was one of dozens of distillers who thrived in the northern colonies and produced millions of gallons in the seven decades prior to the American Revolution.

Rum didn't just fill the holds of merchant ships returning from the West Indies. It was also one of the first mass-market products manufactured in America. By the time of the Revolution, more than half the rum consumed in the northern colonies was produced by local distillers. Indeed, rum distilling was the second most important manufacturing industry at the time, trailing only shipbuilding.

Like every grammar school student, I learned that the American Revolution was the story of thirteen aggrieved colonies rising up as one against an oppressive throne. But the rebellion was more interesting and complex than that. England actually had twenty-six colonies in the New World. Only half rose up in rebellion. To understand why, one needs to start with molasses.

The first distillery producing of any kind of liquor in the northern colonies dates to about 1640—roughly the same time rum was first produced in the West Indies. It was on Staten Island and was operated by William Kieft, a director of the Dutch colony of New Netherland. Kieft restricted the sale of wines and liquor to those sold at his tavern, the first such establishment in Manhattan. It's likely Kieft distilled brandy, and probably a coarse whiskey made of the dregs from beer making—a not uncommon way to wring extra profits from a brewery. But grain was scarce, and colonists lived in the shadow of hunger. In 1676, twelve years after the British assumed control of the colony, the governor sharply limited grain available for brewing and distilling.

What to use to make spirits? Molasses—a trash product—

remained astoundingly cheap in the West Indies. This was especially true in newly settled British island colonies like Jamaica, where a rum industry hadn't been established. But island planters—who had dedicated virtually every acre of arable land to sugar cultivation—needed to import all manner of food and provisions to feed themselves and their slaves. So timber, rope, livestock, dried cod, and fresh produce sailed south. Molasses, in turn, sailed north.

Reports of rum distilling surface in Providence, Rhode Island, as early as 1684. But not until the first years of the eighteenth century did colonial rum hit its stride. Growth in rum distilling was aided by the immigration of experienced distillers to the colonies, both from England, where competition and high taxation made liquor profits hard to come by, and from Barbados and other British West Indian islands, where freed indentured servants found themselves displaced from the scarce land and the demand for their labor greatly lessened by the new reliance on African slaves. Of those servants who sailed north, many were well versed in the craft of rum making.

Distilleries were built wherever molasses could be unloaded and stored, often by merchants who comprehended that a still or two, while an expensive investment, had a very agreeable effect on the value of imported molasses. It was modern-day alchemy—through distillation, the dull, treacly dross of molasses was converted into the gold of rum.

A colonist referring to rum prior to 1700 was likely talking about imported rum; by the first decade of the eighteenth century, he would just as likely be referring to the domestically distilled stuff. With its great trading fleet, Boston quickly moved to the forefront of the continental rum industry. Records show that in just six months of 1688, Massachusetts imported 156,000 gallons of molasses from the British West Indies, of which about half was converted into rum and the other half used for flavoring such staples as baked beans and brown bread. By 1717, a customs officer in Boston reported that the colony was producing 200,000 gallons of rum annually, which is almost certainly an underestimate. Boston had at least twenty-five distilleries operating within the city by 1750; at least another ten distilleries were producing rum in other settlements of the Massachusetts Bay colony.

Massachusetts didn't have a monopoly on the rum industry. Rhode Island was home to 20 rum distilleries, New York to 17, and Philadelphia to 14. (A merchant with the splendid name of Peacock Bigger built successful distilleries in both Philadelphia and Charlestown, Maryland.) The smell of fermenting molasses could also be detected in New Hampshire (3 distilleries), Connecticut (5), and Maryland (4). The southern colonies, with their tobacco plantation economy, didn't have as active a merchant class. But even there 4 rum distilleries were built (in the Carolinas and Virginia). In 1763, by some estimates, New England alone had a total of 159 distilleries producing rum. (A more conservative tally finds maybe half that number in New England, but around 140 distilleries on the continent as a whole.) In any event, by 1770, the North American colonists were importing some 6.5 million gallons of molasses from the islands, which was distilled into about 5 million gallons of rum.

The New England merchants who took up distilling were not rum connoisseurs. They bought molasses cheap and sold the rum equally cheaply. "New England rum" was widely regarded as a low-priced, low-quality version of better-regarded West Indian product. (Domestic rum typically cost one-half to two-thirds the price of rum imported from the West Indies.) One Baltimore merchant, William Lux, noted that "people seem to be more inclin'd to encourage the [local] country rum as it is so much cheaper," so he sensibly changed his trade from rum importer to rum distiller.

The quality of the rum was determined by the whims of the market. Rising demand for molasses to make rum led to periodic shortages. Distillers could make do by using less in the fermentation process, but this resulted in a harsher rum. (Connecticut banned such hurried distillation, noting that "by said practice molasses is made scarce and dear, and the spirits drawn off . . . are usually very unwholesome, and of little value.") In flush times, the price of rum would drop and likewise create an incentive to reduce costs by cutting back on the molasses.

Such economy was not uncommon. One visitor wrote that New England distillers were "more famous for the quantity and cheapness than for the excellency of their rum." There were even efforts to doctor domestic rum to make it pass for imported. One eighteenth-century advertisement promised to teach "the invaluable secret of changing the quality of Philadelphia and New-England rum to that of West India . . . at the trifling expense of only your honour and veracity . . ." Philadelphia merchant Isaac Norris wrote to a companion in 1702 that the local rum "only wants to age to taste well," but lamented that his customers could not be persuaded to pay more for it, as it lacked "the right rum stink."

As Boston grew and became more costly, industries migrated to communities with large tracts of cheap land: shipbuilding to Portsmouth, New Hampshire; Newburyport, Massachusetts; and elsewhere; butchers and tanners to Lynn, Massachusetts. Newport absorbed much of Boston's rum business, the profits from which it used in part to finance slave-trading voyages to Africa. A distillery was built on the island of Nantucket, whose experienced ship captains were well positioned to benefit from the Newfoundland trade. A former Bostonian moved to Halifax, Nova Scotia, and there erected a "large distillery works," putting it in good position to divert much of the rum trade in the Maritimes.

Boston also lost business closer to home. Watertown, Haverhill, Salem, and Charlestown soon were home to thriving distilleries. But only one town rose to uncommon prominence in the rum world: the riverside village of Medford, the fourth oldest in Massachusetts, founded in 1630.

You could go hunting for traces of Medford's once-bustling distillery industry today—as I recently did—but you would find little. A couple of copper kettles gather dust atop a tall shelf at the local historical society. And what's quaintly called Distiller's Row in downtown Medford—where a half-dozen distilleries once filled the air with the aroma of casked rum and fermenting molasses—you'll now find a parking garage and a charmless strip of shops that includes the Wound Healing Center, a CVS drugstore, and a Korean restaurant. The city's Web site notes, with commendable candor, that today "Medford is probably the most untalked about city in the United States."

Yet at its peak in the mid-eighteenth century, Medford was very much talked about. The rum industry first took root sometime between 1715 and 1720, when John Hall constructed a still near the village spring, which bubbled up with sweet, abundant water. Other distilleries followed, often on higher ground less subject to flooding from the river, but still near enough to the wharves for carting the imported molasses. Enough came out of Medford's stills that fishermen complained that the waste dumped in the river wiped out the oyster beds. If true, it was an early instance of industrial pollution destroying a natural resource.

Medford rum became known for its superior quality compared to most New England rums (an advantage that could have been had with the barest attention to quality control), becoming one of the first brand names to emerge from the northern colonies, along with the United Company of Spermaceti Chandler's candles and some milled grains branded with the "best marks." Published recipes in the nineteenth century often call specifically for "Medford Rum."

Medford rum's superior quality was rumored to stem from the excellence of the water—but if that was the secret, it was not one the distillers would have been eager to promote. The spring that gave rise to Medford's first rum distillery couldn't accommodate the expanding industry, and water had to be piped in from Pasture Hill, north of the village, and might well have been infused with cow dung. As the West

Indians proved, however, that extra ingredient might actually have aided fermentation and imbued a certain zest.

Whatever its secret, word of Medford rum spread far, some of it less than truthful. Boosters said that it never left the bonded warehouse "until it had passed a severe test, and was shipped across the Atlantic and back again, in wood, to age it." The most noted was Old Medford Rum, produced well into the nineteenth century by the Lawrence family. Local fans claimed, rather grandly, that it "carried the name and fame of the early town to the snowcapped region of the Rockies and to India's coral strand," and improbable accounts have been published of barrels turning up atop mountains in Switzerland.

It was during the peak of Medford's rum boom that Paul Revere rode through on that fateful night. It was an era of ubiquitous social drinking: a dollop of rum, downed with little ceremony or palaver, was an everyday way of enhancing the bonds of friendship and cementing common purpose in the Republic of Rum. Revere was a typical colonial, fond of playing cards and backgammon at public houses, and his regular lairs in Boston included two taverns, the Green Dragon and The Salutation. His famous midnight ride wasn't novel; the flowery poems and high-blown legends exalting his ride were to come much later. The year earlier he had ridden to Philadelphia to inform Pennsylvanians about the Boston Port Bill, and twice in the two weeks prior to his famous ride he had galloped off with messages—to Concord with word that the redcoats were coming (they weren't), and to Lexington to report that the British grenadiers and light infantry were shifting duties and were evidently up to something. (They were, as the march on Lexington two nights later would prove.) So this particular late-night ride might not have struck Revere as particularly momentous. He might have figured he had time to share a dram with Captain Hall.

Only this much remains certain, as Thomas Convery assured me: Paul Revere did *not* have a Pepsi-Cola.

DISTILLERS IN THE early eighteenth century could acquire molasses from any number of West Indian plantations—British, Spanish, and Dutch islands all had excess to export, as did Portuguese and Dutch colonies along the mainland of South America. (New England merchants had been fond of Dutch molasses from Surinam since at least the late 1600s.) But when New England traders set off in search of West Indian molasses, they increasingly headed for the French islands.

The reason was simple: French molasses was astoundingly cheap. The French were slower than the British to develop great sugar estates, but they hastily made up for their late start, and production was bountiful on their vast acreages of virgin soils. By the 1720s, the French sugar industry was expanding at an impressive clip; at the time of the American Revolution, Haiti alone could produce more sugar than all of the British islands combined. At the same time, the French sugar islands—which also included Guadeloupe, Grenada, and Martinique—had a limited home market for their molasses, since French winemakers and brandy distillers had blocked exports of molasses and rum, fearful that cheap liquor would undermine their monopoly on drink. As a result, molasses was practically free for the taking if you but troubled to stop by one of the French islands

The New England traders and the French sugar estates thus developed a nicely symbiotic relationship. The New Englanders had barrel staves, horses, and dried trash fish, the last of which was impossible to sell in Europe. The French had molasses. While figures on French imports are hard to come by, it's known that Boston in 1688 imported 156,000 gallons of British island molasses. By 1716, with the North American rum industry growing rapidly, imports from the British islands had dropped by more than half, to 72,000 gallons. That gap was undoubtedly made up by the French. It was a similar story elsewhere; one New Yorker reported that the city's distilleries appeared to be "wholly supplied with molasses from Martinique."

The British islands' planters watched balefully as northern merchants sailed past. As a further affront, New England traders who called at the British islands often refused to accept molasses in trade, knowing they could do better elsewhere. This did not escape notice of mercantilists in England. The general theory of colonies at the time was that they existed for the sole purpose of enriching the mother country. And yet here were colonial ships sailing to French ports to purchase molasses to make rum that would likely be traded for other non-British goods. How did England benefit from all this? This was easy to answer: It didn't.

British mercantilists and irritated planters—notably those from Barbados and Antigua—trudged to Parliament and agitated for laws to remedy their situation. The first weapon they suggested was too large and blunt: the outright banning of trade with the French islands. This failed, so instead they asked for heavy tariffs to be imposed on all French sugar products shipped to the northern colonies. Parliament went along and passed the Molasses Act of 1733.

This act did not please the North American merchants. It permitted the northern colonies to continue to ship outbound loads of grain, timber, and horses to non-British markets, but the sugar or molasses they returned with were slapped with hefty duties. This made French molasses far more expensive than British molasses. (Imports of all French-made rum were banned under the act.) New England rum was, in effect, sacrificed to appease the politically powerful British sugar planters. Some fifty thousand white British island residents would benefit at the expense of a half-million northern colonists.

The North American colonists had a choice: They could openly rebel against the assault on this vital colonial industry, or they could simply ignore it and continue business as usual. They chose the latter path: The Molasses Act was the fifty-five-mile per hour speed limit of the era. Molasses continued to flow north into the colonies from the French islands, and New England rum was distilled, consumed, and traded. Duties collected on all molasses imported into the northern colonies in 1735—two years after the act was passed—amounted to the unprincely sum of £2. During the entire three-decade period in which the act was on the books, the Crown collected just £13,702 on a half-million gallons of officially imported foreign molasses. Meanwhile, the French molasses trade was abetted by corrupt British customs officers, who could convert it to British molasses through the alchemy of paperwork. Although these extralegal measures made molasses slightly more costly, avoidance of the act wasn't nearly as expensive as compliance. The New England rum trade continued to flourish. And the planters of the British sugar islands continued to fume.

The Seven Years War (called the French and Indian War in North America), which pitted European countries in elaborate conflicts among one another between 1756 and 1763, is often regarded as the first of the great world wars. Longtime foes England and France were especially bitter enemies, and their enmity carried over into the colonies. This had an impact on New England's traditional West Indian trade, since traders were now fearful that their ships might be seized in French harbors. Instead of sailing directly to the French islands, New England traders now headed for free-trade ports like the Dutch colony of St. Eustatius and the Spanish port of Monte Cristi. This inconvenience didn't last long. The powerful British navy quickly overran the poorly defended French and added Martinique and Guadeloupe to the constellation of British-controlled West Indian islands.

This was good news for the northern traders. Merchants could now, under generous terms of surrender extended by the British, trade legally with French suppliers and avoid both high tariffs *and* the hassles of smuggling. The celebration was short-lived, however. The war drew to a close, and the islands were returned to France under the Treaty of Paris. (This was in part the doing of the British sugar barons. The last thing they wanted was a flood of new sugar into London markets driving down prices, so they encouraged negotiators to give back the islands and keep control of Canada, widely considered the lesser prize.) The New England ship captains, watching from afar, figured that in a few months they could return to the smuggling trade with their old French partners.

It was not to be. To understand why, consider England's mood. The country had just concluded a long and pricey war that had drained the treasury and now found itself saddled with the added expense of managing the vast new territories in Canada. What's more, England believed, no doubt rightly, that North American colonists were the prime beneficiaries of the war, since the threat of French invasion from the north had been vanquished, opening up the possibility of expanded westward settlement. And the British were still peeved about the colonial smuggling that had helped the French finance their army. The newly installed British prime minister, George Grenville, concluded that England's global finances needed revamping and that the northern colonies should pay more of the freight. England discarded the ineffectual Molasses Act, and replaced it with the Sugar Act.

While the old Molasses Act was an attempt to restrict trade among the New World colonies, the new imperial law was designed chiefly to raise revenues. In fact, the new law actually *lowered* colonial tariffs on imported molasses, from six pence to three pence per gallon, with the English figuring they could make up on volume what they lost in price. In contrast to its lassitude on the Molasses Act, England enforced the Sugar Act with uncommon zeal. The admiralty courts were given authority to prosecute offenders. The navy was given orders to pursue violators on the high seas. The Crown diverted twenty-seven navy ships to the task of enforcement. And British customs officers who failed to demonstrate sufficient vigor were abruptly dismissed. After decades of turning a blind eye to New England smuggling, England set about clamping down.

IN LATE SEPTEMBER 1763, news of the Sugar Act began to circulate through the colonies. It traveled along the coast by schooner and scow, and into the backlands by horseback. It was carried by newspapers and pamphlets. And it whipped like wildfire through the taverns in the Republic of Rum—first prompting lively banter, then forging a comity of purpose. The Crown had announced that it would, in effect, apply a tourniquet to the lifeblood of the colonies.

At first, the colonists did not direct their venom at Parliament, but at the West Indian planters whose fingerprints were all over the Sugar Act. The islands had suffered deeply during the Seven Years War, because trade dropped off as traders stayed at home. To jump-start the island economies, planters worked to expand their rum trade. This could be done in two ways: eliminating exports from the French and Dutch colonies and squeezing the New England rum industry by raising the cost of molasses. As a letter writer to the *Providence Gazette* noted in 1764, "in the present declining State of the Sugar-Islands, nothing could tend more effectually to restore the West India Trade from Ruin, than putting a Stop to the further Distillation of Rum in the British Colonies of North America." Two weeks later, another of the paper's correspondents lamented: "The Northern Colonies are to be made the Dupes, Hewers of Wood, and Drawers of Water to a few West-India planters!"

The Sugar Act of 1764 met with wide disapproval in the north. In Massachusetts (where a paltry 3 percent of imported molasses came from the British islands the year before the Sugar Act was passed), the governor wrote that the news of the Sugar Act "caused greater alarm . . . than the taking of Fort William Henry did in 1757." (The bellicose French had captured this Champlain Valley fort just northwest of western Massachusetts.) Rhode Island had imported some fourteen thousand hogsheads of molasses annually before the Sugar Act, less than 20 percent of it from the British islands. A customs officer noted that "everybody with us wears a most heavy Countenance, things being in a much worse way than when the war continued." The act even brought despair to Philadelphia, where a prominent merchant lamented that "nothing but ruine seems to hang over our heads."

A handful of colonial rum distillers went out of business under the burden of the newly enforced tariffs. But most managed to bump along, absorbing higher expenses and the increased costs of smuggling. Yet throughout the colonies, from major metropolises to up-river towns, the Sugar Act was viewed as a great injustice. It was clear that the "rich, proud, and overbearing Planters of the West Indies," were behind it, and the clamor to act grew from whispers to a din.

The assemblies of Rhode Island, Massachusetts, Connecticut, New York, and Pennsylvania took their complaints directly to Parliament. They drew up petitions and circulated pamphlets, including one published in Boston in 1764 with a comprehensive title: *Reasons Against the Renewal of the Sugar Act as It Will Be Prejudicial to the Trade Not Only of the Northern Colonies But to Those of Great Britain Also.*

The most damning argument in favor of repealing the Sugar Act, as the pamphlet's title suggested, was that the loss of New England's trade with foreign islands would boomerang and cause economic hardship to old England. Without cheap molasses, the thriving New England distilleries would be shuttered. Without income from rum, the newly impoverished northern colonies would purchase fewer manufactured goods from England. The northern colonies would begin manufacturing their own goods, further spoiling profits of British manufacturers and merchants. This argument found an unusually attentive audience among English manufacturers, who were already casting a wary eye abroad. English hat manufacturers, for instance, were grousing about the expanded production in New York, where enterprising hatmakers had an endless supply of beaver pelts for fashionable felt hats.

Against the odds, the arguments of the colonials eventually prevailed. The English Parliament revised the Sugar Act in 1766, and the tariffs on foreign molasses dropped to one penny per gallon, or so low that smuggling was more expensive than obeying the law. The Sugar Act had been watered down before any open resistance or rebellion surfaced. No one died over efforts to control molasses or rum. The dispute had been resolved with quiet but determined politicking.

In the process, however, a colonial Rubicon had been crossed. The resistance to the Sugar Act marked the first time the North American colonies, which were administered as separate entities, had effectively joined together to resist British meddling. Resistance went from amorphous to organized. In 1763, a letter writer to the *Boston Post* called for the creation of a new committee "to open a correspondence with the principal merchants in all our sister colonies, endeavoring to promote a union, and a coalition of all their councils." This network was soon established, laying the foundation for the influential Committees of Correspondence that would play such a central role leading up to the Revolution.

England feared that the colonial success in rolling back the Sugar Act would be viewed as a wholesale victory for the colonists and embolden them further. So the Crown was quick to assert its right to impose other taxes. In one of history's more striking instances of political tone deafness, England replaced the Sugar Act with new taxes on imported tea, a product chosen in part to help out the financially troubled and politically well-connected East India Company. Worse yet, the English passed an even more reviled bit of legislation: the Stamp Act, which put an onerous tax on all printed matter, from newspapers to liquor licenses to legal papers to almanacs. While the Sugar Act chiefly affected the New England colonies—the center of rum production—the Stamp Act antagonized all colonists, forging an even more encompassing coalition. And so was born "No taxation without representation."

When the British officials moved to enforce the Stamp Act, the colonies were primed to resist. Colonists launched a boycott of British goods. The tea went into Boston harbor. Paul Revere set off on his ride. In Lexington, a shot was heard 'round the world. And the thirteen North American colonies declared as one their independence from England and took up arms to defend it. The scattered colonial militias became an army of resistance.

The war had begun.

IN FEBRUARY 1775, two months before the battles at Lexington and Concord, a group of British soldiers approached Salem from Boston. Their plan was to seize munitions stored in Salem that might eventually be used against them. At a bridge just outside town, an impassioned group of colonists gathered in front of the advancing troops and stood their ground, barring the way and taunting the British for being cowards, "lobster coats," and "red-jackets." In the heat of the encounter, a man named Joseph Whicher, the foreman of a local rum distillery, pushed to the front of the crowd and challenged the troops to attack him. One British soldier obliged by lunging forward with a bayonet, nicking the colonist's chest and drawing blood.

It was the first blood spilled in a long and bloody war.

It's no coincidence that distillers and rum merchants were in the forefront of the political and armed resistance. As we've seen, taverns had become de facto community centers, virtual petri dishes for the breeding of a discontent that taverners learned to channel. About ninety taverns were licensed in Boston in 1769; of these, twenty license holders were members of the Sons of Liberty, the rebel group behind the Boston Tea Party. Tavern keepers had allies among the wealthy merchant-distillers, who were among those with the most to lose if the English overseers were to dictate terms of their trade. Of Boston's twenty-eight distillers and wine merchants, only seven remained loyal to the Crown, while nearly half were involved with the Sons of Liberty. As historian David Conroy notes, "The manufacturers and importers of the most controversial commodity in the province and the colonial world stood at the very helm of the resistance movement."

In backing this rebellion, the tavern keepers and, more so, the distillers put their livelihoods at risk. As British troops blockaded the harbors against colonial trade, West Indian rum and molasses dried up. One colonial estimated that distillers in the city of Boston alone lost £6,000 in income each week. As a result, rum was increasingly unavailable—unless one had connections to the British military, which continued to import goods from the West Indies though British-held New York and other ports.

This would prove to be not a small matter for the Continental Army. Rum was currency, and its disappearance made it even more difficult for the Continental Congress to fund an army. (Continental specie was in a state of constant crisis and distrusted by local farmers and merchants.) In one small example of rum's role in the American Revolution, prominent New Hampshire politician John Langdon donated to the state some 150 hogsheads of rum to raise a militia. That militia defeated the British forces advancing from Canada under General John Burgoyne and dashed their strategy of dividing the colonies and conquering each half in turn. So at this turning point in the war, rum put the militia in motion.

On a more practical level, rum was a provision of war, as essential in the field as black powder or barrels of salt pork. In November 1775, the Continental Congress in Philadelphia established rules for the newly formed American Continental Navy and followed the British model in issuing a "halfpint of rum per man every day, and a discretionary allowance for extra duty and in time of engagement." Foot soldiers were also to get rum, to be distributed by mess officers. In 1778, one observer suggested that "the moment your army enters an enemy's country, you must seize on all the brewers of beer and spirituous liquor in your neighborhood . . . that the army may never stand in need of a beverage which it cannot do without."

AS THE SIX-YEAR war dragged on, from the late 1770s into the 1780s, rum became increasingly hard to come by, which undermined the morale and effectiveness of the struggling troops. In December 1778, even before the lashing snows and rains had begun at the winter encampment at Valley Forge, a soldier lamented in his diary that rum was always in short supply, and was sorely needed. The poorly clothed and ill-fed troops slowly starved and lost their feet to frostbite. General George Washington sent out imploring appeals for supplies, noting that critical absence of vegetables, salt, vinegar (a poor substitute for vegetables), and drink: ". . . beer or cyder seldom comes within the verge of the camp," he wrote, "and rum in much too small quantities."

The lack of rum even had small consequences on the battlefields. In 1780, the colonial forces under Brigadier General Horatio Gates positioned themselves to attack a British encampment under General Charles Cornwallis in South Carolina. Then the commanders made an unfortunate discovery: Their rum casks were dry. The mess officers, bizarrely, decided to pass out quantities of raw molasses, apparently unaware of its properties as a laxative. The following day, instead of girding for battle, the men scrambled into the bushes grabbing their guts. The British took advantage and routed the colonials.

A year later in South Carolina, at the Battle of Eutaw Springs, colonial troops surprised a British encampment in an early morning raid. The redcoats fled with breakfast uneaten. The hungry and ill-disciplined colonial troops found quantities of food and rum, and wasted little time in availing themselves of both. The British merely waited for the rum to take effect and then counterattacked, driving the colonials back into the forest in disarray.

Among those who suffered from the molasses shortages was Captain Isaac Hall, the Medford militia captain who might have tippled with Paul Revere. Hall provisioned the Continental Army with rum as best he could, accepting debased currency in exchange. His rum business scarcely survived a flood in 1777, which wiped out his stocks of molasses. Sales continued to falter as the war dragged on and molasses remained scarce. In 1787, Isaac sold the distillery to his brother, Ebenezer, and quit the business. (By 1830, Hall's was the only distillery to produce rum in once-redolent Medford. Under various owners, the distillery managed to continue producing traditional New England rum until 1905, when it was finally shuttered.)

Out of the war, a new republic was born. But the old Republic of Rum had begun to totter.

[PUNCH]

Squeeze juice of *one-half* LIME into glass.
Add *one tablespoon* sugar, *one-and-one-half ounces*
RUM, and *two ounces* WATER. Mix well.
Add ice. Grate NUTMEG lightly on top, and
make festive with one or more additions: lemon
slice, papaya chunks, fresh mint, pomegranate,
pineapple spears, cherries, orange peel or slice,
lime wedge, dash of bitters.

Chapter 5

[PLANTER'S PUNCH]

*New England I know little about, except it be the trade
and people. . . . They import large quantities of molasses
from the West Indies, which they distill and sell to
Africa and the other Colonies, which goes by the name
of Yankee rum or Stink-e-buss.*

—NICHOLAS CRESSWELL, CA. 1777

T HE MOST POPULAR and most democratic beverage in colonial America—consumed in more seasons and in more places
than flip—was rum punch.

Punch could be found wherever rum was found—which is to say,
everywhere in America within horse cart distance of the West Indian
trade. As early as 1682, John Winthrop, the first governor of the Massachusetts Bay colony, noted in his records the sale of a punch bowl,
which turned out to be a harbinger of the great era of West Indian rum
imports and later domestic manufacture. Accounts of eighteenth-
century travelers suggest that punch was especially popular in New
York, Virginia, and Pennsylvania. William Penn said that the consumption of punch in his colony rivaled that of beer, and when
William Black of Virginia traveled to Philadelphia in 1744, he mar-

veled that local dignitaries feted him with "a Bowl of fine Lemon Punch big enough to have Swimm'd a half a dozen of young Geese."

Benjamin Franklin, who periodically fretted about the overly exuberant drinking habits of his countrymen, penned a small ode to the pleasant ritual of punch drinking:

> *Boy, bring a bowl of China here,*
> *Fill it with water cool and clear:*
> *Decanter with Jamaica right*
> *And spoon of silver, clean and bright.*
> *Sugar twice-fin'd in piece cut,*
> *Kni[ff]e, sieve and glass in order put,*
> *Bring forth the fragrant fruit and then.*
> *We're happy till the clock strikes ten.*

Before the melting pot, America had the punch bowl. A bowl would be ceremonially placed on the table with sufficient cups and a ladle, which in the better homes was crafted with a handle of whalebone or wood. Early punch bowls were typically ceramic, although those wealthy enough might commission a silversmith to fashion an intricate and gleaming bowl. (After 1780, the cheaper glass punch bowls became more common than the ceramic.) Some punch bowls even achieved a small bit of celebrity. The most famous was made by Paul Revere in 1767 to honor a group of rebellious Massachussetts colony legislators. The local legislature had been ordered by the British Crown to rescind a letter they had sent protesting the onerous Townshend Acts. By a vote of 92 to 17, the legislators refused. The "Glorious 92" were honored with an elegant and graceful silver punch bowl, which is today enshrined at Boston's Museum of Fine Arts.

Punch wasn't only for swells who could afford the fancy trappings; it was also a drink of ruffians and commoners. Pirates and their hangers-on enjoyed a nice bowl of punch between sackings and pillagings. When Captain Kidd and Captain Hewetson met up in 1689, they prepared a punch of "rum, water, lime-juice, egg yolk, sugar with a little nutmeg scrap'd on top." The owners of the most rustic North American taverns in the eighteenth century concocted proprietary recipes for rum punch, which they touted, like their flip, to gain a marketing edge. Early tax inventories suggest that at taverns, punch bowls and cups were almost as common as benches and tankards.

Punch was the first global cocktail, a concoction born in the distant ports of India, England, and the West Indies. Some say the name *punch* evolved from *puncheon,* the small barrel from which sailors received grog rations. But it's more likely that the word came from the Hindustani word *panch,* meaning "five." John Fryer, a British traveler suggested why in 1673: The "English on this coast [of India] make their enervating liquor called Paunch from five ingredients." These five were traditionally tea, lemon, sugar, water, and arrack. The last was a liquor distilled from fermented palm sap and was generally considered nasty enough to make even the most fiery rum taste like cognac. Arrack screamed for dilution and sweetening. Punch was the answer.

As the recipe for punch worked its way westward along trade routes, to Europe and on to the New World, an astonishing number of variations surfaced. Sailors substituted new ingredients when they couldn't obtain the old, and so punch was made with Madeira wine in the eastern Atlantic islands and with rum in the West Indies and North America. The traditional five-part punch was adapted to local conditions; punch recipes called for as few as three or as many as six ingredients. Punch was sometimes made with milk, sometimes with a mix of green and pekoe tea, sometimes with egg yolks, and almost always with citrus. Fresh batches of imported lemons, limes, and oranges were advertised in North American cities for use as punch "sowrings." On Barbados as early as 1694, Father Labat noted that punch consisted of two parts rum, one part water, sugar, lemon or lime juice, cinnamon, clove, and nutmeg. A nineteenth-century recipe for "the established corrective of West Indian languor" was to mix "a compound of rum, sugar, lime juice, and Angostura bitters," which accordingly would be "frisked into effervescence by a stick"—a precursor to the swizzle stick. Pineapple often made it into punch, and at least one Barbados planter preferred his punch made with guava juice.

The most streamlined and enduring recipe for punch called for just four basic ingredients, the recipe distilled to a compact quatrain: "One of sour, two of sweet, three of strong, four of weak." The sour was usually lemon or lime juice; the sweet, sugar; the strong, rum; and the weak, water. This recipe was then modified to taste with spices (nutmeg is especially good) or enjoyed as is. It's a timeless concoction, and still the basis of the best rum punches you'll be served at Caribbean resorts.

The ships that carried sailors and their rum-punch recipes to the New World didn't travel just one way. Once emptied of their westbound freight in the ports of North America, they loaded up with fresh cargo, including locally distilled rum, and set off for the southern mainland colonies and beyond. Rum had found a comfortable and prosperous home from New England to Delaware, but shrewd colonists were certain that if a market could be cultivated in distant lands, America's fortunes could only grow.

This is the story of where rum went when it left New England, and what happened when it got there.

THE SUMMER OF 1764 was busy for the Brown brothers of Providence, Rhode Island. John and Nicholas had recently become signatories on the charter for the new Rhode Island College in Warren. (It later moved to Providence and, in 1804, was renamed Brown University.) And much of the summer was given over to preparing the brig *Sally* for a trading voyage to the African coast. Nicholas—the head of

Nicholas Brown and Company—oversaw business in Providence, but sent frequent instructions to John and their two other brothers, Joseph and Moses, who were at Newport helping to outfit the ship. Among the stores loaded aboard were tobacco, brown sugar, tar, candles, and rice. The ship's manifest also suggests the human cargo it planned to collect when it arrived: a cask of gunpowder, seven swivel guns, eight small arms, thirteen cutlasses, a pair of blunderbusses, a dozen padlocks, three chains, and forty pairs each of handcuffs and shackles. The chief cargo aboard the *Sally* on the outbound voyage to the West African coast was rum, and dozens of casks were rolled aboard—some 159 hogsheads, plus another six smaller barrels, for a total of 17,274 gallons.

This wasn't the Brown family's first venture in the slave trade. Nearly three decades earlier, in 1736, the family patriarch, James Brown, was the first merchant in Providence to sign on with a consortium that backed a slaving voyage to Africa, then onward to the West Indies to trade for coffee and other goods. In 1759, the Browns sent another schooner to Africa, but it was lost, most likely captured by French privateers. At any rate, the Browns certainly had company that summer in the harbors of Rhode Island, where local sea captains were near the peak of their reputation in the booming slave trade.

Rhode Island had little choice but to develop into a trading entrepôt. The southern colonies had their tobacco plantations, and cities like Baltimore, Philadelphia, and New York had great rivers and bays that opened to fertile farmlands, making them centers for the export of grain and produce. But like the rest of New England, Rhode Island had long, bitter winters and rocky, inhospitable soils. So Rhode Islanders turned to the thick forests that provided wood for ships and found the sheltered harbors were perfect for warehouses and anchorages. Rhode Island merchants soon became the Dutch of the English colonies, the masters of trade, first to the West Indies and then beyond.

Merchants or their agents on the islands might have gotten the idea to trade rum for slaves after noticing how much of the West Indian liquor was destined for Africa's coast. The Royal African Company shipped 182,347 gallons of rum from Barbados, Antigua, and Jamaica to Africa between 1700 and 1727. And Rhode Island traders were no doubt aware that rum costing a shilling on the islands could fetch five times that when sent to West Africa.

So the rum and slave trade began to bend northward, as if through some implacable economic magnetism. New England had plenty of rum to trade, and abundant ships to move it. By 1772, about 75 percent of rum exported to Africa came from Boston and Rhode Island.

The Browns had signed a longtime employee (and later Revolutionary War hero), Esek Hopkins, as captain of the *Sally* and, as was customary on such voyages, had given him a free hand in trading. He was instructed to exchange rum for African slaves or any other goods that he thought might net a profit and then sail for the West Indies— precisely which island was left to his own judgment—where he would sell the slaves and other cargo for "hard cash or good bills of exchange." (The Browns also requested that Hopkins return with four slaves for their own use.) They asked Hopkins to "dew as you Shall Think Best for our Interest."

Hopkins and his cargo of rum arrived on the African coast in early November 1764. He discovered he was not alone—it was a busy year for slave traders, hustling to load their cargo because provincial duties on slaves were soon to be imposed in some of the North American colonies. Hopkins had at least one advantage. New England rum had been popular with African chieftains for two decades. "Guinea rum," as it was called, was produced in New England specifically for the African trade, and was usually double-distilled and sometimes triple-distilled. As with Jamaican rum produced for England, the higher proof made it cheaper to ship. Guinea rum was meant to be watered down before being sold. Watering rum was an art, for too much water would make it of little interest to the Africans. Another trader, a Captain Burton, noted that African traders would visit with his ship between seven and ten each morning for negotiations and drinking rum. "If a glass of watered rum, which they detect more easily than we do watered milk, be offered them," wrote the captain, "it will be thrown in the donor's face."

Hopkins spent nine months trading along the African coast—a long time, but not unusually so. (It commonly took six to twelve months to fill a ship with slaves.) His first trade was on November 10, when he swapped one gallon of rum for some wood. The next day, Hopkins brought three gallons of rum to the local tribal official to begin talks, and three days later he traded one hundred fifty-six gallons of rum and some flour, taking a pair of slaves in return. From then on, the ship's trade manifest shows that rum left the *Sally* by the gallon and the hogshead. One hundred ninety-five gallons were traded for a boy and a girl slave in early December. Seventy-five were delivered as a tribute to an African king whom he met "under the palaver tree." One hundred twelve gallons were traded with the king for a single slave; forty-eight gallons for a girl slave; fifty-two gallons for a boy slave; ten flasks for "country cloths;" three flasks as a reward for the return of a runaway slave; three hundred twenty-eight gallons for three slaves, some cloth, and one hundred sixty-five pounds of beeswax. And rum was distributed liberally as gratuities—a flask to the man who owned a spring and four flasks provided to another functionary to expedite an unspecified task.

As Hopkins learned, slaves could be acquired singly or in lots. Trading along the southern coast of west Africa was often quick and efficient, and enough slaves for a westward voyage to the islands could be acquired within a month or two. Other captains in other years might have acquired slaves in lots of a hundred or more at a single trade. But these tended to be weaker, less desirable slaves. The slaves that brought the best prices in the West Indies were found along the Gold Coast—roughly between Cape Verde and the Bight of Benin—

where captains might spend as long as a year trading before the ship was full and readied for the West Indies.

Rum wasn't the only product in demand at African trading posts. Slave sellers also wanted hardware—copper basins, tankards, and unworked brass—and kegs of tallow. Bolts of cloth were much esteemed, and for some reason African traders clamored for red blankets. Guns and gunpowder—the role of which is often overblown in modern accounts of the slave trade—were useful in tribal raids and for capturing more slaves. Guns were not of the highest quality, as the French learned in 1759. They had purchased a lot of muskets from traders on the island of St. Eustatius to defend against an anticipated British invasion. About three-quarters of the guns exploded violently upon the first shot—the French had made the novice's error of buying munitions intended for barter in Africa.

Hopkins sold nine of his slaves before he left the African coast, believing he could fetch a better profit with other goods. He traded four young slaves for 270 bars of iron one month, and four old slaves for 240 bars the next; he also traded away a "man slave with his foot bitt of by a shark." Hopkins hoisted his sails and departed the African coast in late August. He had on board 167 slaves along with his miscellaneous cargo.

New England sailors hated the Africa trade. Malaria, yellow fever, and dysentery were endemic along the Guinea coast, with the summer months especially fatal. While at anchor, the New England ships were a target for vengeful Africans and roaming pirates. And when the trading was completed, the outbound voyages were full of hazard; the chances of slaves rising in revolt in the first few days was considerable. Some slaves were convinced that their fate was to be fed, fattened, and devoured, and they had little incentive to remain docile. At least fifty-five slave uprisings on slave ships were recorded during the slave trade era, with possibly another hundred that went unremarked. Slave ships often departed the African coast with mounted guns aimed inboard and loaded with loose shot, ready to quell unrest. Not until the sight of land vanished over the horizon did the prisoners lose hope. Then the guns were swiveled around for action against pirates.

The *Sally* was among those ships struck by revolt. A week after departure, the captain and crew had to put down an uprising, when, Hopkins recorded, "Slaves Rose on us [and we were] obliged to fire on them and Destroyed 8 and several more wounded badly." Another slave died of the wounds he received during a second, smaller revolt three weeks later.

The voyage, of course, was far more dreadful for the captives than the crew. The shortest crossing, from western Africa to Barbados, could be done in as little as three weeks, but it was the rare ship that could arrive with such haste. If hampered by slack winds and dismal conditions, the crossing might take three months. Slave ship captains at first debated whether tight packing or loose packing worked best. The tight packers had higher fatalities during the voyage owing to the less healthful conditions, but a trip with relatively little disease could yield a greater profit. By the middle of the eighteenth century, tight packing was the norm. The space allotted the slaves below deck was cramped beyond imagination. ("Not so much room as a man in his coffin," wrote a ship's doctor about a ship in 1788.) On average, about one in eight slaves died on the crossing; many deaths were ascribed to "fixed melancholy," in which slaves simply lost the will to live and could not even be forced to eat.

Hopkins's crossing took about a month and a half, and conditions were worse than average. His slaves had been dying for months— about twenty succumbed before he even left Africa. And the voyage was uncommonly deadly—scarcely a day passed that he didn't record another fatality. After the failure of the revolts, many of the slaves simply gave up hope. Hopkins wrote that "some drowned themselves, some starved, and others sickened and died." On at least two days, Hopkins recorded four deaths each. In all, some eighty-eight slaves perished during the voyage—about half his cargo. Those who survived were reported to be in a "very sickly and disordered manner."

And for them, their arrival in the islands meant one nightmare would end and another would begin.

IF NOT FOR slavery, sugar might have been a minor economic footnote in the rise of North America. Growing, harvesting, and processing sugar demanded an army of laborers, and planters wouldn't have cultivated as many fields or reaped a fraction of the profits if they'd had to pay their workers. In any event, the indentured servants shipped over from England and other European countries proved ill-suited for dreary field work under the harsh tropical sun. Africans were less prone to tropical diseases (they died at one-quarter the rate of European immigrants), could be forced to work long hours and, while more expensive than indentured servants to acquire, cost less over time. Without the slaves, sugar would not have been produced in such heroic quantities; and without the molasses from the sugar, rum would not have become such a vital instrument of exchange between the colonies and Africa. Slaves made the rum, and rum made the slaves.

The number of slaves imported to the islands was staggering. They outnumbered Europeans immigrating to the New World throughout the whole of the eighteenth century and nearly half of the nineteenth. The population of Europeans on Barbados peaked at about 20,000 from 1650 into the 1770s. The number of slaves, meanwhile, grew to about 50,000 by the 1680s—about 2 per arable acre—a number that would hold steady for more than a century. The typical West Indian sugar plantation had at least 50 slaves, but more commonly had 200 to 300. (Compare that to the United States: In the 1850s, fewer than half worked on plantations with more than 30 slaves.)

For the planters, life on a sugar plantation was, not surprisingly, very agreeable. Father Antoine Biet visited Barbados in 1654 and noted that a great bowl of punch was often brought out after the midday meal, and toasts were offered all around until the punch bowl was dry. "The afternoon passes thus, in drinking and smoking, but quite often one is so drunk that he cannot return home," Biet reported. "Our gentlemen found this life extremely pleasant."

Life was not so pleasant outside the walls of the great houses. (The perimeter was often planted with lime trees, which not only provided fruit for punch, but had thorns that kept the slaves at a distance.) Slaves planted and harvested the sugar fields and ran the boiling houses and distilling operations, working long hours in conditions that ranged from almost tolerable to beyond wretched. Slaves on Jamaica typically had Saturday and Sunday off, but they were expected to farm their own food during those days. On Barbados, they had only one day off, but at least got most of their food from their overseers. That food, however, was dreadful. Slaves were often fed the worst of the salt cod from Newfoundland (the best went to Europe), and the salted pork from the southern mainland colonies was generally ill prepared. It was customary on the English islands for slaves to get the carcasses of cattle and horses that had died of disease. They were also given about a gallon and a half of molasses each year, although that ration was gradually eliminated as molasses became more valuable for export and distillation.

For the slaves, rum provided nutrition, currency, and entertainment. At some plantations, they were expected to barter their allowance of rum for food, but many typically drank it and suffered, as a result, from malnutrition. Rum could also be a reward. Slaves that turned in other slaves for stealing might be paid, as one plantation visitor noted in 1833, a "trifle in money, flesh, fish or rum." At Codrington Plantation on Barbados, a captured runaway slave would earn the capturer a gallon of plantation rum.

The rum rations given to the slaves varied from plantation to plantation, and from island to island. If the weather was especially disagreeable or the work unusually hard (such as digging the holes for cane planting), an overseer with a reputation for some humanity might take pity and provide an extra ration or two. Among the more generous plantations was Worthy Park, in St. John's Parish on Jamaica.

Each week some of the slaves—including the three drivers, three carpenters, four sugar boilers, the cooper, the blacksmith, and the watchman—were given a full quart of rum. The children's field nurse, the midwife, and the potter got a pint each week. In 1796, some 922 gallons went to Worthy Park slaves over the Christmas season—about two quarts each, which might have made for a merrier Christmas than usual. (Frederick Douglass, who grew up a slave in eastern Maryland in the early nineteenth century, observed that holiday debauches in which liquor was liberally provided to slaves were "useful in keeping down the spirit of insurrection" by allowing the slaves to equate freedom with an incapacitating hangover. "When the holidays ended, we staggered up from the filth of our wallowing, took a long breath, and marched to the field—feeling upon the whole rather glad to go, from what our master had deceived us into a belief was freedom.")

While a little rum might keep the slaves content, a lot could have the opposite effect, provoking rebellion. And island colonists, who were greatly outnumbered by Africans, lived in constant fear of being awakened in their bedrooms by a band of slaves bent on retribution. Among the early laws on Barbados was one that required a planter to hire one white servant for every ten slaves, to ensure that enough free men were available to respond to uprisings. One of the great reasons the British West Indies didn't join their cousins to the north in rebelling against the English Crown—after all, they, too, labored under heavy-handed taxation without representation—was the planters' desperate need of the British navy. Whereas the northern colonists resented the redcoats on their soil, the planters knew that without a heavily armed navy prowling the islands, slaves would be more liable to rise up against their European masters.

And rebellions did occur—they're listed and dated in island histories like notable hurricanes: in Barbados in 1685, 1692, 1702, and 1818; in Antigua in 1736; at Demerara in 1823 (twice); in Jamaica in 1831 and 1832. As many as seventy-five rebellions broke out in the British West Indies before 1837.

The year 1736, for instance, was uncommonly dry in the Caribbean, and this resulted in shortages of water and food on Antigua.
The slaves suffered most, naturally. Outnumbering the whites eight to
one—24,000 to 3,000—slave leaders plotted to pack gunpowder beneath the floor of a ballroom, then, during the king's birthday ball on
the evening of October 20, blow the island's elite into the blue
Caribbean sky. The explosion that echoed around the island would
serve as a signal to slaves on other plantations to slay all the whites
they encountered.

October came and a bloodbath ensued, but it wasn't the one slaves
had envisioned. Planters got wind of the conspiracy and launched a
brutal campaign of torture to root out every slave involved. Slaves were
wrapped in chains and left to die, broken on the rack, and burned
alive. In all, eighty-eight slaves were killed. More would likely have
died had not the island treasury exhausted its funds to reimburse
planters for slaves who were executed or died during questioning.

The great arrows of the Triangle Trade depicted in history text-
books—New England to Africa to the West Indies and back to New
England again—serve as a simple illustration of how the rum trade
kept the great mechanism of colonial economic development hum-
ming along. The rum-to-slaves-to-molasses trade brought untold fortunes to merchants and sugar planters, as well as African chieftains
selling captured slaves. H. F. Willkie noted the triangle's perpetual-
motion-like quality in 1947, when he wrote, "Slaves worked in the
sugar-cane plantations, preparing the molasses from which rum was
made to buy more slaves." Another historian called the trade "the
backbone of New England prosperity," and yet another wrote that it's
"probably not an exaggeration to say that the slave trade was the lu-
bricating oil that kept the machinery of the colonial [New England]
economy moving smoothly." The Triangle Trade even left its mark on
popular culture, most memorably in the 1969 Broadway musical
1776, whose hit song was "Molasses to Rum." ("Molasses to rum to

slaves, Oh what a beautiful waltz, You dance with us, We dance with you, Molasses and rum and slaves . . .")

The Triangle Trade was horrifically elegant, easy for teachers to explain to students, and readily comprehended by sixth-graders. As an historical fact, it lacks only one thing: truth. The smooth-running and sinister New England Triangle Trade is, in large part, an overblown myth.

For starters, no New England traders are known to have completed a single circuit of that triangle. Historian Clifford Shipton spent years of sifting through hundreds of New England shipping records, yet couldn't recall "a single example of a ship engaged in such a triangular trade." (Another historian drew the same conclusion after an exhaustive review of Philadelphia shipping records.) Even the *Sally* was engaged in just two legs of the trade. She failed to load up on molasses in the West Indies. Instead, the Browns demanded cash.

An historian taking a longer view might look at the larger picture and conclude that a variation of the Triangle Trade did exist. After all, some ships brought New England rum to Africa to trade for slaves, other ships brought slaves to the West Indies to trade for molasses, and some other ships—many, actually—traded for molasses to bring back to New England. But did this amount to a powerful economic engine that fueled the emerging economy?

Not likely. Compared to overall global trade, between the colonies and with the greater world beyond, the value of the rum-for-slaves trade was minimal. It didn't come close to providing an economic engine for early New England. More molasses went into pudding, beer making, and baked beans than into rum for the slave trade. As rum historian John McCusker puts it, "the involvement of the Continental Colonies in the slave trade [during the later colonial period] was insignificant by every measure we can apply but a human one."

Rum, it turns out, was welcome but not terrifically esteemed at

African slave stations. It was useful in African ceremonies commemorating the dead and in tribal rites where it was poured down the throat of the corpse. (This was typically followed by a three-day celebration in which the tribesmen would consume it freely to remember—or forget—the past.) But there's little evidence that the Africans took to guzzling rum with anything like the zeal of their North American counterparts. If rum had been the central engine of the slave trade, the quantities exported would have turned the African coast into an alcoholic swamp. As it was, traders complained about temporary rum surpluses on the slave coast, as in 1777 when the price went so low as to make trade untenable. (This was during the Revolutionary War and was likely the result of West Indian rum being diverted to Africa after North American markets were largely closed off.) In the end, exports from New England to Africa accounted for less than 4 percent of all rum produced in and imported to the northern colonies.

Even if one takes rum out of the triangle, the New England involvement in the slave trade was relatively limited. Historian Jay Coughtry identified 934 voyages, carrying more than 106,000 Africans, from Rhode Island to Africa between 1709 and 1807. That's a large number, but still less than 1 percent of all the slaves brought across the Atlantic. British ships alone carried 2.5 million. Rhode Island was a bit player. Indeed, fewer than 1 percent of cargo ships sailing from the northern colonies were destined for Africa and the slave trade.

The simple truth is that the slave trade wasn't very profitable, with or without rum. It was risky, and the money made from a successful voyage wasn't enough to compensate. Rhode Island's Nicholas Brown sent two other ships to Africa in addition to the money-losing *Sally*. One was lost at sea and the other managed only a very slight profit. Brown abandoned the slave trade and looked for business elsewhere.

So where did this notion of a vast, smoothly ticking Triangle Trade originate, and how did it become so ingrained in popular history? As with many legends, it started small, first suggested (vaguely and inconclusively) in an 1866 book by George H. Moore on the history of slavery in Massachusetts. In 1872, it was picked up by another historian, George C. Mason. But the idea didn't come into full flower until 1887, when American businessman and historian William B. Weeden presented a lecture that creatively interpreted the previous two studies. Weeden held up a few isolated examples of the New England slave trade and, in the absence of other records, extrapolated from them aggressively. "We have seen molasses and alcohol, rum and slaves, gold and iron, in a perpetual and unwholesome round of commerce," Weeden wrote. "All society was fouled in this lust; it was inflamed by the passion for wealth . . ." His argument found a receptive audience, and McCusker suspects this was because of a "morbid and somewhat flagellant fascination on the part of late nineteenth century New Englanders with the sins of their forefathers."

The myth found further traction thanks to various political and social movements of the time. Southerners who fought against the abolition of slavery hauled out the idea of the Triangle Trade to show the rank hypocrisy of New England abolitionists. Their argument went like this: Northerners could criticize slavery and call for its end, but only because they had already made *their* fortunes with slavery and the rum trade. Abolition was thus only a matter of economic selfishness. One southern magazine in 1855 referred to the "morbid sensibility evinced in the northern section of our Union upon the subject of slavery," noting that northerners liked to ignore "the substantial fact" that Rhode Islanders were as late as 1808 "trading rum on the coast of Africa for negroes!"

The temperance movement later exploited the Triangle Trade in its crusade against Demon Rum. Booze could be presented as the instrument of enslavement for millions of unfortunates. An investigator with the Church Missionary Society in Africa in the 1880s reported solemnly that he'd seen churches with pews made of liquor boxes, and "canoes in hundreds coming down by river laden with the most precious products of the interior and returning with nothing but filthy drink."

Rum is not untarnished in the long, sour history of the slave trade, but neither is it the kill-devil so often portrayed. As so often is the case, the shadow proved more alarming than the object that cast it.

LIKE FLIP, THE classic punch—whether made from rum, brandy, or wine—began to fall out of fashion in the nineteenth century and was consigned to live out its retirement at regimental reunions and college dances. The working class increasingly took up beer, and the upper classes became enamored of a new breed of sophisticated cocktail that included the Manhattan, the sidecar, and the whiskey old-fashioned. The punch bowl was stashed away in the closet, to be replaced by collins and fizz glasses.

But punch wasn't out yet. A small punch craze surfaced in the 1930s, following Prohibition, when planter's punch emerged as a wildly popular new drink. It actually wasn't all that new; variants of it had appeared decades earlier. The Planter's Hotel (now defunct) in St. Louis claimed credit for the invention of planter's punch based, not implausibly, on its connection with Jerry Thomas, head bartender at the hotel in the mid-1800s and the author of the first bartender's manual. But the hotels' proprietors also claimed credit for the Tom Collins, forcing one to discount their credibility. In fact, Thomas included a great many punch recipes in his early cocktail books, but none for planter's punch. (Another Planter's Hotel in South Carolina has also claimed credit for the punch.)

At any rate, planter's punch is a class of drink rather than a single cocktail, with hundreds of variations floating around, and more invented daily. Each bartender and each generation has variously added to, subtracted from, improved, and spoiled the drink.

Here's the starting point. The *New York Times* ran this ditty in 1908 under the title "Planter's Punch," providing a somewhat modified classic punch recipe.

This recipe I give to thee,
Dear brother in the heat.
Take two of sour (lime let it be)
To one and a half of sweet.
Of Old Jamaica pour three strong,
And add four parts of weak.
Then mix and drink. "I do no wrong—
I know whereof I speak."

The drink had been around long enough that as early as 1920, a writer in a Jamaican paper groused that the planter's punch "has fallen off in strength from what it was in the great days of old when it comes to drinking." Yet few agreed on what went into one. During Prohibition, a writer insisted planter's punch needed to have grenadine and should be topped off with soda water and served in a tall, frosted glass. Most recipes called for lime juice. Others called for the addition of grapefruit juice, orange juice, or both. Varied and assorted fruits have joined the parade. Charles Baker's cocktail guide (1939) abandons any pretense of sorting it all out and lists ten recipes for planter's punch. Island resorts today have their own recipes, and many are quick to claim their own as the original.

If there's a standard planter's punch, I'm guessing it can trace its origins back to the 1920s and to the Myrtle Bank Hotel in Kingston, Jamaica, arguably the most elegant hotel on the island in its day. "I soon found myself in the Myrtle Bank Hotel, and a planter's punch soon found itself in me," wrote a theater columnist for the *New York World* of his visit to Kingston in 1921. He went on: "A planter's punch is made of pure Jamaica rum, a little cane syrup, cracked ice along with a slice of native pineapple and orange to make it more attractive. If one is at all fussy one can have a cherry in it too. The price is the same with or without the cherry at the Myrtle Bank bar."

The drink was popular enough that the Jamaican distiller who made Myers's rum went on to label its as "Planter's Punch Rum," words still emblazoned on some bottles today. The popularity of dark Jamaican rum was such that even distillers in Puerto Rico and Cuba, famous for their lighter rums, started producing a dark rum specifically to meet the demand for planter's punch cocktails.

To my mind, the final word on planter's punch appeared in 1936 in the *New York Times.* "For many people seem to feel that there are only two recipes—the right one and the wrong," wrote Jane Cobb of the ongoing controversy. "In the Ritz-Carlton [in New York], for example, Planter's Punch may appear made with lime juice or lemon juice, white sugar or brown, a dash of brandy or a dash of Angostura bitters, all depending on which of the three bars it is served at. The chances are ten to one that most people who drink the punches like them very much, no matter which version is served. Anyway the sensible thing to do is to drink slowly and stop fussing."

If rum is the archetypal New World drink—protean, varied, inconsistent—planter's punch is its cocktail equivalent. Try inventing one yourself. Start with something basic—one of sour, two of sweet, three of strong, four of weak. Then adapt it: Give it a college degree and better clothes. Try exotic fruit or maybe some bitters. It doesn't really matter what you do. Planter's punch can be constantly reinvented. It's owned by whomever wants to claim it.

[PRUNE WATER]

In three cups of water, *cook slowly* for one half-hour *one-quarter pound* of PRUNES and a thin strip of LEMON PEEL. Add JUICE of one-half LEMON. *Strain* and *sweeten* to taste. Do *not* add RUM.

[FROM *On Uncle Sam's Water Wagon*, A 1919 GUIDE TO "DELICIOUS, APPETIZING, AND WHOLESOME DRINKS, FREE FROM THE ALCOHOLIC TAINT."]

Chapter 6

[DEMON RUM]

Hear the happy voices ringing,
As "King Rum" is downward hurled,
Shouting vict'ry and hosanna,
In their march to save the world.

—WOMAN'S CHRISTIAN TEMPERANCE
UNION SONG, LATE NINETEENTH CENTURY

IN OCTOBER 1884, a small but vocal group of Protestant clergymen gathered at a rally in New York City to show their support for the Republican presidential candidate, James G. Blaine of Maine. It was an impromptu meeting without an official sponsor or much of an agenda, and Blaine attended mostly to show his face and make a few encouraging comments to the pious group. Before Blaine rose to speak, though, an elderly, unremarkable Presbyterian minister named Samuel Burchard made his way to the podium. Little is known about Burchard, and by some accounts he didn't even have the full attention of the assembled when he spoke. But one of Burchard's lines would enter the lexicon. "We are Republicans," he said, "and don't propose to leave our party and identify ourselves with the party whose antecedents have been rum, Romanism, and rebellion."

What came to be known as the "Burchard Alliteration" was not atypical for the times: Politicians and temperance leaders loved to set off a string of rhetorical firecrackers to get the attention of a crowd. In 1888, a temperance crusader attacked liquor dealers as those who destroyed society with "bombast, beer, and bombs," and who were happy to substitute "anarchy for order, lawlessness for law, license for liberty."

Burchard's remarks caught the ear of at least one man, a journalist from the *New York World*. He jotted down Burchard's remark and published it the next day in his account of the meeting.

"Rum, Romanism, and rebellion" turned out to be a hand grenade, an unexpected gift from Burchard to the Democratic Party. Blaine did not instantly distance himself from the comment, lending the impression that the Republican candidate would bring to Washington his elitist and bigoted friends who had little tolerance for Catholics—those Romanists—and their drinking, rabble-rousing ways. Large numbers of Catholics had immigrated in recent years, and most were fervent Democrats. The comment had the effect, in modern terms, of motivating the party's base. Blaine struggled to control the damage, claiming that he had been weary after a long campaign swing through the West, that his attention was focused on preparing his own remarks during Burchard's talk. He never even heard Burchard make his comment, Blaine said. The tepid disavowals didn't slow the thunderhead of Democratic criticism from building. Three days later, Blaine finally stepped forward to loudly repudiate the remark, saying, "I am the last man in the United States who would make a disrespectful allusion to another man's religion."

His response came too late, and offered up too little. When voters went to the polls a few weeks later, James G. Blaine lost New York to Grover Cleveland by a little more than a thousand votes. The electoral college race was extremely close nationally—a situation familiar to those who voted in 2000 and 2004. Had Blaine won New York, he would have moved into the White House.

The meek Burchard was ever after known as "the man who opened his mouth and swallowed a presidency."

To the drink historian, the most interesting question is, exactly *what rum* was Burchard referring to? Because by the late nineteenth century, rum had fallen so far out of fashion as to be all but forgotten. It was rarely found in a proper home; and when it was, it was likely stashed in a hallway closet or under the front stairs, hunted up only when someone had bronchitis, or for holiday mince pie or eggnog.

By the late 1800s, rum was no longer just the stuff made from sugarcane and its leavings. It was a name used to describe all drink—whiskey and gin and cordials and beer and Madeira wine. Anything that got you drunk was "rum."

And "rum" was much, much more. It was evil in a glass—a dark force that infiltrated families and tore them asunder, that broke good men and left them derelict, that had seeped into the underpinnings of American democracy and was working to rot it from below.

In the nineteenth century, rum had become the devil incarnate.

IN TRUTH, RUM hadn't been quite itself since the American Revolution. The conclusion of the rebellion in 1783 and the return to a fitful peace was at first good news for the war-ravaged rum industry. Trading ships could resume their West Indian trade routes, and distillers could again import barrels of molasses to feed their stills. Rum soon flowed out of the northern distilleries, headed to taverns in the new nation and to traders sailing for coastal West Africa. Rhode Island, in particular, wasted little time in reclaiming its role as a center for the rum trade, and the treacly aroma of fermenting molasses again filled the seaports.

Rum's recovery was brief. The chief problem was molasses—or the lack of it. Molasses proved harder to get after the war than before, and more expensive when it could be had. The trade with the British colonies never fully recovered after hostilities ended. The West Indian planters, who had remained loyal to the Crown when their northern compatriots rebelled, were still bound by the Navigation Acts, which prohibited direct trade between British colonies and nations other than England—which now included the newly minted United States. U.S. distillers could at first direct ships to obtain molasses from French and Spanish islands, but these doors, too, began to close. In 1783, Spain abruptly shut its Cuban ports to Americans and seized two U.S. ships in a spat over American settlers in Spanish Florida. French ports were also soon off limits, the fallout of Byzantine political intrigue involving the British. In any event, the French islands had by then invested more in its own rum industry, and molasses was no longer viewed as something to be cheaply bartered away for a few sticks of lumber. In what must have sounded like a death knell to North American rum distillers, in 1807 the United States passed the Embargo Act, which banned American trade with England and France. The rum industry couldn't catch a break.

Trade opened up between the United States and the West Indies after the War of 1812, but by then the soils on the British islands were worn and depleted after two centuries of sugar production, and great amounts of manure were needed to maintain a decent yield. What's more, the British had begun emancipating its slaves. Without a ready supply of forced labor, the once immensely profitable sugar plantations became uneconomical and tipped into a long decline. Rum soon lost its historic role as the cheap spirit that fueled international commerce and returned to its roots: a local commodity, produced by islanders and for islanders. By the mid-nineteenth century, a melancholy traveler to the British West Indies colonies wrote of the abandoned sugar estates, "It is difficult to exaggerate, and yet more difficult to define, the poverty and industrial prostration. . . ." The islands at the center of the world for two centuries were consigned to the forgotten margins.

FINDING ENOUGH MOLASSES to keep the North American stills running was only part of the problem. There was also the matter of changing tastes, fueled by an animated American nationalism. American consumers had come to regard rum as an artifact of the ancient régime, a product associated with the imperious British, their fussy teas, and their high-handed ways. Rum had little role in the shaping of a new national political culture. Prior to the Revolution, drinking rum was a sign of the growing affluence and independence of the colonists. It demonstrated they were prosperous enough to purchase rum made abroad—and later to manufacture their own rum from raw materials acquired through trade of their lumber and livestock. But following the war, rum took on a whiff of national weakness and vulnerability, and became a small emblem of financial imprisonment. Why drink an imported product that aided one's enemy when you could purchase a local product and advance your own economy?

Throughout the colonies, drinkers made the switch to other drinks. Some shrewdly saw opportunity for gain. Boston brewer Samuel Adams ran advertising that noted, "It is to be hoped, that the Gentlemen of the Town will endeavor to bring our own October Beer into Fashion again, by that most prevailing Motive, Example, so that we may no longer be beholden to Foreigners for a Credible Liquor, which may be as successfully manufactured in this Country."

New Englanders in the business of distilling rum did what Americans often do best in times of economic change: They retooled. The more adept distillers switched to other products. In Providence, the illustrious Brown family had constructed a new rum distillery after the war in an attempt to revive their business. But they abandoned that endeavor by 1791, and regrouped to open one of the nation's first gin distilleries, placing ads in newspapers to reach growers of rye, barley, buckwheat, and juniper berries. Rum, they concluded, was a relic of the old economy, like sperm whale candles or coarse red-clay pottery.

Rum makers who lacked the capital or desire to retool simply shuttered their distilleries and walked away. By 1794, the number of distilleries in once-thriving Boston had dwindled to a handful, and of those not many were operating at even half capacity; by 1800, American distilleries were producing only 45 percent of rum made just a decade earlier. The trend was inexorable; by 1888, Boston was down to three rum distilleries.

If rum was of the spirit of the past, what was the spirit of the future? Without question, it was whiskey.

WHISKEY WASN'T WHOLLY unfamiliar to the taverngoers of the early nineteenth century, but it was rare compared to rum. The first native whiskey had been produced in the northern colonies in the seventeenth century, but was made out of valuable grain that had to be transported by inefficient wagons from inland farms. Molasses was produced a much greater distance away, but cheap shipping ensured that it was far less expensive.

After the Revolution, Americans emigrated in increasing numbers from crowded seaboard cities, across the Appalachians, to the Ohio River Valley and beyond. Here they found fertile soils and ideal growing conditions for grains and corn. Forests fell, crops blossomed, and the new settlers found they could produce more than they could consume or sell locally. This presented a logistical problem. Americans had two markets for agricultural commodities such as wheat and corn. One was east of the Appalachians at the seaboard cities. The other was far downriver in New Orleans. Shipping barrels of wheat or corn by buckboard overland across the mountains was expensive and impractical. (This was ameliorated somewhat in 1825, when the Erie Canal opened between the Great Lakes and the Atlantic.) New Orleans was a much greater distance away, but it was cheaper to ship bulk products by boat.

One other alternative existed. With a modest investment, farmers could convert their grain to a commodity that could be more affordably shipped east.

The arithmetic was appealing. One horse might be able to haul four bushels of wheat milled into flour. But if that grain or corn were run through a still and the whiskey put in casks, the same horse could haul the equivalent of twenty-four bushels. So farmers bought and built stills in great number. One traveler in western Pennsylvania observed that at least one farm in thirty had an operating still. Great torrents of whiskey flooded across the mountains and began to inundate the cities along the eastern coast.

THE SURPLUS OF grain and corn was an essential ingredient in the nineteenth-century whiskey boom, but the new liquor was greatly aided by technology. As America embarked on its industrial revolution, inventors tinkered endlessly to improve the old ways of doing things. Americans were especially keen to advance the science of distillation. Between 1802 and 1815, more than a hundred patents were granted by the government for distillation devices—or about one in every twenty patents issued. Printers published articles and pamphlets to aid journeyman distillers, with titles like the 1824 "Essay on the Importance and the Best Mode of Converting Grain into Spirit."

The most radical change came with the invention of new stills that could run continuously. The process and equipment used to separate alcohol from water had been largely unchanged for five hundred years. A distiller placed a fermented, low-alcohol brew into a pot, boiled it, captured the steam, condensed it, emptied out the pot, and then ran another batch. This was time-consuming and slow, since the pot had to be cleaned between each batch to avoid spoiling the spirit.

The new stills changed all that. The first variation was the "perpetual still," an ingenious device involving a condensing globe (rather than a copper cooling coil) housed *inside* a sealed tank. The wash was continually piped into the tank and around the globe. This still not only could be run nonstop, but it used the wash to cool the condensate, thereby preheating it and reducing the need for fuel in boiling off the alcohol.

The perpetual still was a precursor to an even more magnificent breakthrough—the continuous column still. Around 1826, Aeneas Coffey, a distillery worker in Dublin, Ireland, separated alcohol from water using two tall copper columns, each divided horizontally by a series of perforated plates. Steam was piped into the bottom of each column, and this heated the upper plates enough to boil off alcohol but not water. So the wash was pumped in to the top of the first column, and then trickled down through the heated plates. Vapors rich with alcohol evaporated first and were piped into the second column, where it went through the process again. The highly alcoholic steam was then captured and condensed. The less-alcoholic water vapors would condense lower in the column and would flow as waste out the bottom.

One problem arose with the brilliant efficiency of this process. The alcohol that emerged from the column still was so astoundingly pure, and so devoid of the trace elements that lent each liquor its distinctive taste, that whiskey and rum and other spirits from these stills proved all but impervious to aging. A distiller could put the liquor into a barrel and age it, and five years later it came out as hot and harsh as it went in. Coffey had, it turned out, invented the process for distilling neutral spirits—pure alcohol. All but the most committed topers found it medicinal and unpleasant. Some years later, a workaround was devised when a distiller figured out that he could mix the pure alcohol from a column still with a smaller amount of heavier, and more aromatic, pot-stilled liquor and put the blend up in barrels. The resulting liquor aged nicely. This discovery gave the ancient pot still a new lease on life. To this day, many rums are made with a blend of rums from pot stills and column stills. (Modern column stills have also been fine-tuned so that more of the spirit's essential elements can be captured, reducing the need for the pot still.)

THE YEAR 1802 was a good one for American liquor, especially whiskey. An ill-advised whiskey tax imposed some years earlier by

Treasury Secretary Alexander Hamilton—which triggered the short-lived Whiskey Rebellion in western Pennsylvania—was at last repealed. Americans now had the tacit blessing of their government to produce and consume more liquor. The United States was home to an estimated eighteen thousand distilleries, and over the next three decades American consumers found themselves awash in whiskey. It was available everywhere, from country stores to city taverns, and made by everyone from large producers to one's neighbors. Ever pragmatic, Americans made an even stronger commitment to drink than their besotted colonial ancestors. And few Americans were too poor to drink. "During the first third of the nineteenth century the typical American annually drank more distilled liquor than at any other time in our history," writes liquor historian W. J. Rorabaugh. Americans of the era outdrank the English, the Irish, and the Prussians. (They fell short, however, of the Swedes.) By conservative estimates, the average American in 1830 drank the equivalent of five gallons of absolute alcohol annually—close to three times current levels. The average American didn't really exist, of course. Those doing the drinking were mostly over fifteen years old, and mostly male. And even within this group, not all drank. So the drinkers *really* drank. Rorabaugh estimates that half of the adult males in the nation were responsible for downing about two-thirds of the spirits. Historian Norman Clark estimates that in the early nineteenth century, drinkers actually swilled about ten gallons of pure alcohol each year—or more than two bottles of 90 proof liquor each and every week.

America's love affair with strong drink fascinated and scandalized visiting Europeans. An Englishman who traveled down the Mississippi in the 1820s noted that in every corner he visited, "north or south, east or west," he found "the universal practice of sipping a little at a time, but frequently." In 1824, essayist Samuel Morewood noted the impact of inexpensive whiskey: "From the extraordinary cheapness with which spirits can be procured in the United States, averaging scarcely more than thirty-eight cents the gallon, the people indulge themselves to excess, and run into all the extravagancies of inebriety." Drink permeated all levels of society, from the gutter to the ballroom. At Andrew Jackson's 1829 inaugural gala, the guests guzzled booze with such ardor that the White House staff feared the official residence would be trampled into a ruin. They devised a simple solution: The staff hauled the whiskey out to the lawn, and when the great herd of guests followed, closed and bolted the doors behind them. Frances Trollope's *Domestic Manners of the Americans,* first published in 1832, noted that for all the exalted talk of democracy's promise, she most often heard it "in accents that breathe less of freedom than onions and whiskey."

Liquor-fueled troubles swelled in small towns and large cities alike, from drunken street clashes to heads of households abandoning wives and children. Drinking invaded hallowed churches; one New England magazine was compelled to note in 1812 that "the selling of spirituous liquors at a place of worship should be discouraged and that a man who indulges in the use of ardent spirits is in a poor situation to either hear or preach the gospel."

The unseemly and unproductive behavior of drunkards was increasingly at odds with a new generation of can-do Americans, who saw their nation as full of promise and plenty. Drink was a tax on the sober, stuck with the tab for the wreckage left by drinkers in their wake. Upright citizens began organizing to reform the morals of their neighbors. Amid a besotted society, a backlash started to brew.

And while rum now served as second fiddle to whiskey in all aspects of American life, from economic to cultural, in one sphere rum remained supreme: the temperance movement.

IN 1785, the great patriot named Benjamin Rush published a small book on the perils of drink. Rush was a Philadelphia doctor, as learned as he was restless. A signer of the Declaration of Independence, he had served as the first surgeon general of the Continental Army, opposed the ownership of slaves, and advocated the development of a large-scale maple sugar industry to create "a source of sugar that would be free from the taint of slavery." He distributed watermelons to Philadelphia prisoners in summer. But most notably, Rush was the first physician to challenge the medicinal benefits of alcohol—no small feat given distillation's long alliance with alchemists and apothecaries, and the persistent belief that alcohol was the cure for nearly every disease. While Rush allowed that beer and wine consumed moderately were good for one's health, his observations of his countrymen led him to wonder about the merits of consuming "ardent spirits." Indeed, Rush was among the first to identify alcoholism as a disease, one in which drinkers became victim to a "craving" or "appetite" that lured them to the edge of a cliff and then pushed them over. Rush was nothing if not a careful observer. In his *Inquiry into the Effect of Ardent Spirits,* Rush outlined the eight stages of drunkenness with unsettling accuracy: First, "unusual garrulity." Second, "unusual silence." Third, "a disposition to quarrel." Fourth, "uncommon good humor and an insipid simpering, or laugh." Fifth, "profane swearing and cursing." Sixth, "a disclosure of his or other people's secrets." Seventh, "a rude disposition to tell those persons in company whom they know, their faults." And eighth, "certain immodest actions." Rush called for Americans to resist the siren song of liquor as they built their new nation.

At first, the sentiments in Rush's tract found only a small audience. But with alcohol consumption at historic highs in the early nineteenth century, the scattered brigade of concerned Americans began to coalesce. Individual protests against drink in isolated communities grew into small but organized units, which in turn became broader campaigns. The Union Temperance Society of Moreau and Northumberland, founded in Saratoga, New York, in 1808, prohibited members from drinking "rum, gin, whiskey, wine, or any distilled spirits" except when sick or at public dinners. The following year the Total Abstinence Society was founded in nearby Greenfield, New York. The Massachusetts Society for the Suppression of Intemperance, which would become one of the most influential groups nationally, was founded in 1813. Dozens of other societies would follow, among them the powerful Washington Temperance Society, the American Temperance Society, the Congressional Total Abstinence Society, the Sons of Temperance, the United Order of the Golden Cross and Sons of Jonadab, the Marblehead Union Moral Society, the Order of the Templars of Honor and Temperance, the National Temperance Society and Publication House, and Catholic Total Abstinence. By 1833, a million Americans had signed pledges for temperance through six thousand temperance associations around the nation.

The attack on intoxicating liquors was more than a crusade in name—it had the trappings of a full-out war. Books like Charles Jewett's *Forty Years' Fight with the Drink Demon* (1877), and J. A. Dacus's *Battling with the Demon* (1872) urged followers to take up arms against an insidious foe. Rev. W. W. Hicks said of drink, "It has no regard for honor. It knows no truce. It hears no cry of remonstrance—no appeal for quarter." A letter to the *New York Tribune* following the Civil War noted that "the people in this part of Ohio honestly think the next war in this country will be between women and whiskey; and though there may not be much blood shed, you may rest assured rum will flow freely in the gutter."

The most powerful weapon in the temperance arsenal, at least in its crude firepower, were the temperance tracts—the booklets and pamphlets that decried drink and urged the reader to follow the more righteous path of sobriety. Crusaders embraced the doctrine of overwhelming force, as if the weight of the printed word could overcome the evils of alcohol. Between 1829 and 1834, temperance societies in New York—the most active state in the nation in the war on drink—churned out 5.5 million tracts; by 1839, fifteen temperance journals were published in the United States; in 1851, the American Tract

Society alone had distributed another 5 million tracts nationwide. Other temperance groups published their own screeds, or ordered them in bulk from National Temperance Society, which had dozens of titles available at wholesale for between $4 and $8 per thousand.

The tracts informed readers exactly what would happen to those who succumbed to drink. The best they could hope for was impeded digestion or clogged brains. At worst, they could expect cheerless haggardness, physical collapse, and, in the final stages, the horrors of the delirium tremens. In libraries and reading rooms, visitors could peruse *Sewall's Stomach Plates,* a set of eight lithographs nearly two-by-three-feet each, which showed the deterioration of the stomach of a drunk. "Not the production of mere fancy," the promotions claimed, but "the result of actual scientific research and investigation." One 1877 tract noted that "scientific men agree . . . that all diseases arising from intoxicating drinks are liable to become hereditary to the third generation, increasing, if the cause be continued, till the family becomes extinct." The Woman's Christian Temperance Union, founded in 1874, oversaw its own Department of Scientific Temperance Instruction, which produced schoolbooks detailing the effect of alcohol on the body, such as the thinning of the walls of blood vessels, which could result in abrupt bursting. (The WCTU didn't limit its antipathy to drink; they also had a Department of Suppression of Social Evil that promoted blue laws, a department to end bigamy among Mormons, and a department that advocated the eating of bland foods, since spicy foods were believed to provoke a thirst for strong drink.)

Violent deaths were a natural by-product of drink in the temperance tracts, an early variant of the "scared-straight" approach to dissuasion. Children were left destitute by swilling fathers, and young men once brimming with promise died early. M. L. Weems, best known for inventing the legend of George Washington and the cherry tree, wrote in *The Drunkard's Looking Glass* (1812) of a young Dred Drake, who, in his cups, agreed to a horseback race through a piney wood. He scarcely made it a hundred yards before falling from his horse and dashing out his brains. "There was not a sign of a nose remaining on his face," Weems wrote, "the violence of the blow had crushed it flat, miserably battering his mouth and teeth, and completely scalping the right side of his face and head—the flesh, skin, and ear torn off to the back of his skull. One of his eyes, meeting a snag on the trunk of a tree, was clearly knocked out of its socket; and held only by a string of skin, there lay naked on his bloody cheek."

If the trees didn't get you, the literal fires of damnation would. Temperance tracts reported that the blood or perspiration of a drunk would flare up when he or she got near an open flame. Even if no flame were present, there was the distinct possibility of spontaneous combustion. The first reports of boozers coming to an abrupt and fiery end surfaced in Europe and found a keen audience among Americans, who already had a large appetite for spectacle. Vanishing in a puff of smoke crossed from rumor into popular culture in 1853 when Charles Dickens, in *Bleak House,* depicted a character reeking of gin abruptly dematerializing into "a smouldering suffocating vapor in the room, and a dark and greasy coating on the walls and ceilings." In a subsequent edition, Dickens defended the veracity of the scene in a preface that cited nearly three dozen cases of spontaneous combustion among heavy drinkers.

If the prospect of a fiery end didn't frighten one off drink, there was always the relatively mundane fear of poisoning. Temperance leaders averred that distillers weren't content merely to poison their customers with alcohol alone; they added toxic ingredients to encourage addiction and slowly kill off the drinker. (No explanation was offered as to why a liquor vendor would want to kill off his client base.) "The adulteration and manufacture of villainous and maddening decoctions have become common," wrote one temperance sympathizer. Another fretted that the "addition of some actively poisonous substances to alcohol, in order to produce a new luxury, is the evil most disastrous." The new liquors "do not satisfy as the genuine liquors of the past were wont to do," wrote an oddly nostalgic third, "but instead to incite further indulgence."

Some of these reports of poisonings took root in the thin soil of a partial truth—the less scrupulous rum sellers were long known to stretch a supply of Jamaican rum by wiles and deceit, cutting it with harsh domestic rum and more. An 1829 work entitled *Wine and Spirit Adulteration Unmasked* included several recipes for making "old Jamaican rum" with nontraditional ingredients including birch-oil tincture, oak bark, "new-scraped leather," tar, and oil of clove. A later account noted even less appetizing ingredients to give fresh-made alcohol the sophistication of mature liquor: logwood, brazil-wood, green vitriol, opium, tobacco, aloes, bitter orange, henbane, nux vomica, sugar of lead, oil of bitter almonds, poison hemlock, bark of tartar. Spirit sellers, increasingly under attack, defended the whole-someness of their products by advertising that their wines and liquors were, in the words of one Philadelphia tavern keeper, "warranted pure and unadulterated."

THE TEMPERANCE CRUSADE was more of a guerrilla uprising than a traditional battle with a well-defined front. Scattered, far-flung groups went after the local and state liquor trade in isolated skirmishes; group leaders came together at conclaves and conventions to ex-change ideas and beat the drums to maintain the fervor. The enemy was always out there, in kegs and bottles and tankards. Crusaders often railed against "intoxicating liquors" when among themselves, but that terminology was ungainly and lacked punch on pennants and posters and in podium-pounding speeches. "Ardent Spirits," another favorite, seemed too genteel, and "King Alcohol" lacked absoluteness— alcohol, after all, was useful in industry and for medical reasons. The Drys needed a villain, one that had resonance, was memorable, and could command the attention of distracted crowds.

And so was born Demon Rum. The omnipresent liquor of the colonial era was now back, a symbol of everything odious that plagued the new republic, the windmill at which temperance crusaders would tilt.

By what curious process did rum come to exemplify the worst elements of liquor? In the 1830s, whiskey was by far the dominant drink. Why didn't temperance leaders put whiskey squarely in their crosshairs? (To be fair, some tracts did go after whiskey, like the 1878 *National Temperance Almanac,* which asked, "What key will unlock the door to hell? Whis-*key.*")

Whiskey was inconvenient in small ways, not the least that it was hard to rhyme. Yet anyone could find a rhyme for rum. In the 1900 presidential campaign, Republican supporters of William McKinley were given to chanting, "McKinley drinks soda water, Bryan drinks rum; McKinley is a gentleman, Bryan is a bum." Rum was also pliable and could append itself nicely to other words. The mid-nineteenth century was the glory days for rum words: *Rummy* surfaced in 1834, *rum-hole* in 1836, *rum-mill* in 1849, and *rum-dealer* in 1860. Orators assailed the "rum interests" and made references to the "rum tax."

Samuel Smith, a temperance poet, put this informal use of rum into more formal terms:

> *Hail, mighty rum! and by this general name*
> *I call each species—whiskey, gin or brandy:*
> *(The kinds are various—but th' effect's the same,*
> *And so I choose a name that's short and handy;*
> *For reader, know it takes a deal of time*
> *To make a crooked word lie smooth in rhyme . . .*

This sturdy, three-letter word—the very epitome of Anglo-Saxon vigor—packed a vast amount of power, lore, and tradition into its small frame. As historian J. C. Furnas noted, rum made for a "fine, short disreputable-sounding syllable, admirable for rhetorical uses."

Yet rum could also sound a charge. Its sound was to temperance troops like the sound of a bagpipe to a Scot or a bugle to a western infantryman. It evoked memories of pioneers like Benjamin Rush, or early crusaders in the Republic of Rum. Never mind that few now *drank* rum—it was a name infused with the sacrifice of early heroes.

To fight Demon Rum was to fight the fiercest and most formidable dragon terrorizing the countryside. Some posters featured Demon Rum personified, with horns and a rictus grin, its evil tail wrapped around bodies of the dead and dying drinkers. One tract offered helpful hints on child raising: "If you must some times scare them in the room of telling them that bears will catch them, that hobgoblins or ghosts will catch them, tell them that *Rum* will catch them."

Demon Rum helped pull together a decentralized movement that was often at cross-purposes. Goals varied: some called for complete abstention from drink, others just for moderation. Some wanted all forms of alcohol, including beer and wine, driven from the country; others focused their wrath on ardent spirits. But they all could share a vivid loathing for the great demon itself. Rum was a uniter, not a divider.

And it had come full circle: In colonial times, rum was a symbol of freedom and independence—not only from the mother country, but also freedom from the dour Puritan elites. Now rum stood in the way of true freedom and so became the focus of one of the most persistent campaigns in American history.

SUCH TECHNIQUES AS public browbeating and extraction of signed sobriety pledges were remarkably successful—for a while. Personal consumption of alcohol dropped, in one estimate, by three-quarters, the boozy 1830s becoming the relatively dry 1840s. But the ocean of temperance pamphlets, plays, and poems failed to have a more enduring effect. A signature on a temperance pledge was hardly binding, and backsliding was endemic. And for every person who signed the pledge, hundreds refused. An influx of European immigrants from Ireland, Germany, and Scandinavia brought with them entrenched tippling habits and changed the demographics. By the late 1840s, drinking was again on the upswing. A new approach was needed.

So the temperance crusade turned its attention away from the rum drinker and toward the rum seller. The campaign to shut down the Rum Traffic started small, embracing the "local option" that allowed localities to ban liquor sales. In Massachusetts, for instance, whole counties went dry. Emboldened, the movement went for larger quarry and sought to ban sales at the state level. Success was spotty at first. In 1838, Massachusetts effectively banned the retail sale of liquor with the "fifteen-gallon law," which permitted sales of liquor only in amounts of fifteen gallons or more—effectively shutting down taverns and dramshops. Creative interpretations of the law cropped up, among them the famous "striped pig." A liquor dealer painted up a pig with colorful stripes and announced that for a mere six cents a citizen could marvel at this freak of nature—and enjoy a complimentary glass of whiskey while doing so. The fifteen-gallon law, riddled with loopholes, was soon repealed.

In 1851, Maine was the first to pass a state prohibition, thanks to a short, tenacious businessman turned politician named Neal Dow. With its population of fishermen, farmers, and lumbermen, Maine had long been home to serious drinkers, whose habits offended the abstemious and hardworking Dow. His conversion from passive disgust to open activism occurred in the 1840s, when he sought to aid a destitute relative who drank to excess. Dow went into the shop where the besotted relative bought his liquor and asked the rum seller to refuse the poor, broken man. The rum seller curtly brushed off Dow's suggestion by noting that he was licensed by the city and he could sell to whomsoever he pleased. Dow took this as a challenge.

With increasing fanaticism, Dow pursued his vision of a liquor-free society. He agitated successfully for a citywide law banning liquor sales in his hometown of Portland. Drinking slowed but didn't stop.

Frustrated by the flow of liquor from adjoining towns, Dow badgered the state legislature into considering a statewide liquor ban. His arguments and sheer personal force proved irresistible, and what came to be known as "Maine law" carried the legislature. Dow brought the document to the governor for his signature and then set about enforcing its provisions. Just months after the law's passage, Dow himself oversaw the destruction of $2,000 worth of liquor in Portland, and boasted that "in Portland there were between three and four hundred rum-shops, and immediately after the enactment of the law not one." Dow portrayed alcohol as a quarry that needed to be hunted and slain: Liquor "stands in the same category with wild beasts and noxious reptiles," he said, "which no one can claim as property and which every one may destroy, and in so doing any one is a public benefactor."

The success of the 1851 law came as a revelation to temperance movements nationwide. Dow traveled widely to promote Maine's triumphs and assisted other states in passing similar laws. Within four years, thirteen states had banned liquor sales, and the trade was passing into its first miniature ice age.

Sadly for temperance leaders, the chill proved temporary. Wets successfully lobbied for amendments to weaken dry laws in several states, making the sale of wine and beer legal. Court challenges in eight states found the liquor bans at odds with the state constitution and repealed them altogether. And Wets in all states soon made a discovery: The laws were easy to evade. The striped pig became a "blind pig," and a nickel bought a viewing of a sightless hog and a dram of free liquor. The first coming of Prohibition stumbled and fell.

The temperance movement faced further setbacks in the run-up to the Civil War and the four-year bloodletting that followed. After the South fired on Fort Sumter, social activists shifted their energies from social betterment to the emancipation of slaves—except for a handful of temperance camp followers who traveled with the troops and forced tracts upon them. (The temperance crusaders marked up one small success during the war: They had a law passed in 1862 that banned liquor aboard "vessels of war, except as medicine and upon the order and under the control of the medical officer and to be used only for medical purposes.") After Robert E. Lee's surrender at Appomattox, Virginia, and the postwar rebuilding of a nation, liquor prohibition seemed a distant and quaint memory. America resumed drinking habits not from the more moderate 1850s but the harder-drinking 1830s.

Temperance leaders charged, possibly with some accuracy, that the Civil War had changed the social landscape. The country came out of the war with a more dominant masculine culture, in which the ability to hold one's drink became a mark of status. Many states renounced their earlier flings with prohibition, and no states showed any interest in curbing drinking anew. Not one state passed a law banning liquor sales between the years of 1856 and 1879.

DRINK WAS BACK. H. L. Mencken dubbed the decades following the war—roughly from 1865 to 1900—the "Golden Age of American Drinking." Bartenders concocted their own bitters, infused their own cordials, and brought a high level of skill to their craft. This era saw the invention of such classic cocktails as the Manhattan, the old-fashioned, and the martini. The highball—liquor enlivened with a splash of soda water—came into fashion in 1895, although purists groused that the liquor was "robbed of authority" by diluting it with the "cheap fluid which they put under bridges or use in sprinkling the lawn." The rickey, a cocktail made with a fresh-squeezed lime, surfaced around 1880, possibly at a bar in Washington, D.C. The Tom Collins, basically a rickey with the addition of sugar, followed soon after. Even flip resurfaced, although considerably altered from its colonial incarnation: Hot water was used in the place of the red-hot loggerhead.

The cobbler, the fizz, and the sour also appeared in this heady era, and Scotch, brought into fashion by the golf craze that swept the nation in the 1890s, began its decades-long fling with popularity.

Cities large and not so large were suddenly home to a surfeit of fancy hotel bars, as famous for their drinks as for the opulence of their surroundings. Among the more notable were the Waldorf, the Hoffman House, and the Knickerbocker in New York City; the Palace in San Francisco; the Antlers in San Antonio; and the Touraine in Boston. The trend was abetted by the invention of the modern ice-maker, which could produce ice in bulk and on demand, without the mess of cutting ice from a February pond and packing it in sawdust. Cocktails on the rocks went from a luxury to a necessity. Jerry Thomas became the first modern bartender and authored a now-revered book for both bartenders and home drinkers. The ungainly word *mixologist* was coined in 1856. By 1870, W. F. Rae noted, "The most delicate fancy drinks are compounded by skillful mixologists in a style that captivates the public."

The embrace of elaborate concoctions, flavored and mixed with an array of bitters and tonics and infusions, was one of America's most visible cultural exports in the 1890s. "American bars" appeared throughout Europe, with the fanciful drinks inspiring curiosity among many and revulsion among a few. *Harper's* magazine in 1890 noted the rise of American bars in London, dispensing "various mixtures that taste like hair oil, but . . . cost[ing] twice the price of English liquor." Among the cocktails of note were the Sustainer, the Silent Cobbler, the Square Meal, the Alabazam, the Bosom Caresser, the Flash of Lightning, the Corpse Reviver, the Heap of Comfort, and the Prairie Oyster.

And where was rum in all this? It made the occasional cameo in bar guides but for the most part was relegated to cold-weather drinks and cough medicine. Its most notable incarnation was in the Tom and Jerry cocktail, invented by Jerry Thomas himself: An egg (the yolk and white beaten separately) was mixed in a china mug with Jamaican rum, powdered sugar, and brandy. Hot water was added, and nutmeg grated over the top. This cocktail has not remained in fashion.

WHILE SWELLS IN derbies elbowed their way up to the modern hotel bars, rough-edged drinkers congregated in saloons, which proliferated in the years following the Civil War. Saloons ranged from rank hellholes in urban slums to fancier establishments in prosperous downtowns, complete with hand-carved back bars and brass railings and original artworks, often of female nudes. Saloons could be found on main streets and in back alleys, and various estimates put the number nationwide at one to every three hundred to four hundred Americans. San Francisco might have been the most pickled city, with one saloon for every ninety-six inhabitants. A saloon was not the place for the fancy drinks of hotel bars. Here, patrons ordered their whiskey straight or beer by the tall glass.

Especially beer. Known as "the poor man's clubs," saloons attracted immigrants who brought to their new country a love of malt and hops. German immigrants established breweries in Milwaukee and St. Louis, and beers made by the Coors, Pabst, Schlitz, Schmidt, Anheuser, and Busch families became household names. Whiskey found its popularity eroding against the cheaper, easier-to-quaff beer, the consumption of which increased fourfold between 1880 and 1913. By the turn of the century, more than 60 percent of the alcohol consumed by Americans was beer—a reversal for spirits, which had accounted for 60 percent of the alcohol consumed in 1830.

Saloons were often owned and operated by the largest breweries and boosted their beer sales with aggressive promotions and free (and salty) lunch buffets. The world of the saloon was increasingly seen as one of extravagant excess—not only of drink, but of gambling, sex, and petty crime. While old-fashioned temperance tracts flogged the "rum seller," a new breed of activist turned his or her sights on the saloon as the nation's chief distribution center of evil. The charge had resonance, since Americans increasingly associated saloons with the wave of immigrants that had fetched up on its shores. Their unfamiliar accents sounded a note of alarm to established Americans already unsettled by the social and economic changes of the late nineteenth and early twentieth centuries.

Temperance had found a new demon.

In May 1893, Howard Hyde Russell founded the Anti-Saloon League of Ohio, which was soon followed by nine other state chapters. Two years later, these groups and dozens of local affiliates merged to form the Anti-Saloon League of America. Deft at political assassination and ready to carpet bomb with its screeds—the ASL printed and distributed more than 100 million copies of antidrinking tracts in the early twentieth century—the ASL became politically influential in short order. A new wave of state prohibitions on liquor sales soon swept the nation.

This time, temperance leaders—many of whom happened to be women—viewed the battle against drink as more than a metaphor. Perhaps none embraced the fight as fervently as the six-foot-tall and sourpussed Carry Nation, a Kansas resident who lost one husband to alcohol and a second to her activism. She concluded, not incorrectly, that prayer at the doorstep of a saloon did little to reverse the evils of alcohol. It would require weaponry. (Suffrage also played a role: "You refused me the vote," she explained simply to the Kansas legislature, "and I had to use a rock.") In the spring of 1900, following the Lord's instructions—conveyed to her in a dream—she loaded a wagon with brickbats, bottles, bits of scrap metal, and chunks of wood, then traveled twenty-five miles from her home in Medicine Lodge to Kiowa and proceeded to lay to waste three saloons, smashing windows, glassware, and artwork. Efforts to arrest her came to nothing, since Kansas was a "dry" state. The mayor and town council needed arresting, Nation thundered, and then continued on her way unmolested.

Her armaments grew less cumbersome. She adopted the hatchet as her weapon of choice and ravaged saloons in Kansas and other dry states, smashing bottles and glasses, and hacking at the polished bars. (Her efforts in wet states were limited to loud hectoring, since she didn't have carte blanche to cause actual damage to legal enterprises.)

Carry Nation launched her final crusade in Butte, Montana, in 1910. She was sixty-three. It did not go well. She crossed swords with a woman saloon proprietor whose determination equaled her own. Her cloak of invincibility, already frayed, was in tatters. She died a year later of "nervous trouble," and was buried, largely forgotten, next to her mother in a small cemetery in Missouri.

The Anti-Saloon League soldiered on, turning its attention to Congress and pushing for a nationwide ban on alcohol sales. They found growing support in Washington. Heavy drink and its attendant problems were again on the upswing. The league proved agile in corralling politicians into supporting its cause, especially through the determined efforts of Wayne Wheeler, who began his career on a bicycle lobbying for antidrinking statutes along Lake Erie in Ohio. Wheeler raised vast amounts of money from the industrial leaders, including Henry Ford, Andrew Carnegie, Pierre du Pont, Cyrus McCormick, and both John D. Rockefeller Jr. and Sr. The corporate titans, who believed that drinking was hurting productivity among their workers, contributed more than money. They were visible supporters of temperance, believing a sober workforce would yield more profits.

By the second decade of the twentieth century, there was a groundswell of support for a broader prohibition. In 1907, another round of state prohibition laws were passed. In 1915, whiskey and brandy were eliminated as medically approved drugs, and the American Medical Association condemned the drinking of spirits. An effort to pass a national prohibition through constitutional amendment in 1914 fell 61 votes short of the two-thirds majority required. The movement regrouped, and in 1916 the ASL succeeded in getting numerous antidrink legislators into office. A constitutional amendment banning the sale of drink was introduced again the following year, and this time quickly passed in both the House and the Senate.

The amendment moved to the states. Thirty-three were dry when the voting began; the Drys had seven years to convince thirty-six states to ratify the amendment and change the Constitution. The Wets had been lax in fighting the amendment, in part because they were convinced that states would refuse to tinker with the constitution over such a small matter. They were wrong. Mississippi was first to ratify the amendment in January 1918, and fourteen other states followed by the end of the year. Then came the deluge. In early January 1919, twenty states signed on to the ban on liquor sales, and on January 16—less than one year after Congress had voted on the amendment—Nebraska became the thirty-sixth state to ratify the amendment. (In all, forty-six states would go along, with only Connecticut and Rhode Island declining.) As saloon historian George Ade saw it, "The non-drinkers had been organizing for fifty years, and the drinker had no organization whatever. They had been too busy, drinking."

The Volstead Act created the mechanisms that would actually end the liquor trade, and Congress passed it quickly. Americans poured themselves a last legal drink. The temperance crusade, which began in the 1830s, was an eighty-year thunderstorm that concluded with a single thunderclap. On midnight, January 16, 1920, any American involved in the production, transfer, or sale of any liquor, beer, or wine would be jailed and his or her property confiscated.

The Republic of Rum had fallen at last.

[DAIQUIRI]

Mix *two ounces* LIGHT RUM with juice of *one-half* LIME and *one to two teaspoons* of SUGAR or sugar syrup, to taste. Shake in cocktail shaker with *half cubed ice, half crushed ice,* with no la-dee-da, until shaker is *too icy* to hold. *Strain* into chilled cocktail glass.

Chapter 7

[DAIQUIRI]

The moment had arrived for a Daiquiri. It was a delicate compound; it elevated my contentment to an even higher pitch. Unquestionably, the cocktail on my table was a dangerous agent, for it held in its shallow glass bowl slightly encrusted with undissolved sugar the power of a contemptuous indifference to fate; it set the mind free of responsibility; obliterating both memory and tomorrow, it gave the heart an adventitious feeling of superiority and momentarily vanquished all the celebrated, the eternal fears.

—Joseph Hergesheimer,
San Cristóbal de la Habana, 1920

It was 1932, and Ernest Hemingway was looking for a way to avoid his home in Key West, Florida. His celebrity as a writer had soared after the publication of *Death in the Afternoon,* and a constant stream of friends, well-wishers, and the idle curious flowed to the Whitehead Street house where he lived with his wife, Pauline. Hemingway tried to write in his office off the backyard pool, but the constant splashing and merrymaking put him in a state of great distraction. So he packed his bags, headed to the ferry terminal, and bought a ticket for Cuba. A few hours later, he made his way through narrow streets of old Havana to a small hotel called the Ambos Mundos. Here, he paid for a corner room on the quiet fifth floor and settled in to write. He said that the cool breezes of a Havana morning allowed him "to work as well there . . . [as] anywhere in the world."

But then came the stifling Havana afternoons. Hemingway would rise from his desk and set off to explore the city. He went deep-sea fishing, swimming in the Caribbean, and wagering at the jai alai fronton. And, increasingly, he haunted Havana's bars, of which there were no shortage in the waning years of American Prohibition. He grew fond of one in particular, El Floridita, just a few blocks up Obisbo Street from his hotel. He discovered here a delightful drink and a consummate bartender, both of which he would make famous. The bartender was named Constantino. The drink was called the daiquiri.

Prohibition had a number of far-reaching effects on American society, virtually none of which the antibooze crusaders had anticipated or desired. "The Noble Experiment," in large part, served mostly to prove the law of unintended consequences.

For starters, instead of stigmatizing the drinking of alcohol, Prohibition actually made it more respectable. While the Volstead Act did succeed in shuttering the lower-class saloons, it gave rise to the speakeasy, which soon became the habitat of women and the middle class. As Prohibition historian Thomas Pegram noted, the liquor ban "broke down the saloon culture of male drinking and replaced it with a culture of youthful, recreational drinking which emphasized social contact between men and women." Not every drinker welcomed this change. Hollywood gossip Heywood Broun groused that the old saloons may have been rotten and coarse, but a visit to the bartender didn't require elbowing through a crowd of schoolgirls.

Prohibition also transformed what America drank and how it drank it. In particular, it gave rise to the cloying cocktail, which arose in part to mask the medicinal-tasting homemade liquors that flooded the underground market. "Everyone with a bottle of bathtub gin, a basket of fruit, and some icebox leftovers invented a new cocktail," wrote David Embury in 1948. "Almost any liquid short of gasoline, added to the liquor of that era, would help conceal its raw alcohol taste and would therefore improve it. Eggs and cream, in particular, smooth out the taste and disguise the alcoholic strength of liquor. And so dawned the day of the poultry and dairy cocktails."

And then there was the Dry's influence on West Indian rum. By banning the sale of all beverage alcohol in the United States, prohibitionists did what no island distiller could have dared hope for: They pulled weary old rum out of its shallow grave, not only infusing it with life, but giving it a bit of swagger and a touch of class.

Prohibition, it turned out, was the best thing to happen to rum since the first barrels rolled ashore on the docks of the northern colonies in the mid-seventeenth century.

When the ban on liquor went into effect in January 1920, hundreds of American distilleries went dark. (A few dozen were granted permits to manufacture industrial alcohol.) This, in turn, triggered the largest coast-to-coast home science project in American history. Americans were suddenly fascinated by the obscure habits of yeast. In 1919, even the august Scientific American Publishing Company printed a booklet entitled *Home Made Beverages: The Manufacture of Non-Alcoholic and Alcoholic Drinks in the Household*. Vendors sold small barrels for aging homemade spirits, along with simple stills that could process one- or five-gallon batches. Those who couldn't afford a fancy apparatus adopted a simpler approach: They would ferment a mash from corn (or grain) and sugar, then set it in a large pot on the kitchen stove and bring it to a low simmer. When the mixture reached 180 degrees, above the boiling point of alcohol but below that of water, they draped a cloth over the top and patiently squeezed out the captured vapors. With the addition of a few juniper berries, an almost potable gin could be fashioned from the rag's wringings.

More ambitious moonshiners fired up backcountry stills to meet demand. Small puffs of smoke blossomed like dogwood in rural hills across the country, and white lightning and "corn likker" moved from the hollows to homes and speakeasies under the cover of night. (Federal agents found and destroyed 696,933 stills in the first five years of Prohibition, but the liquor kept on coming.)

The stuff sold in speakeasies often wasn't much better than the stuff wrung out of rags. Enterprising owners would smuggle in perfectly good liquor from Canada or the Bahamas, and then cut one bottle of good liquor to make five bottles of bad. The good stuff would be diluted with whatever cheap industrial-grade alcohol could be bought or stolen. If that wasn't available, antifreeze, hair tonic, and aftershave could be employed. The product could then be colored with caramel and flavored (sometimes with creosote) to hide the raw taste.

The powerful urge to find a drink that wouldn't mercilessly assail the palate led to one other unintended impact of Prohibition. It promoted travel and tourism. In particular, it promoted travel to nations where liquor was still available. This left an impressively large choice—in fact, every country except Finland, which had imposed its own prohibition in 1919. (Canada flirted with prohibition in some provinces early on, but came to its senses when it realized the vast size of the American market for contraband liquor.)

Of the many overseas choices, Cuba stood out. The largest of the Caribbean islands, Cuba was just a short hop from Florida and was redolent of romance, adventure, and fermenting molasses. The *New York Times* noted that not only was the sunshine and the Old World charm of Havana alluring, but that "nowhere . . . does the Eighteenth Amendment run or the Volstead Act have jurisdiction." The paper added that " 'swizzles,' 'Daiquiris,' 'planters' punches' and other drinks may be consumed without subterfuge or fear of poisoning." Ships soon disgorged thousands of parched American passengers on Cuban shores. At least twenty made weekly runs to Havana, and far more ferries shuttled Americans from Miami and Key West.

Drinking began early in a journey south. When foreign-registered steamships crossed into international waters while still within sight of the American shoreline, armies of stewards invaded the staterooms bearing trays of cocktails. And even before passengers disembarked to fill the nightclubs of Havana, a flotilla of small "bumboats" would besiege arriving ships, with locals offering up bottles of cheap rum for sale. Ship captains hoping to keep their crews sober (and passengers buying onboard cocktails) turned the fire hoses on the floating vendors. The hapless boats filled and capsized, leaving the liquor salesmen to swim to shore with their bobbing bottles. The flotilla developed techniques to counteract these attacks, including sending out more bumboats than the ship had fire hoses. The craftiest entrepreneurs would dodge under the overhanging stern, from which the conspiring crew would lower a basket and exchange a few dollars for liquor.

New transportation networks arose to meet demand for travel to Cuba. In November 1920, just ten months after Prohibition went into effect, Aeromarine Airways took its first passengers to Cuba in eleven-seat "flying boats"—the first international airline service ever offered from the United States. In 1927, Pan American Airways (better known later as Pan Am) first took off: its seaplanes lifted off from the blue-green waters at Coconut Grove, then banked over the Keys and landed in Cuba an hour later, well in time for afternoon cocktails. Business boomed; Pan Am flew Amelia Earhart to Havana for the gala opening of the airline's new terminal, and in Miami, airline salesmen swarmed the sidewalks, handing out flyers promising passersby they could "bathe in Bacardi tonight." "Havana," *Fortune* magazine noted, "became the unofficial United States saloon."

The city was touted in travel magazines as a sort of licentious Paris with palm trees, a city of smoky nightclubs overflowing with sultry music, liquor, and more than a hint of romance. (Havana's reputation was not new; as early as 1911, the *Cleveland Press* reported that "Havana is World's Wickedest City, Press Man Finds," noting that naked women actually performed on stage.) Havana had everything you couldn't get at home, including syphilis cures that were advertised in tourist magazines. Even the Shriners and the Elks were drawn here for conventions in the 1920s; the Cubans got along famously with the Shriners, but were puzzled by the more taciturn Elks.

Most of all, Havana attracted the affluent and socially prominent. Basil Woon, writing in *When It's Cocktail Time in Cuba* (1928), insisted that the city's fashionable watering holes were on par with the best of Europe. " 'Have one in Havana' seems to have become the winter slogan of the wealthy," he wrote, adding that the city attracted society visitors along the lines of Charles Lindbergh, Anita Loos, Cyrus Curtis, and William K. Vanderbilt. Havana's season ran from the opening of the horse track in early December to the closing of the casino in March. "Havana is not, like Palm Beach, a parrot-cage of ostentation," Woon wrote. "It is rather, like Paris, a city of definite attraction where smart people go to be amused."

American hoteliers scrambled to cater to the new breed of seasonal immigrant, and in 1928 a travel writer reported that "Havana is studded with very new and painfully expensive English-spoken hotels, which are jammed to the billiard tables from January to April." Among them was the Biltmore chain, which already had hotels catering to the well-off in New York, Atlanta, Los Angeles, and Coral Gables. The chain bought the Hotel Sevilla in downtown Havana just before Prohibition took effect, adding a ten-story tower and a roof garden, and rechristening it the Sevilla-Biltmore. They added new services to lure visiting Americans—like long-distance phone calling and two orchestras to play the ballroom—and they ensured that the extensive bar was amply stocked.

Just across from the Sevilla-Biltmore was the Telégrafo Hotel. Inside was Donovan's bar, operated by an Irishman from Newark, New Jersey. When Prohibition was enacted, other bartenders in Newark either padlocked their doors or switched to soft drinks. Donovan had a grander plan. He wrenched out his entire bar—stools and signs and mirrors and chairs—and shipped everything to Havana. He installed it in the Telégrafo and reopened to his new clientele, business as usual.

Among the more popular haunts of visiting Americans was a bar on Zulueta Street called Sloppy Joe's, whose slogan was "Where the Wet Begins." It was originally called La Victoria, but a local newspaper reporter, irked at the owner's refusal to advance him a $50 loan, penned an editorial attacking the bar and called for local officials to look into its unsanitary conditions. The article snidely suggested that it be called "Sloppy Joe's." The infamy brought more business, especially with Americans. So the bar's owner officially changed the name of the place and catered increasingly to the tourist trade, even selling belts crafted with holsters to hide small bottles of smuggled rum beneath jackets. The bar became famous among gawking tourists, and infamous among those who sought to avoid them. "It is not a very pretty picture to see a half a dozen grey-haired American ladies clinging to the bar rail in Sloppy Joe's," reported one traveler in the *New Republic,* "shouting maudlin ditties to the tropic night and their bored and slick-haired gigolos."

The visitors to Cuba discovered something else that pleased them greatly: a light, crisp rum that tasted nothing at all like the medicinal, rough, dark New England rum of decades past. As Basil Woon put it, "Rum, by the grace of a family named Bacardi and of American prohibition, had become, in fact, a gentleman's drink."

Rum had been reinvented. Again.

THE NEW RUM traced its history to 1836, the year that a fifteen-year-old Catalonian immigrant named Facundo Bacardi y Maso arrived with his family at the elegant colonial city of Santiago de Cuba on the island's southeast coast. Facundo set himself up as an importer of wines and seller of spirits and, in 1862, purchased with one of his brothers the modest Santiago distillery of an Englishman named John

Nunes. Depending on which company legend one subscribes to, a colony of bats either lived in the rafters of the distillery or occupied a tree in the backyard. They fluttered around the distillery in the evenings, and locals started calling Bacardi's rum "the bat drink." Bacardi smelled opportunity. Rural Cubans were largely illiterate, and a graphic logo allowed the drink stand out among so many incomprehensible words of other brands. So Bacardi introduced the bat trademark, plastering it on his labels. The logo caught on, and never left. One magazine recently ranked it as one of the ten most valuable logos in the world, in league with those of Kodak, McDonald's, and Coca-Cola. (There's another explanation for the bat: Bacardi may have lifted the idea from the civic heraldry of his native city of Valencia, which features a bat with wings spread atop a crown. Legend has it that in 1238, moments before King Jaume stormed Valencia to reclaim it from the Moors, a bat hovered overhead and landed atop his standard, and forever after the bat was seen as a harbinger of luck.)

Bacardi's success as a distiller left little to luck and much to technological innovation. He set about looking for a way to make the harsh, often disagreeable spirit lighter, smoother, and more palatable to a broader array of drinkers. His breakthrough was a filtering system, which removed the heavier, oilier impurities that often made rum such a rank bit of business. (The filter, which remains a family secret, probably involved a combination of charcoal and sand.) Bacardi toyed with different woods for his casks and tinkered with the blending process, mixing rums from different batches to create a consistently smooth product. Bacardi entered his rum in international competitions; at the Philadelphia Centennial Exhibition in 1876, Bacardi's light rum won a gold medal.

In 1892, Bacardi was rewarded with another welcome piece of publicity. Spain's ailing six-year-old King Alfonso XIII was faring poorly—feverish and with dim prospects for survival. Not knowing what else to do, the king's keepers administered a dollop of Bacardi's rum, which knocked him into a deep slumber. When Alfonso awoke, his fever had broken and he was on the mend. Spain's royal secretary wrote the distiller to thank Bacardi "for making a product that has saved the life of His Majesty." Bacardi did not keep this letter a secret.

Bacardi's rise was blessed by another accident of history—the outbreak of the Spanish-American War in 1898. The war is remembered mostly for the historic shift in American foreign policy, from isolationism to a more bellicose interventionism. Less well known is the effect the war had in introducing Americans to a new rum. When Teddy Roosevelt charged up Cuba's San Juan Hill with his Rough Riders, he established a beachhead for a wave of American immigrants, initially in the mining and the sugar industry, and later in tourism. The new arrivals quickly embraced Bacardi's rum. In 1899, a reporter for a New England newspaper concluded that the Santiago region's charms were not overly impressive. ("The country houses around Santiago are infested with mice and lizards.") But he did commend a restaurant where he was served "a native rum, called bacardi [sic], which is made from molasses, and which, well mixed with water and cooled with ice, makes a very smooth sort of beverage and a somewhat insidious one. A quart bottle of this rum costs only fifty cents, and as a good deal of it is usually drunk at the midday meal it is not to be wondered at that a nap immediately follows it."

Bacardi's light rum, in fact, mixed well with about everything—carbonated water, lime juice, pineapple juice, orange juice—and new cocktails were born, sometimes by design and sometimes not. In 1899, Santiago was swept by a craze for a new drink called the "mismo." It arose when a group of Cubans and Americans got together at the Cosmopolitan Club, and one of the Cubans ordered a Bacardi and seltzer. The next Cuban said, *"Lo mismo,"* which is to say, "The same." The Americans, eager to try something novel, also ordered *los mismos,* and found them much to their liking. When they returned to the bar the next day, they ordered another round of mismos. The same waiter was fortunately on duty and served them their mismos without missing a beat. "It spread with remarkable rapidity," reported the *New*

York Tribune, "until now every barkeeper in Santiago knows what you are after if you ask for a 'mismo.' In fact, you rarely ever hear Bacardi rum and seltzer spoken of in any other way now."

Bacardi saw a welcome increase in orders to the United States during World War I, when supplies of European spirits were disrupted. But Prohibition gave Bacardi its greatest windfall: an estimated $50 million in sales to dry Americans. Not only did Bacardi sell vast quantities to Americans visiting Cuba, but its shipments to the smuggling ports of Saint-Pierre—a French island off Newfoundland—and the Bahamas tripled. In 1924, flush with profits, the Bacardi family commissioned the noted American illustrator Maxfield Parrish to design an office building in Havana, a fanciful construct of modern lines and old world whimsy. The eight-story tower, just a block from the Parque Central and a short walk to the presidential palace, had an oversized ground floor clad in a chocolaty marble, with the upper floors in a pale yellow brick capped by fanciful friezes and colorful cornices and crenellations.

Edificio Bacardi became one of the city's chief attractions for Prohibition pilgrims. Few were interested in the architecture, however. To promote its rum, Bacardi gave away free drinks weekdays to any tourist who wandered up to the second floor bar, where bartenders crafted perfect cocktails. "We took rum, an unsophisticated drink, and made it a sophisticated drink," company patriarch Jose Argamasilla-Bacardi recalled to the *Wall Street Journal.* "All the people who liked rum but were ashamed to ask for it aren't ashamed anymore."

Travelers touring the West Indies during Prohibition quickly learned that the world could be wonderfully exotic when viewed through the bottom of a cocktail glass. Adolph Schmitt, a bartender on the Hamburg-American liner *Reliance,* groused about the extra work: "No passenger wanted the same drink twice," he said. "Instead of ordering Scotch or rye they insisted on clover clubs, orange blossoms, gin fizzes, gin rickeys, mint juleps, and old-fashioned cocktails. Then they learned about Daiquiri cocktails at Havana, rum swizzles at Trinidad, and punch at Kingston. On the way home they wanted all of these. I worked twelve hours a day trying to keep pace with the demand and at night I used to dream that new drinks had been invented."

AMONG THE NEW drinks, the daiquiri cocktail was a standout. A perfect blend of lime, sugar, rum, and ice, the daiquiri cuts through the humidity, heat, and haze of the tropics with an uncanny precision. It has an invitingly translucent appearance when made well, as cool and lustrous as alabaster.

How was it invented? Two origin myths have surfaced, both involving Americans. The most common involves an American engineer, Jennings Cox, who managed mines near the town of Daiquirí, not far from Santiago. In one telling, Cox and another foreign engineer spent a dusty afternoon touring abandoned mines near Cobre in 1896. The day's work over, they retired to Cox's home for a drink, where the host was mortified to discover that he lacked imported gin or whiskey to serve his guest. With only local rum that he wouldn't serve straight, he improvised: He put lime juice and sugar into a cocktail shaker and gave it a lively shaking. The result was surprisingly delicious. "What is this cocktail?" asked the marveling visitor. Cox admitted that it hadn't been properly christened, but allowed that it was probably a rum sour or something of the sort. The guest found this name insufficiently laudatory. "This name isn't worthy of such a fine and delicious cocktail," he exclaimed. "We'll call it a daiquiri!"

Other variants of this story surface now and again. Cox's granddaughter claims that when he served the proto-daiquiri he was entertaining not another engineer, but a group of American dignitaries. In another account, Facundo Bacardi was present and reported that Cox exclaimed, "I'll tell you what, lads—we all work at Daiquirí and we all drank this drink first there. Let's call it a daiquiri!"

The second myth involves an American military officer named

William Shafter, who came ashore during the Spanish-American War in 1898 near Santiago. He was not shy of girth and in poor health, and he liked food and drink more than the tedious chore of battle. When he sampled the drink of the Cuban patriot—rum, lime juice, and sugar muddled together—he found it to his liking and declared, "Only one ingredient is missing—ice." He set about remedying that omission, and, lo, the daiquiri was born.

Which tale is correct? Who knows? Cocktail archives are lamentably scarce. Connoisseurs of spurious tales will appreciate both stories for the precise, often stilted quotes rendered verbatim (the "lads" is a nice touch). But it's a bit odd that anyone would claim credit for a cocktail whose ingredients had been mixed well and often since at least 1740, when Admiral Edward Vernon issued his order to distribute limes and sugar with grog rations. Limes had mingled with rum for centuries aboard ships, and it wasn't much of a secret that the puckery tartness of limes and the underlying sweetness of rum were born to marry. The pair were the Astaire and Rogers of the cocktail world, every bit as perfect as gin and vermouth.

At heart, the daiquiri is simply a variation of the ageless punch recipe: one of sour, two of sweet, three of strong, four of weak. The chief difference between a daiquiri and punch—and the real stroke of brilliance, to which the General Shafter origin myth gives a nod—was the use of ice as the "weak."

The cocktail culture that blossomed in the tropics in the 1920s was abetted by the wide availability of ice. In the steamier counties, ice had long been a luxury—captured most vividly in the opening chapter of Gabriel García Márquez's *A Hundred Years of Solitude,* in which gypsies bring a block of glimmering ice to a small village in South America, a jewel in a sawdust-filled chest, and the protagonist, Colonel Aureliano Buendía proclaims it to be "the great invention of our time." The inconvenience and expense of cutting ice in winter near northern ports and shipping it south ended around 1870, when the invention of artificial refrigeration meant that even the most sultry

cities could produce their own frosty diamonds. By the early twentieth century, ice was an everyday commodity.

What makes the daiquiri an enduring classic is its perfect simplicity. It doesn't require an off-putting list of unfamiliar ingredients, and
the techniques for making one can be easily learned. Yet it requires a
nuanced pouring hand to get just the right proportions—not too
sweet nor too sour, not too icy nor too warm. A proper daiquiri may
be either shaken or stirred. Recipes typically call for shaking the lime
juice, sugar, and rum until the shaker frosts over, then straining and
serving. In 1909, a naval medical officer named Lucius W. Johnson
met the engineer Jennings Cox, who served him one of his famous
daiquiris. "He mixed in each glass a jigger of rum, the juice of half a
lime, and a teaspoon of sugar," Johnson wrote. "He then filled the
glass with finely shaved ice and stirred it well. In that hot, humid
weather the ice melted rapidly and the glass quickly became frosted."

Johnson brought his daiquiri recipe to the United States, where
he introduced it to the Army and Navy Club on Farragut Square in
downtown Washington, D.C. The drink caught on, and the club soon
opened the Daiquiri Lounge. (Officers still order up daiquiris here.)
This was the first step to making the daiquiri a proper cocktail in the
eyes of Americans.

It took Ernest Hemingway to give the daiquiri a more literary glow.

CONSTANTINO RIBALAIGUA VERT was the chief bartender and
owner of El Floridita, a popular establishment just a few minutes'
walk from Hemingway's hotel. With its long bar, dim interior, and
grocery stocked with basic cooking supplies, it had the congeniality
of a bodega combined with the sophistication of a hotel bar. Constantino had first learned about daiquiris from Emilio Gonzalez, a bartender at the nearby Plaza Hotel. But Constantino wasn't content to
leave the concoction alone, and he tinkered endlessly, mixing daiquiris
with the chipped ice from the Flak Mark chipper he had imported

from the United States. He created at least four different versions of the daiquiri, all excellent. One popular variant included five drops of Marasquin, a cherry-flavored liqueur. He dubbed it the "Daiquiri Floridita."

Constantino's technique involved equal parts precision and flamboyance. He would fill stemmed cocktail glasses with ice to chill them, pour the ingredients (often for several drinks) into a cocktail shaker, and then shake vigorously, reportedly then sending the contents in a great arc from one half of the shaker to the other. He'd empty out the ice from the now-chilled glasses, line these up in a row on the bar, and fill them with a fluid sweep of his arm. Awed visitors said that every glass was filled to the brim, and not a drop was left in the shaker. To watch Constantino was to watch a master craftsman at work.

As he presided over his bar one day, a scruffy, bearish man entered and asked to use the toilet. According to one account, when the man emerged from the bathroom and saw the daiquiris lined up on the bar, his curiosity was piqued. He asked for a sip. "That's good, but I prefer it without sugar and double rum," the man said. Constantino mixed one up to those specifications, and the man declared it *very* good. He was, of course, Ernest Hemingway. This modified version of the daiquiri became known ever after as the "Papa Doble." (A later variation also enjoyed by Hemingway included a splash of grapefruit juice and a dash of maraschino liqueur: the "Hemingway Special.")

It was Hemingway's first but by no means last visit to El Floridita. About a third of his life was spent in Cuba, a measurable portion at El Floridita. One of the waiters later recalled that Hemingway would often slide into his usual seat in a shadowy corner of the bar, far to the left, where he would read or write, and remain so still as to attract no more attention than a painting. "If you didn't see him you didn't know he was there," the waiter said. Hemingway made no effort to stand out; one of the things he liked best about Havana was that he could let his beard go long, wear ratty blue swimming trunks and a dirty guayabera shirt, and sit barefoot at El Floridita while downing Constantino's double daiquiris.

And down them he did. Hemingway drank long and deeply, sometimes breaking up a drinking session with a trip to the jai alai fronton, only to end up back at El Floridita, where he'd have four or five more drinks before calling it a night. He maintained his drinking habits even after his third wife, journalist Martha Gellhorn, persuaded him to leave his downtown hotel room and purchase a small farm, which they called Finca Vigía, a few miles southeast of Havana. Hemingway said the marathon sessions with the bottle were essential to combat the fatigue that plagued him after writing. Biographer Carlos Baker notes that his binges were the only aspect of Hemingway's Cuban life that really annoyed Gellhorn. And as their fights over his drinking increased, Baker wrote, he spent more time "at the Floridita while the tall daiquiris came and went in seemingly inexhaustible supply."

During his fourth marriage, to Mary Welsh, Hemingway still sought out El Floridita while awaiting her return from her frequent travels, keeping at bay what he called the "black lonelies" by staying out until two in the morning. A consummate competitor, Hemingway managed to set a house record, consuming sixteen daiquiris in one sitting. Yet he had a heroic capacity for drink. He rarely became a nasty or sloppy drunk, but rather tended to grow sullen and remote. He chief problem, he said, was the "mastodon hangovers" that made it all but impossible to work the next day.

The daiquiri became nearly as large a part of the Hemingway legend as bullfights in Spain and the woods of northern Michigan. He worked the daiquiri into his fiction, most notably in his posthumously published *Islands in the Stream*. "The Floridita was now open," Hemingway wrote, and his protagonist Thomas Hudson entered and ordered "a double frozen daiquiri with no sugar from Pedrico, who smiled his smile which was almost like the rictus on a dead man who had died from a suddenly broken back, and yet was a true and legiti-mate smile." Hemingway later turned uncharacteristically rhapsodic about his favored drink: "This frozen daiquiri, so well beaten as it is, looks like the sea where the wave falls away from the bow of a ship when she is doing thirty knots." (Hemingway can't claim credit for in-troducing the daiquiri to the literate American public. That honor goes to F. Scott Fitzgerald, who produced the first known published reference to it in 1920, when the daiquiri made a fleeting cameo in *This Side of Paradise.*)

The daiquiri was by no means Hemingway's only drink—he was not especially picky when it came to alcohol. He often knocked back three Scotches when he finished writing. He liked absinthe and red wine and white wine and champagne and vodka and whiskey. On the *Pilar,* his thirty-eight-foot fishing boat, Hemingway had a customized bar built high on the flying bridge to keep drink at hand when piloting the boat; he called tequila his "steering liquor." Hemingway stead-fastly refused to admit that he had a drinking problem. ("Have spent my life straightening out rummies and all my life drinking," Heming-way wrote to A. E. Hotchner in 1949, "but since writing is my true love I never get the two things mixed up.") But his drinking began to poach on his skills, and his output lessened and grew less compelling after the publication of *The Old Man and the Sea* in 1952. Even FBI di-rector J. Edgar Hoover noted, apropos of Hemingway's fruitless hunts for German submarines off the Cuban coast during World War II, that "Hemingway's judgment is not of the best, and if his sobriety is the same as it was some years ago, that is certainly questionable."

Hemingway managed to curb his thirst after being hectored by his friends, but like Captain Morgan four centuries earlier, his present love of drink began to overshadow the exploits of his youth. He was often in pain as a result of injuries suffered during his last African sa-fari, and drink proved a balm for the body as well as the mind. Work-ers at Finca Vigía remember the afternoon he learned he had won the 1954 Nobel Prize for literature. He brought out tray after tray of drinks and served them up to the nearly dozen employees who maintained the house and grounds. "By the time we were done drinking, I could barely find the door," one recalled. By the late 1950s, the writer George Plimpton said he could see Hemingway's distended liver through his shirt, standing out "from his body like a long fat leech." The writer's mental state deteriorated, and he submitted to electroshock treatments in 1960 and 1961. Then one day in Ketchum, Idaho, two days after being released from treatment, he took out a shotgun he used for hunting partridge, loaded it, put it to his head and pulled the trigger. It was July 2, 1961, and Ernest Hemingway was sixty-one years old.

THE BELLS OF Repeal rang out on December 5, 1933, the day that Utah became the thirty-sixth state to ratify the Twenty-first Amendment to the U.S. Constitution. With noteworthy brevity, the amendment stated, "The eighteenth article of amendment to the Constitution of the United States is hereby repealed." The Eighteenth Amendment, which banned liquor sales, remains the only constitutional amendment ever to be rolled back. The reasons for the reversal were many. The Drys had largely expended themselves in the long and hard-fought battle to ban liquor, and thereafter lost much of their drive, focus, and ardor. It turned out that they were better crusaders than administrators. What's more, in the early 1930s, the nation was slouching through the Great Depression, and any effort to revive manufacturing was welcome. Firing up the shuttered distilleries would light a spark in the more depressed regions of the country, and beleaguered farmers would find new corn markets for bourbon and grain markets for beer, thereby shoring up flagging commodity prices. ("Beer for Prosperity" neckties were fashionable among advocates for repeal.)

And, in the end, Prohibition didn't achieve its goal of eliminating liquor consumption—not by a long shot. Drinking did decline: By most accounts, Americans drank about a third less at the end of Prohibition than the beginning, not so much because they couldn't obtain booze but because drinking cost more. Yet the tax bill for reducing America's alcohol consumption by one beer out of three was staggering. Not only was enforcement expensive—by some estimates, the government spent more than $10 billion (in current dollars)—but the government also lost huge amounts of tax revenues to bootleggers and the black market.

More significantly, Prohibition undermined respect for the law. Crime became endemic in the cities as turf battles erupted in the shadowy demimonde of bootleggers and organized crime bosses. (Some 550 died in liquor-related clashes in Prohibition Chicago alone.) More insidiously, common citizens who otherwise considered themselves law-abiding thought nothing of filling a hip flask with illegal hooch or spending an evening at a speakeasy. When the nation's most esteemed citizens openly flouted the nation's guiding charter, other cracks in the foundation were inevitable. Even John D. Rockefeller Jr., a firm Prohibition advocate who put his money into lobbying for the liquor ban, reconsidered his stand. "Many of our best citizens, piqued by what they regarded as an infringement of the private rights, have openly and unabashedly disregarded the Eighteenth Amendment," he wrote. "As an inevitable result respect for all law has been greatly lessened."

Faced with growing crime, a floundering economy, a mixed track record, and the impossibility of eradicating liquor consumption, the tide began to turn. The amendment to repeal the ban was introduced, passed, and ratified, and less than a year into his first term, Franklin D. Roosevelt signed Presidential Proclamation 2065. Roosevelt reportedly then mixed the nation's first legal martini in nearly fourteen years.

With drinks once again on the table, customers rushed to the bars, and bartenders hustled to stock the shelves. Although Prohibition had rendered the saloon extinct, its role was quickly filled by nightclubs and other entertainment venues, which proved to be a breed apart from the beery watering holes of the past.

The new places were, however, a distant cry from the grand hotel bars of the cocktail's golden era: The knowledge of how and what to drink had been lost to a generation. For drinkers, Prohibition was akin to the burning of the library at Alexandria.

Serious imbibers who recalled the stylish cocktails served up prior to Prohibition were disheartened by unschooled hordes that filled the new bars to overflowing. These were young people who saw drink as a mere intoxicant rather than a centerpiece to a social ritual. "Those who had mastered the art [of drinking] somewhat before Prohibition, have been slow to reappear, whereas the new crop would put to shame the uncouth ecstasies of South Sea Islander or the Indians of New Mexico," wrote H. G. Moody in *American Mercury* in 1936. "Let the modern American who wishes to drink be made to know that he is starting from scratch, that he has to acquire a form of culture to do the trick even half well." A drinker old enough to remember better days told a reporter that she hoped only that her grandchildren would one day "know the difference between drinking like gentlemen and lapping it up like puppies."

NO SPIRIT BENEFITED from the long national drought as much as rum. With ample supplies in the islands and a newly developed taste for the stuff among everyday Americans, this three-hundred-year-old spirit emerged from its century-long slumber into a bright new day. Approximately 2.5 million gallons of rum were readied at the shipping docks of the West Indies on the eve of Repeal. The island of Trinidad sent off America's first legal consignment—one hundred cases—and gave away thousands of free drinks to American visitors in the hope that they would carry their newfound tastes back home.

"While a great deal of inferior 'fire water' rum is likely to be sold in the United States for several years," reported *Literary Digest* in early 1934, "the better quality rum made from genuine sugar cane should be obtainable in increasing measure . . . and the industry is confident of restoring the taste for a liquor that was once inextricably woven with the romantic history of early America."

Rum was back in fashion. "Perhaps the fanatical dry will object to the latest discovery the drinking public of America is making—the discovery of rum," reported *New Outlook* magazine in 1934. "The American public has been a little delayed in discovering this beverage, but according to reports from the West Indies and other Caribbean isles, a rum boom is under way, after many years of sad decline. . . . Perhaps because it was impossible to imitate, the years of Prohibition had made us forget just how efficient and tasty a beverage it is. But now the public taste is turning back to the memory of its ancestors, and rum is arriving, or about to arrive, on our shores in staggering quantity."

The rum that made its way to these shores, of course, landed in a very different America than the rustic colonies it had left behind. Advances in the chemistry, sanitation, engineering, fermentation, and distillation had brought major changes to the liquor industry. Production was no longer undertaken by a motley assortment of small-scale producers—like the approximately two thousand whiskey distilleries that flourished in the hills and hollows of Kentucky just prior to Prohibition. It was increasingly dominated by fewer, larger firms with enough capital to take advantage of new technological efficiencies. Among the largest and best known of the companies was National Distillers, dubbed "the United States Steel of liquor," which had seven plants running night and day to meet booming post-Repeal demand. To compete effectively, rum manufacturing began the process of consolidation. Larger, better-funded companies like Cuba's Bacardi, Jamaica's Wray & Nephew, and Barbados's Mount Gay would come to dominate international rum markets.

An even more sweeping change came in marketing and branding. Early rum producers could ship a passable product in plain barrels to an undemanding market. That world had passed. To attract attention on crowded shelves and anticipate (or manufacture) consumer needs, rum manufacturers had to learn the craft of advertising and marketing.

Many rum distillers quickly realized that what the consumer wanted was "Cuban rum"—an almost generic term referring to any light, crisp rum. Like Bacardi, which started it all, Cuban rum went down easily and mixed well with everything. Cuban competitors had long ago sought to copy Bacardi's production methods, filtering and blending to produce a less cloying product. The Matusalem family produced a similar rum as early as 1872, and Havana Club rolled out its improved rum in 1878.

During and after Prohibition, other West Indian distillers also retooled to meet the clamor. Puerto Rico made the transition best, its rum becaming synonymous with Cuba's in the public mind. The government pushed hard to improve quality, banning island distillers from blending their rum with neutral spirits, then decreeing that all Puerto Rican rum be aged at least one year. Puerto Rican rums were further aided by its status as a United States territory, meaning that most exports, including rum, were exempt from import duties. In 1936, Cuba's Bacardi family, rightly concerned about its financial disadvantage, became licensed to distill in Puerto Rico, and then invested more than a half-million dollars to buy an empty building near the seawall in San Juan's old city. This was a seed from which the world's largest rum distillery would one day grow.

For the smaller island distillers, Bacardi wasn't the most worrisome competitor. It was an unexpected heavyweight: the U.S. government. In 1934, the administration of Franklin D. Roosevelt moved to improve the living conditions in another U.S. territory, the Virgin Islands, which the United States had acquired from Denmark twenty years earlier. President Herbert Hoover visited in 1931 and described it as an "effective poorhouse," an island devastated by the back-to-back economic hurricanes of Prohibition and the Depression. To make the islands self-sufficient, the U.S. government invested a million dollars to set up the Virgin Islands Company, which was chaired by the U.S. interior secretary. The money was used to buy sugarcane lands, sugar factories, and shuttered rum distilleries. The old stills were fired up. The goal of the government—in a striking departure from its recent role as liquor cop—was to produce "as fine a rum as distilling science knows how to produce." Not all greeted this project with enthusiasm. U.S. distillers didn't relish the idea of competing directly with the U.S. government in home markets. And feral Drys took affront that government was getting into the rum trade. Roosevelt ignored the bawling and put this on his list of pet projects. He suggested that the new rum be called "Colonial" and even sketched out a possible label. In the end, Roosevelt didn't get his way. The rum was sold as "Government House," and its label featured a palm tree, a harbor, and a sailing ship.

The first fifty thousand cases of Government House rum arrived in New York in April 1937. To the relief of other West Indian distillers, it did not cause much of a stir among the new class of rum aficionado. "I have never yet tasted a good Virgin Island rum," David Embury would later write in his 1948 bible of bartending, "but Old St. Croix and Cruzan are probably the best I have tried and Government House the worst."

BACARDI REMAINED THE rum to beat: It was so dominant that drinkers in the United States often used "Bacardi" interchangeably with "rum," and would often order Bacardi and soda, or Bacardi and tonic. This was good news for a company in a market that increasingly depended on branding. But it was bad news in another way: "Bacardi" threatened to become a generic term—like Kleenex or FedEx—and bartenders increasingly felt free to substitute any rum on hand, even if a customer specifically ordered "Bacardi."

Things were further muddied by the popularity of a cocktail

called, simply, the bacardi—in essence a daiquiri made with a splash of grenadine syrup instead of sugar. American bars sold plenty of bacardi cocktails without a trace of actual Bacardi. This put the Bacardi family in an unpleasant mood. In 1936, Bacardi took the unusual step of suing two transgressors—the Barbizon Plaza Hotel and Wivel's Restaurant, both in New York City—in an effort to get them to stop selling another company's product under their name. The stakes were high, and the company flew in bartenders from around the globe to testify that, yes, any bartender worth knowing would put authentic Bacardi rum in a bacardi cocktail. The appellate division of the New York Supreme Court eventually agreed, ruling that a bacardi cocktail *must* contain Bacardi rum. And so it was. In 1946, the *Stork Club Bar Book,* among others, began specifying "Bacardi rum" in its recipe for the bacardi cocktail. (The company victory didn't come without some backsliding. "Though bearing the proprietary Bacardi name," reported *Holiday* magazine cheerfully in 1962, "it is not improper, or even adulterous, when made with any of the excellent dry Puerto Rican or Cuban brands.") Hoping to eliminate the confusion altogether, Bacardi eventually launched a campaign to rename the cocktail the "grenadine daiquiri." That didn't catch on, but the crisis had passed. The bacardi cocktail followed the path of so many fine drinks and eventually slipped from favor, to live on mostly in musty bar books.

The daiquiri, happily, stuck around, although often in a form that Constantino and Hemingway would scarcely recognize. Havana's El Floridita bar has changed considerably since Hemingway's day, and customers now enter under a graceful neon sign that declares the bar to be El Cuna Del Daiquiri, or "the cradle of the daiquiri." Tour buses crammed with Italian and Spanish tourists fresh off cruise ships idle outside the door. Inside, El Floridita has been nicely cleaned up, with bartenders in crimson vests and towering mirrors that give the place a sense of spacious elegance. (In the 1960s, large murals of Fidel and his colleagues in their field uniforms were installed behind the bar;

they came out and the mirrors went in when Cuba decided to embrace tourism again after the Soviet Union collapsed.)

El Floridita has long capitalized on its connection with its most famous habitué. A bust of Hemingway was commissioned and installed above the bar while the great man still came in to order daiquiris. Giddy tourists often insisted he sit beneath the statue so they might take his picture. Hemingway, not surprisingly, found this odious. "How can you look at a bust of yourself in a bar?" he groused in 1957.

A long, graceful bar curves around the wall, ending in the cul-de-sac where Hemingway was said to perch. His bar stool was chained off and "reserved" for him for years after his death; in 2003, the bar replaced the bust of Hemingway and his stool with a life-sized bronze statue of the author leaning against the bar. A memorial daiquiri usually sits in front of him, along with a bronze book with a pair of bronze reading glasses. Photos cover the wall, most notably a shot of Hemingway sharing a light moment with a wispily bearded Castro. A steady stream of tourists line up to have their photos taken with Hemingway's simulacrum.

At today's El Floridita, Hemingway's beloved daiquiris are served frozen and dispensed from a blender. The drinks are served in a gracefully tapered cocktail glass and cost $6—or twice as much as daiquiris in bars in the surrounding neighborhood. Blender daiquiris are no doubt the only way to accommodate the crowds that come and go by the busload; the old-style shaken daiquiri required an undeniable amount of labor. There was the squeezing of the fresh lime, the measuring of the sugar, and the shaking of the drink. (Cocktail authority David Embury even insisted on moistening the rim with lime and dipping it into powdered sugar.) Shortcuts naturally appeared to accommodate bartenders pressed for time and talent. In 1937, the Seven-Eleven mix was created—a first step toward the mass-marketing of the bartending craft. Bartenders, like workers everywhere, had become assembly workers rather than individual artisans.

The same year that Seven-Eleven mix was introduced, the Waring Blender, named after and promoted by a popular big-band leader (Fred Waring of Fred Waring and the Pennsylvanians), premiered at the National Restaurant Show in Chicago. It proved wildly popular as a time-saver. But it also led to the misguided belief that a proper daiquiri should have the consistency of a sherbet, something to be eaten with a spoon. Daiquiris were "improved." Some New York bartenders not only whipped their daiquiris into a fine slurry with their mechanical aids, they also added egg whites such that "these frosted Daiquiris could stand up in an ice cream cone to the last nub," wrote Hugh Foster in 1962. Foster noted the chief defect of the sherbet daiquiri was that the extreme cold "anesthetizes the whole apparatus of taste, and markedly that of smell." This effectively removes the alcohol taste from an alcoholic drink, and leads drinkers down an old and familiar path to intemperance.

Busy bars now feature apparatuses the size of small washing machines that dispense frozen daiquiris at the tug of a lever. Prior to Hurricane Katrina, the New Orleans Original Daiquiri chain had forty-one company-owned bars plus twelve franchises in and around Louisiana (twenty-seven alone in the city of New Orleans). Most had reopened by the end of 2005. The chain also sells trademarked Blend-A-Paks packs to other restaurants. "Each pak makes one blender of frozen drinks," says the advertising, "so you get three times the fun."

Or not. Those who succumb to the easy, slushy charms of the premixed, frozen daiquiri miss out on the subtle, complex quality of a gently made original, shaken briefly but vigorously with crushed ice— just enough to chill it thoroughly and dilute it slightly. Small, sharp crystals of ice persist for those first two or three sips. The daiquiri should always be served in a stemmed cocktail glass, like a martini, so that the heat of one's fingertips doesn't warm the drink. A well-made daiquiri does not produce an ice-cream headache.

If one needs an example of how to drink a proper daiquiri, one need only go back to the 1960s. On the night he was elected president in 1960, John F. Kennedy sat sipping daiquiris in the dining room of his house in Hyannis Port, Massachusetts. When dinner was over, Kennedy rose and walked to a nearby room to watch a small television with bad reception. Here, he checked in on the election returns, and here—infused with the glow of a daiquiri—he learned he would be the next inhabitant of the White House.

This, to my mind, was the perfect daiquiri moment: a blend of power and understatement, edged with upper-crustiness like sugar on a rim. From these heights, rum had only one direction to go.

Rum and Coca-Cola would escort it into the netherworld.

[RUM AND COKE]

Place *one-and-a-half ounces* RUM into tall glass with ice cubes. *Fill* with COCA-COLA. *Garnish* with slice of LIME. Repeat until well intoxicated.

Chapter 8

[RUM AND COCA-COLA]

*Our American public has an eccentric habit of jumping
from one extreme to another. One year the whole
population goes daft over the teasing perplexities of
midget golf and becomes wildly excited while trying to
wham the ball through hollow logs and gas-pipes and
around sharp curves and over all kinds of misplaced
bumps. Next year the Tom Thumb pleasure grounds
are as dead as night clubs.*

—GEORGE ADE, *THE OLD TIME SALOON:
THE NOT WET—NOT DRY JUST HISTORY* [1931]

WAR IS HELL on liquor. Just when the citizenry finds itself
in need of a stiff drink, drink becomes scarce.

On November 1, 1942—less than a year after the
Japanese bombed Pearl Harbor—the U.S. government banned domestic production of gin and whiskey at the nation's 128 distilleries.
(The domestic production of brandy and rum, both inconsequential,
was permitted to continue.) Distilleries were ordered to produce
high-grade, 190 proof industrial alcohol, a vital ingredient in producing butadiene, used to manufacture aviation fuel essential to the war
effort.

The government sought to assure Americans that diverting distillery production to the war effort would not unduly inconvenience them. Domestically, 500 million gallons of whiskey remained at bonded warehouses as a sort of strategic whiskey reserve. At the prewar rates of consumption, the government said, whiskey reserves were expected to last for four years, by which time the war would be concluded. Imported Scotch was also available from time to time, although it was becoming more rare and expensive. Scotch was shipped only when chance permitted from Great Britain, in the holds of otherwise empty homebound Liberty ships that had ferried wartime supplies to England. Prowling German submarines in North Atlantic shipping lanes made the export of Scotch unpredictable at best, and it fell from 7 percent of the American market prior to the war to about 5 percent during the war.

With imports down and domestic production sharply curbed, liquor soon found itself subject to rationing, like nylons and rubber tires. The seventeen states with state-regulated liquor sales all rationed sales—in Washington State, customers were entitled to just one pint of liquor per week; in Iowa, topers were allowed a quart. In noncontrol states, prices rose as supplies shrank, and shortages made it hard for liquor vendors to survive. About a thousand package stores, taverns, and bars closed in Ohio alone; an equal number were shuttered in San Francisco.

Faced with the shortfalls of bourbon and Scotch, American tastes proved fungible. Whiskey bottlers stretched out their inventory of aged liquor by ramping up production of blended whiskeys, using imported neutral spirits distilled from molasses and potatoes. This was not without problems. Alcohol hastily distilled from molasses sometimes retained the heavy aroma of rum, prompting consumers to grouse about the off-smell. Seagram—the big Canadian distiller—sensed an opportunity, their ads bellowing about "ersatz" whiskeys flooding the market while boasting that their own blends were made of pure grain spirits. Prior to 1941, blended whiskey accounted for less than 40 percent of the U.S. whiskey market; in 1946, the peak year for blends, they accounted for 87 percent.

United States consumers faced with declining stocks and a diminished quality of whiskey retooled their palates. Retailers reintroduced their customers to a spirit from Mexico that had been smuggled in during Prohibition, made from fermented agave cactus. Tequila made a reasonable replacement for now-scarce gin but was generally regarded as a nasty bit of business, something to be consumed only in grave emergencies. ("In general," wrote David Embury in 1948, "the only liquor I have ever tasted that I regard worse than tequila is slivovitz.") Tequila had a rank, rotten-egg odor, displacing old-time rum as the most evil-smelling of liquors. According to Embury, the overpowering tequila aroma could be partially offset by first downing a dilute acid, which helped to counteract its foul taste and smell. Such an acid could be concocted simply by mixing salt and the juice from a citrus fruit. A routine called the "Mexican Itch" arose, which involved first licking salt from the back of one's hand, then sucking on a lemon before downing the tequila, usually with one's face twisted into a look of extreme distress. Tequila has improved immeasurably, yet the routine persists in college bars and elsewhere. Why the routine has shifted to the present order of salt, tequila, *then* lemon or lime is unknown.

THE WEST INDIAN rum industry worked overtime to fill empty U.S. liquor cabinets. Distilleries produced more rum and neutral spirits for blending, and Cuba even started distilling gin—although Cuban gin was regarded as generally unpotable.

The renewed demand for West Indian alcohol came at a welcome time for the islands, as the war had proved devastating to distillers. Barbados had seen its exports to Europe and Great Britain plummet, and Jamaica, which had found a niche supplying Germany with heavy rum to be blended with alcohol from sugar beet, watched helplessly as this profitable market imploded.

The thirsty United States made up for the evaporation of the German market and then some. Rum came flooding north in quantities unimagined prior to the war. The production of beverage alcohol increased fivefold in Puerto Rico, Barbados, and Trinidad. In 1944, Puerto Rico exported 3 million cases of rum to the United States. Cuba sent 5 million. And even the struggling Virgin Islands accounted for 1 million cases. (The U.S. War Production Board had mandated that distilleries in the U.S. territories, like those on the mainland, produce only industrial alcohol during the war. But the outcry from Puerto Rico—which stood to lose $12 million in taxes alone—forced the feds to relax the decree, so that distillers were permitted to produce 90 percent of their previous year's rum output.)

The war aided rum distillers in other unexpected ways. The London blitz sent more than a quarter million gallons of rum up in flames at the Deptford storage yards, and the Admiralty scrambled to contract for emergency supplies from Cuba and Martinique—which scrambled to meet the demand.

Smaller rum companies, which had closed their doors as the larger companies dominated in the post-Prohibition years, swept out the cobwebs and resumed production. Puerto Rico alone saw seventeen distillers in operation during the war. The newly invigorated rum economy was hampered only by the lack of a merchant fleet to freight the spirit north, since cargo ships had been dragooned into supplying Europe. So the buyers and sellers of West Indian liquor scratched together an improvised fleet, sending retired schooners and fishing vessels of questionable seaworthiness to haul rum from the islands. *Business Week* reported in 1943 that the rum shipping fleet serving Cuba "made rum-running look like a House of Morgan transaction."

Alas, the wartime rum trade bore another similarity to the rum-running era: Much of the product was strikingly bad—unaged and produced hurriedly by out-of-practice distillers. Few drank this rum by choice, so distributors forced wholesalers to buy three cases of it for every one of hard-to-find whiskey. (The practice was both illegal and impossible to stop.) Liquor store owners, who bought from wholesalers, were also required to stock more rum if they wanted whiskey for their shelves. They would sell for $2 rum that cost them $4, but they made up the loss on Scotch or Canadian whiskey, which could bring a profit of $6 or $7 per bottle. Buying cheap, unpalatable rum was simply the cost of doing business. As a result, rum was again dragged into the gutter, consumed by those who couldn't afford better. John Adams would have recognized it.

Consumers who bought the wartime rum struggled to mask the taste. Fortunately, a popular and inexpensive soft drink with elements both bitter and sweet was widely available and eager to rise to the occasion.

THE ANGOSTURA BITTERS plant is in Laventille, Trinidad, on the southwest side of a low ridge that separates it from the sprawling city of Port of Spain. Laventille is an industrial suburb of snarled traffic, dun-colored warehouses, bland factories of concrete block, and hardscrabble hillside homes with galvanized steel roofing. The Angostura compound is large and modern and consists of a great many low buildings; the company's 250 employees attend to inscrutable industrial activities, much of which involves tankers of molasses. Stainless steel columns soar skyward under corrugated tin roofs, and the din of steam being vented is constant. The factory would not be out of place within sight of the New Jersey Turnpike.

This is both unsurprising, because Trinidad is one of the more industrial of the West Indian islands, and surprising, since the flagship product, virtually unchanged for nearly two centuries, is sold mostly in four-ounce bottles and only rarely served more than three drops at a time. It is hard to imagine a business built on a less substantial foundation.

Bitters are made by infusing sharp-tasting herbs, seeds, bark, fruit peels, or roots—like orange peel, hops, calumba, or cascarilla—in alcohol and extracting their essence. Like many ingredients of recreational drinking, bitters were first produced as an elixir and only later embraced for their flavor. The Swiss have been among the most passionate consumers of bitters. Absinthe Suisse, a cordial made with an infusion of wormwood, enjoyed a mania in the late nineteenth century and then was banned for such inconvenient (and largely fictional) side effects as hallucinations, convulsions, tremors, and paralysis.

Angostura bitters are brewed in a room not much bigger than a suburban shoe store. This is the second ring of the bitters inner sanctum, filled with stainless steel tanks and gauges and a tangle of shiny pipes. In the corner is a chute that leads from a room upstairs—the first ring of the inner sanctum, "the Sanctuary." Only five company directors are authorized to enter the Sanctuary, as this is where the secret ingredients of Angostura bitters are actually mixed.

The company orders as many as twenty herbs, roots, seeds, and whatever else from around the world, although how many of these are actually employed is a mystery. Maybe only a half dozen. Maybe more. "Who needs to know?" asked Everard "Chippy" Roberts, fixing me with a long, neutral stare.

Once the directors mix the herbs according to a proprietary formula, the potpourri is sent down the chute, then infused—or "shampooed," in company parlance—in vats of alcohol. Following this, it is filtered, bottled, and exported worldwide, with markets in more than a hundred countries. Every drop sold globally is produced in this one room.

I sniffed the air in the shampooing room. I detected mace, perhaps, and maybe nutmeg or dried orange peel. I asked Roberts about gentian root, and he shrugged, admitting to nothing. I pointed out to him that this is the one and only ingredient listed on the label. Roberts looked at me as if I had greatly underestimated him. He shrugged again.

Whatever it is, the formula has evidently been unchanged since 1824. It was the handiwork of a German named Dr. Johann Gottlieb Benjamin Siegert, an adventurer who became the surgeon general of

Simón Bolívar's rebel army at Bolívar's base of operations, a town called Angostura up the Orinoco River in what's now Venezuela. (The town is now Ciudad Bolívar.)

Siegert was directed to produce salves and potions to treat the troops, especially for various tropical ailments that proved more fatal to the rebel army than wounds suffered in combat. Siegert concocted remedies and tisanes by gathering herbs, bark, and roots. (Exactly which? Who needs to know?) He infused these in bottles of rum. He spent much of his time tinkering and perfecting one of his infusions, which he called *amargo aromatico*, or aromatic bitters. When the fight for independence concluded, Siegert remained in Angostura, and seamen who arrived at the river port started seeking him out and asking for his bitters, which not only relieved gastric discomfort but made most drinks taste better.

Today, the four-ounce dark brown bottle of Angostura bitters has an oddly oversized paper label that extends up to where the bottle's side curves into the bottle's neck. The label has been aptly described as having the appearance of a child unhappily wearing his big brother's jacket. The company ascribes this packaging quirk to miscommunication between the printer and the bottler, but the issue went unresolved long enough for the ill-fitting label to become integral to the product's identity. In 1995, the British Advertising Council voted Angostura bitters as the "world's worst displayed product." In the same announcement, the council urged Angostura never to change it.

ANGOSTURA'S WEREN'T the first or even best known bitters of the nineteenth century. During the Haitian revolution of the 1790s, when slaves overthrew their French masters and established the first black republic in history, the family of a French Haitian named Antoine Peychaud fled the island for New Orleans. In his new home, he became a pharmacist and produced bitters concocted of various Caribbean spices, thought to be the first commercially sold in North

America. Most of his customers presumably bought bitters as a tonic to relieve a queasy stomach, but Peychaud had the imagination to add several drops as a flavoring to a cognac, which he served to customers in an eggcup. The French called the cup a *coquetier,* but it was mangled by English speakers and became "cocktail."

Et voilà: the first cocktail. At least that's one theory behind the name—etymologists only agree only that any reliable documentation about the name's origin is lost. Other explanations include the odd notion that a strong drink was said to "cock your tail," which was a way of telling a show dog to keep its tail up. Some suggested that the remains of various kegs—supposedly called cock-tailings—were mixed together and sold in early taverns. Other accounts include roosters in various forms—that the first mixed drink was stirred with a rooster feather, and that topers once toasted the winner of cockfights. These explanations strain credulity; only the *coquetier* one passes the straight-face test. Unfortunately, recent research by Phillip Greene, one of Peychaud's descendents, found that Peychaud actually left Haiti in 1803, when he was less than a year old. The first known appearance in print of the word *cocktail* referring to an alcoholic drink dates to May 1806, when it appeared in a Hudson, New York, newspaper. "He must have been a precocious little pharmacist at the age of three," Greene notes drily. So the debate over the name's origin goes on.

Cocktail is today a generic term, but in the late nineteenth century it meant just one of many types of intoxicating drinks, among them fizzes, rickeys, slings, juleps, and cobblers. A cocktail *always* included bitters. In its earliest documented use in 1806, a cocktail was defined as "a stimulating liquor, composed of spirits of any kind, sugar, water and bitters." Even as late as the 1880s, more than half the recipes for cocktails in one guide called for bitters.

Bitters were far more common and esteemed then, and discerning drinkers were more sophisticated when it came to using them. Medicinal bitters were particularly popular in nineteenth-century America, especially where local option laws banned liquor sales. Hotstetter's Stomach Bitters contained 44 percent alcohol and was advertised as "harmless as water from a mountain spring." Others included Luther's Temperance Bitters, Drake's Plantation Bitters, Flint's Quaker Bitters, and Faith Whitcom's Nerve Bitters, all of which had an alcohol content somewhere between wine and 90 proof liquor, and none of which probably tasted much worse than bootlegged liquor then available. *Cooling Cups and Dainty Drinks,* published in 1869, provides recipes for the home mixologist to make seven types of bitters. Even in 1939, six years after Prohibition ended, a popular bar guide detailed the "eight main bitters" used in drink preparations. In 1944, when Ernest Hemingway departed Cuba to report on the war in Europe, his luggage consisted of a toothbrush, a comb, and "innumerable two-ounce bottles of Angostura bitters," according to one of his friends, because the novelist had been informed that bitters were in desperately short supply owing to the depredations of German submarines.

Today, one can turn up Peychaud's Bitters (still made by a New Orleans company) in specialty gourmet and liquor shops. It has a bitingly sharp and medicinal orangish-cherry flavor. Regan's Orange Bitters No. 6 began production in 2004, a faithful re-creation of a once-popular style of bitters. But the wide selection of bitters once available to drinkers is much diminished. Today, "bitters" almost always refers to Angostura's.

THE NINETEENTH-CENTURY appetite for bitters grew as the twentieth century neared, and exotic flavorings eventually came to be mixed increasingly with sugar and water and consumed without alcohol as a refreshment. Bitters and today's soft drinks are two branches of the same family tree, although bitters ceased to evolve some time ago and have an archaic appearance, like Ovaltine or Marmite, when spotted on modern, fluorescent-lit supermarket shelves. Early soft drinks were sugary syrups made of infused fruits, nuts, and roots, then diluted with water containing what was then called "fixed air," later "charged water," and today carbonated or soda water. Impressively elaborate soda fountains with marble counters and carved back bars cropped up in big cities to serve beguiling new products to an eager public in the 1870s and 1880s, a process as filled with ritual as the opium dens of the Orient.

An 1876 temperance article about an excursion to a saloon noted, "The only unalcoholic drink found in the shop is that known as soda water or sometimes sold in bottles as mineral water, which owes its slightly exhilarating effects to the carbonic acid gas compressed into the liquid and which throws the water into effervescence when the pressure is removed. The pleasant taste is due to the sirups used, and the gentile excitement to the impression of the carbonic acid on the stomach. This is a wholesome and unalcoholic drink."

The more complex and exotic the ingredients in soda syrups, the more firmly they seized the public's imagination. In 1876, a Philadelphia Quaker named Charles Hires trademarked his now-famous root beer, which he boasted was made from no fewer than sixteen wild roots and berries. In 1885, Dr. Augustin Thompson of Lowell, Massachusetts, introduced the world to Moxie Nerve Food, a fizzy drink with an acrid medicinal taste that was curiously soil-like. Thompson sold oceans of it thanks to a story so wildly implausible that people thought it must have been true. He claimed that an adventurous associate named Lieutenant Moxie had in his jungle wanderings stumbled upon an elusive South American tribe that gained superhuman strength by brewing a beverage from a mysterious root. While coyly insisting that his nerve food was not a medicine, Thompson suggested that four glasses daily would have proven highly beneficial; it would relieve brain and nervous exhaustion, "loss of manhood," paralysis, and mental imbecility, among other afflictions. Like Angostura bitters, Moxie is flavored in part with gentian root; it's still produced today and remains popular in certain precincts of New England.

A glass of iced Moxie, it should be noted, mixes splendidly with a jigger of Jamaican or Demerara rum.

Moxie was the nation's top-selling beverage until the 1920s, when it was overtaken by a soft drink of even more exotic ingredients. Its inventor was a pharmaceutical chemist from Atlanta named John Pemberton. He concocted it with infusions of the coca plant from the Peruvian Andes and the high-caffeine kola nut from Africa, then tempered it with seven secret flavoring agents. Pemberton named the drink after its principal ingredients: Coca-Cola.

Coca-Cola's taste was distinctive, at once bitter and sweet, and it quickly moved ahead of the mob of nerve tonics and soda fountain drinks. The fledgling company distributed thousands of coupons redeemable for free samples and later established a far-flung network of franchisees that bottled and sold its product. But what brought Coca-Cola to the fore and kept it there was its legendary flair in trademarking and marketing. Early on, the company directors understood the power of a memorable brand, a remarkable achievement when many consumer staples were still purchased as bulk goods. The graceful script logo and the slogan "Delicious and Refreshing" were established by 1887, and by 1913 the company started splashing its distinctive script on the sides of buildings. The same year, the company distributed 100 million items, ranging from matchbooks to baseball cards to metal and cardboard signs, emblazoned with the soon-to-be inescapable Coca-Cola script logo. In 1916, the company started selling its product in a sensuous pale green bottle that was as memorable to the touch as the flavor was to the taste.

From its base in Atlanta, Coca-Cola first captured southern markets, then deployed its troops to conquer a nation. Coca-Cola moved from the corner fountain to the bottling plant in 1894, first in Mississippi, and then nationwide in 1899 after setting up a licensing agreement with a pair of Nashville entrepreneurs. About the same time, Coca-Cola also took its first tentative steps abroad. Canada and Germany were among the earliest global markets for the company, as was one other country that had recently gained its independence: Cuba. And when Coca-Cola crossed the Straits of Florida, a dalliance with the local spirit was never in doubt.

"WAR IS PROBABLY the single most powerful instrument of dietary change in human experience," writes historian Sidney Mintz. Shortages force folks on the home front to change their expectations of what's for dinner. Expeditionary forces in distant lands not only sample new and exotic foods, but also contaminate local fare with ingredients they've brought along.

The same may be said for habits of drink. Soldiers abroad find new and appealing means of intoxication and seek to re-create them when they return; at home, consumers adapt to shortages of old favorites by developing a preference for something more widely available. Such a shift might start begrudgingly and evolve into genuine enthusiasm. The English war against Holland introduced gin to the British Isles in the sixteenth century and launched a lethal mania that took two centuries to quell. The American Revolution disrupted the rum trade and helped usher in whiskey as the American tipple. After massive numbers of American troops left for home from Europe following World War II, they brought with them a new taste for French brandy and wine, along with German schnapps. World War II also introduced a generation of American soldiers to a new kind of rum.

One story suggests that like the daiquiri, rum and Coca-Cola has its roots in the Spanish-American War. In the 1960s, a man named Fausto Rodriguez swore out an affidavit that in 1900, while a messenger with the U.S. Army Signal Corps, he and an officer friend (name redacted in the affidavit) went to a local bar, where the officer ordered a Bacardi and Coca-Cola. American soldiers ordered a round for themselves and, finding it to their liking, toasted the officer as the inventor of a new and delightful drink.

It is rare and exciting for a cocktail historian to find a legal affidavit attesting to the invention of a popular drink, but several details render this one suspect. First, it was published in a full-page ad in 1966 by *Life* magazine—and paid for by Bacardi, which was promoting itself as the source of many famous drinks. More troublingly, Rodriguez was well known in spirits circles as the New York–based director of publicity for Bacardi. As such, the document is only slightly more believable than a man dressed as Santa Claus telling you that he is, in fact, Santa Claus.

A slightly more plausible variation of the creation myth involves similar elements: American soldiers in Cuba, the Spanish-American War, a group of Cubans and Americans in a bar. But this one has the soldiers mixing rum and Coca-Cola and toasting their Cuban comrades in arms by calling out, *"Por Cuba libre!"*—"to a free Cuba!"

Whatever its origin (and it is the lot of the cocktail historian never to be fully satisfied), it's clear that the Cuba libre or rum and Coke crossed the Straits of Florida and headed north. It was initially most popular in the American South, like Coca-Cola itself. During Prohibition, Coca-Cola emerged as a handy mixer to mask the taste of the lower grades of rum and other alcohol; after Repeal, rum and Coke continued to gain adherents north and west. Only the most vile and industrial rum can overpower the Coke and spoil the drink. H. L. Mencken noted, presumably in jest, that residents of western South Carolina mixed Coca-Cola with denatured alcohol drawn from automobile radiators: "Connoisseurs reputedly preferred the taste of what had been aged in Model-T Fords," he said. George Jean Nathan— who spent much of the Prohibition editing *Smart Set* with Mencken— introduced a writer for *Gourmet* to the delights of the Cuba libre, evidence that it had also found a home with a swankier crowd.

Rum and Coca-Cola is, by any measure, a drink of inspired blandness, with its two main ingredients both plentiful and cheap. It requires few if any skills to prepare: It is not a cocktail, like the daiquiri, that can be toppled into an overly sweet or tart imbalance with a sloppy pouring hand. It can be made heavy or light on rum, with rum that's either light or heavy. If you have a lime to add a bit of citrusy zest to a rum and Coke, wonderful. If not, no matter. Some early published recipes make lime a mere garnish—a thin slice dropped in at the end—while others call for substantially more. A 1940 recipe calls for filling nearly half a glass with rum, the other half with Coke, and then squeezing in the juice of half a lime. More exotic versions of the Cuba libre include one (popular before Prohibition) that calls for the addition of gin and bitters. But these are mere curiosities. Basic rum and Coca-Cola was the perfect drink for the masses. It would need only the lightning of popular culture to transform it from what cocktail writer William Grimes has called "a harmless invention" into an enduring icon.

THE MAIN ACTION of World War II unfolded in Europe, Asia, and Africa, but another theater of combat had quietly opened in the West Indies. German submarines had taken to sinking cargo ships along trade routes, and they took an especially keen interest in ships carrying oil from the South American coast and bauxite (needed for aluminum production) from island mines.

Not only did the German submarines inconvenience the war effort, they marked the first direct threat to American shores since the British sacked and burned the U.S. Capitol in 1812. Long protected by two oceans from rival powers, the United States found itself suddenly at risk of attack from a foreign power. As historian Fitzroy Baptiste put it, submarines were a first-generation intercontinental ballistic weapon system, able to bring ruin and mayhem around the globe to American soil with a simple coded message from abroad.

In the summer of 1940, Franklin Delano Roosevelt met with Winston Churchill to address the threat. The deal they hammered out was this: the United States would provide England with fifty Liberty ships and a million rifles to aid the war effort. In return, the United States would get ninety-nine-year leases to construct a first line of defense in the form of bases on British controlled islands that included Newfoundland, the Bahamas, Jamaica, St. Lucia, Antigua, Bermuda, and Trinidad. Within months of the agreement, thousands of servicemen had been deployed to beef up national defenses at the United States' extended eastern perimeter.

The impact of the military influx on island life was abrupt and profound. Bermuda's local population of 31,000 soared by 20 percent almost overnight. Trinidad became home to the largest Caribbean naval base, with American military occupying 34,000 acres and the island population of 400,000 swelling with the arrival of 130,000 U.S. soldiers, airmen, and sailors. The great flood of servicemen to the islands resulted in cross-cultural ferment as the soldiers adapted to local flavors and islanders in turn clamored for American products. On Bermuda, bartenders reported in 1941 that rum was now beating out beer as the drink of choice among the soldiers, in large part for economic reasons— beer cost 30 cents a glass and rum 25 cents. When the newfound appreciation for the spirit led to rowdiness near bases, bars were ordered closed between lunch and dinner, and an 11:00 p.m. curfew was mandated. The U.S. military brass did their part to keep servicemen from causing trouble by reducing the price of beer to 10 cents on the base.

On Trinidad, the U.S. military arrived with fistfuls of U.S. dollars, Chiclets chewing gum, and cigarettes. With the soldiers also arrived case after case of Coca-Cola—war being a prime occasion to boost sales. (During World War I, Coca-Cola ran ads slyly associating itself with patriotism, one ad depicting a hand bearing a glass of Coke in front of the Statue of Liberty, bearing a torch.) When America entered World War II, Coca-Cola moved swiftly, starting with a company commitment that servicemen would always be able to buy a bottle of Coke for a nickel, the same price it cost during World War I. Coca-Cola sent its own small army of technical advisers abroad to follow the troops. When a region was secured, the advisers would immediately set up bottling operations to ensure that the soldiers were never without Coca-Cola.

The Coca-Cola Company also commissioned studies to show

that well-rested, well-refreshed soldiers performed better than tired and thirsty soldiers, and that, in short, war went better with Coke. Some 10 *billion* Cokes were served to soldiers around the globe during World War II. An unusually large number of solders wrote home that they were fighting, among other reasons, for the right to drink Coca-Cola. (In *God Is My Co-Pilot,* Colonel Robert L. Scott wrote that his thoughts when shooting down Japanese fighters were of "America, Democracy, Coca-Colas.")

IN 1943, a trained cellist turned comedian arrived in Trinidad on a tour of West Indian military bases. His name was Morey Amsterdam, and he was winding down from a ten-week USO tour. Rubbery-faced and with a memorably nasal voice, Amsterdam is best remembered as Buddy Sorrell, the comedy-writing sidekick on the immensely popular *Dick Van Dyke Show* in the 1960s. In the 1940s, he broadcast twelve radio shows a week and was known as a "human joke machine" who could spit out jokes on any topic with the speed and firepower of a Gatling gun.

While on Trinidad, he overheard sailors and soldiers singing a catchy calypso song around the base. It was a version of a number made popular by an island singer named Lord Invader, who had adapted the lyrics of an earlier tune. The original tune was composed in 1906 by Trinidadian musical prodigy Lionel Belasco and originally entitled "L'Année Passé"; it told in French patois the melancholy story of a young country girl from a good family who fell in love with a cad who cast her aside and left her to fend for herself as a streetwalker. Lord Invader altered the song to make it about American soldiers and their off-duty activities. He had recently visited Point Cumaná—a beach near the naval base at Chaguaramas—and here he watched the American soldiers flirting with the island girls and drinking rum followed by a chaser of Coca-Cola. He wrote a calypso about what he saw.

Since the Yankees came to Trinidad,
They have the young girls going mad,
They young girls say they treat them nice,
And they give them a better price.

They buy rum and Coca-Cola,
Go down Point Koomhana
Both mother and daughter
Workin' for the Yankee dollar.

The song was a great local hit with both Trinidadians and sailors. Amsterdam liked it, too, and figured that he might sing a version of it on one of his radio shows. Back home, he sanitized the lyrics somewhat. Instead of "young girls going mad" around the Yankees, he changed it to "They make you feel so very glad." Yet the mother and daughter remained working for the Yankee dollar, and Amsterdam added some goofy new lyrics, among them:

Native girls all dance and smile
They wear grass-skirts, but that's okay
Yankees like to "hit the hay."

Amsterdam worked with a pair of professionals to polish the song and help with the scoring: Jeri Sullivan, a singer best known for her work with Mel Tormé and the Mel-Tones; and Paul Baron, then the musical director for the CBS broadcast network. Success remained elusive: eight publishers turned the song down. Then, after singing it on one of his shows, Amsterdam received a call from Leo Feist, who said he'd be honored to publish the tune.

The "Lana Turner moment" didn't arrive for "Rum and Coca-Cola" until late 1944. The Andrews Sisters, a popular trio of sisters from Minnesota whose stardom was built on hits like "Boogie Woogie Bugle Boy" and "Don't Sit Under the Apple Tree," were in New

York to record for Decca Records. LaVerne, Patty, and Maxene had finished up half an hour early one afternoon and, rather than break, decided to record a silly song with a catchy beat they heard for the first time just the night before. It was, of course, "Rum and Coca-Cola."

"We just threw it in," Patty Andrews later recalled in *Swing It! The Andrews Sisters Story*. "There was no written background, so we just kind of faked it." The sisters used the same faux-Caribbean accents they had earlier adopted in "Sing a Tropical Song," and the whole recording took less than ten minutes. It was pressed on the flip side of a curiously plaintive ode called "One Meat Ball," a song that Decca expected would be a huge hit.

"One Meat Ball" proved prophetically titled. Although this song edged briefly into the top twenty, it was "Rum and Coca-Cola" that took the single into the stratosphere. This wasn't without complications. Since the song glorified drinking, national radio networks weren't eager to broadcast it to the dry states, making the network a lightning rod for teetotaling critics. Anyway, liquor advertising over the airwaves was illegal, and the song seemed to venture into a murky region between advertising and entertainment. Financial considerations also arose: Why should the networks give the highly profitable Coca-Cola Company a free ride? Shouldn't they be billed for the airtime when the song was broadcast? Then there was the whole mothers-and-daughters-working-for-the-Yankee-dollar thing. That the GIs abroad were hitting the hay with "native peaches" probably wasn't the best morale booster for a nation at war, and no one wanted to be seen as undermining the war effort. (The Andrews Sisters, somewhat disingenuously, said that they never really considered the lyrics, but just liked the rhythm.)

Any objections fell aside as the song proved a force of nature. Sheet music flew off the shelves—by February 1945, nearly a half-million copies had been sold, driven in large part by the exotic place names and oddball lyrics behind the hard-to-discern accents. On

January 6, 1945, the Andrews Sisters's "Rum and Coca-Cola" broke into the Billboard Top 30, where it would remain for twenty weeks, ten of those in the number one spot. It also hit number one on *Variety*'s "Jukebox Hits" list. (Bacon's Grille in Phoenix banned the record from its jukebox following an uprising of waitresses who refused to hear it played eight hours straight.) Decca could scarcely keep up with demand, and the company had to beg other record companies for shellac, which was in short supply during the war, to keep pressing the disk. The song would go on to sell 7 million copies and be the third bestselling hit of the 1940s, topped only by Bing Crosby's "White Christmas" and Patti Page's "Tennessee Waltz."

"Rum and Coca-Cola" was a huge hit with soldiers at military bases, and the most requested Andrews Sisters song during their USO tours. The song was called "the National Anthem of the G.I. camps." And soon rum and Coke became the de facto national drink of many of the troops. During World War II, General George Patton reportedly ensured that the Coca-Cola "technical observers" had unfettered access to get their job done efficiently and quickly, in large part because he demanded a reliable supply of Coca-Cola to mix with his rum.

By 1946, *Gourmet* writer and bon vivant Lucius Beebe would write in his *Stork Club Bar Book* that the Cuba libre, the daiquiri, and the MacArthur Cocktail were as "dominant in their field as Martinis or Scotch and Soda are in theirs." (The MacArthur, sadly forgotten, was made with rum, triple sec, and a dash of egg white.) Rum and Coke had achieved icon status.

MOREY AMSTERDAM HAD "borrowed" the song without permission and profited from it greatly. This did not go unnoticed in Trinidad. After the song became a smash international hit, a lawsuit was brought by Maurice Baron, a music publisher who had recently come out with a collection of West Indian songs that included Lionel

Belasco's "L'Année Passée." Belasco, who was then in his seventies, traveled to New York to testify in the trial. The plaintiffs suggested that Amsterdam brought the song from Trinidad as a tourist might a suitcase full of rum. Amsterdam continued to insist that all the lyrics were his. Yet a number of facts were marshaled to upend his assertion. Among them: The plaintiff's lawyer had soldiers take the stand to testify that throughout the island substantial portions of the song had been sung long before Amsterdam had even arrived. And it didn't help that Amsterdam had earlier boasted to *Time* magazine that he had "imported" the song to the United States. Amsterdam shared the common attitude that calypso, no matter how recently composed, fell under the category of "folk song," and was free to be harvested and exploited by traveling foreigners as they saw fit.

In February 1947, a federal judge prohibited Amsterdam and the other defendants from further profiting. He ordered up an accounting (Amsterdam claimed he had made $60,000 off the song), and said that henceforth all profits would go to Belasco. "There is no doubt in my mind that Amsterdam brought both the words and the music with him from Trinidad, and it was in substantially that form that the song was published," the judge wrote. Amsterdam et al. appealed the verdict, but the courts once more ruled that his "songwriting" was tantamount to theft. The rights and profits from "Rum and Coca-Cola" returned to the island whence it came.

LIKE THE LOSER in a game of musical chairs, the liquor industry found itself stuck with a surfeit of cheap, scarcely potable rum when the war ended. By one estimate, the United States was saddled with a five-year supply in its warehouses and stockrooms. Making things worse, the liquor trade slid into a slump after an initial burst of postwar buying. Rationing on most goods ended, and consumers bought up those things they had long gone without—like stockings and gasoline. Liquor was overlooked, and sales fell from a peak of 231 million gallons in 1946 to 160 million in 1949. Price wars erupted as distillers and distributors struggled to reduce their inventories. As a result, rum was almost always the cheapest spirit on the shelf, often selling for less than the taxes levied on it. Even Scotch could be had for $5 a bottle, half the wartime price. Even with the prices low, rum's share of the liquor market fell—not only from pumped-up wartime levels, but from prewar levels. It now sat at a dismal 1.3 percent.

Puerto Rico was especially hard-hit, since its tax-free status made it the chief exporter of rum to the United States. The island found itself saddled with some 20 million gallons in storage—the equivalent of a ten-year export supply and more than all the other rum-making nations combined. Of the seventeen distillers that produced rum during the war, ten closed soon after.

This brush with mortality led the rum industry to conclude that something had to change. And two things happened. Rum went further in the direction of Bacardi, defining itself as a light and refreshing liquor. And it embraced techniques of modern marketing.

Puerto Rico took the lead. In 1948, it passed the Mature Spirits Act, which required that all Puerto Rican rums had to be aged at least three years. This had a double benefit. It ensured a higher-quality rum that helped the island establish a stronger brand, and it immediately reduced reserves, allowing supply to drift somewhat closer to demand.

Puerto Rican rum makers also tried to increase demand by launching a multimillion dollar advertising campaign in the United States. For an American in the early 1950s, it would have been hard not to know about rum. Some thirty-five hundred liquor dealers put rum promotions in their windows in 1952 (almost twice as many as the prior year), and the Rum Institute, based in Puerto Rico, ran numerous ads in major American magazines and newspapers. Double-page ads touted the merits of thirteen brands of rum from Puerto Rico and the Virgin Islands. Drinkers were encouraged to ask for "free Rumsters!"—brightly colored cardboard cutouts that an easily amused drinker could affix to the rim of his or her glass. Rumsters included a tuxedoed man who appeared to be sipping a drink through a straw and a jockey riding the edge of a glass. On the reverse were jingles design to correct misperceptions. One example: "Some people think all rum is sweet/But that's a silly myth./Smooth Puerto Rican rum's a treat/And dry—just try a fyth!" A million Rumsters were distributed in 1950, and demand among liquor dealers for the free novelties pushed distribution to 3 million by 1952.

The new advertising campaign was funded in part by the U.S. government, which hoped to increase its revenues from taxes on rum. The government also underwrote a film entitled *A Glassful of History,* starring Burgess Meredith, to be shown at liquor sales conventions, and paid for a research facility at the island university to improve both quality and production efficiency.

By 1952, Puerto Rico had started to reclaim its stature among rum exporters, largely by leading the charge toward lighter and lighter rums. They took the Cuban experience—stripped out the more overbearing tastes and aromas—and built on it.

So, tastes moved away from the distinctive toward the unexceptional, from full-flavored to light. "U.S. Taste Buds Want It Bland" read a 1951 headline in *Business Week.* Rum took notice. It was the era of Wonder bread and iceberg lettuce, when complexity of taste gave way to ease and convenience of preparation. The art of mixing a balanced drink, which never fully recovered from the interruption of Prohibition, was further lost as elderly mixologists in short-waisted scarlet jackets retired from hotel bars. Surveys showed that more people were drinking at home than in bars or restaurants. The preferred cocktails shifted with it. Complex drinks lost favor. Make it easy, Americans said, and make it bland and sweet.

Surveys in the 1950s showed that more than half of all drinkers actually didn't like the taste of liquor. This was especially true in two key markets: women and young men. As that *Business Week* story noted in 1951, "from all the available data it looks as though Americans of the 1950s like their drinks well watered down." Sweet fell from fashion and dry came to dominate. The dry martinis started to elbow aside the sweeter Manhattan.

And a new kid appeared on the block: vodka. Given its current ubiquity, it's hard to imagine that until about half a century ago, vodka was all but unknown in the United States. A colorless and nearly tasteless spirit distilled from whatever was available (grain, potatoes, molasses), it was an exotic spirit consumed by few Americans. It got a modest boost during Prohibition, since it was easy to doctor up as a fake whiskey. But as late as 1948, the cocktail writer David Embury noted that no imported vodka was available, only a few domestic brands: "It's not exactly what I have called 'common liquors.' "

Vodka would go perfectly with the austere outlook of modernism. The drive was to get rid of the clutter of the past and welcome the clean lines of modern architecture. Vodka was as invisible as the glass walls now cladding the new skyscrapers, as light as the clean lines of the Scandinavian furniture now in homes. The brown spirits—bourbon and rye and rum—were part of the old regime, the spirituous version of an overblown Victorian home. The future belonged to the transparent.

Foremost among the vodka producers was Smirnoff, produced by Heublein—a company that in 1907 got its start making A.1. Steak Sauce and later introduced the breakfast cereal Maypo and the barbecue accessory Sizzl-Spray. (The latter was a spray-on barbecue sauce that had to be taken off grocery shelves because the cans had an unfortunate propensity to explode.) The original Smirnov vodka was produced by an old-line Russian family and favored by the czars. This lineage put it in bad odor when the Bolsheviks came to town, and the family and business moved to France for a time, without much success, before they sold the company to Heublein—which immediately made the name more American-friendly by replacing the "v" with "ff."

Vodka's glorious rise in the American consumer market can be credited in large part to Heublein's shrewd marketing. It deftly publicized a series of novel vodka drinks, beginning with the Moscow Mule—a mix of lime, ginger beer, and vodka, and served "by tradition" (wholly fabricated) in a five-ounce copper cup. The Moscow Mule was invented by an executive at Heublein, who leveraged its novelty into a hot national trend, especially among younger and more rebellious drinkers not averse to irking their elders by ordering "a Commie drink." (Bartenders even organized and marched in New York with placards that read "Smirnoff Go Home. We Can Do Without the Moscow Mule." Smirnoff reaped the free publicity, and neutered its critics by pointing out that all of its vodka was made at home of patriotic American grain.) Smirnoff later promoted other easy-to-guzzle drinks like the screwdriver, the Bloody Mary, and the bullshot, the latter a mix of vodka and beef bouillon.

Vodka had much to commend it. It not only had the lighter, nearly undetectable taste for which Americans now clamored, but it could be produced and sold right from the still, with no inconvenient aging or prescient market demand forecasts. And it didn't impart a common stigma of a problem drinker—booze breath. Smirnoff's advertising slogan was "It leaves you breathless," which suggested that an executive might suck back five vodka martinis at lunch without being detected back at work. When distillers of other liquors disputed the claim, Smirnoff hired a lab to run tests. The lab concluded that vodka actually couldn't be detected on the breath just five minutes after consumption, compared to the half hour required for the dissipation of other liquors. Sales of vodka boomed, nearly rivaling gin by the late 1950s. Vodka sales weren't tracked in the 1940s, but by 1955 they had risen to 3.5 million cases. And by 1960, they had soared to 18 million cases, with Heublein's Smirnoff accounting for 30 percent of the market.

Lighter Puerto Rican rum distillers wasted little time in chasing after vodka, claiming in ubiquitous ads that their spirit was "as different from dark rums as Scotch is from brandy." Rum would go with anything: It was "a regular one-bottle bar!" the ads crooned, adding that "Puerto Rican rum mixes better with everything from coffee to cola to fruit juices." The distillers' efforts paid off. The island soon exported to the United States more rum than all other Caribbean producers combined. The improved quality helped, and equally helpful was the island's tax-free status on rum exports. Puerto Rico's Don Q retailed for just over $4 a fifth, or about 30 percent less than Myers's from Jamaica. At a 1952 tasting in New York hosted by the Wine and Food Society, the eleven rums from Puerto Rican far outpaced the entries from other producers—six from Jamaica, and one or two each from islands like Cuba and Barbados.

But a backlash had been quietly brewing against the cult of the bland, the cult of the transparent. The beatnik and the bongo drum were first appearing in smoky clubs and urban parks. And in faux Polynesian bars, rum would find a new and unusual life.

[MAI TAI]

Mix in cocktail shaker *one ounce* good JAMAICAN STYLE RUM, *one ounce* good MEDIUM-BODIED RUM [Cuban or Barbados], *three-quarters-ounce* ORANGE CURAÇAO, *three-quarters-ounce* fresh LIME JUICE, *one-quarter-ounce* ORGEAT. Shake and strain into tumbler with crushed ice. *Garnish* with fruit and fresh mint.

Chapter 9

[MAI TAI]

*And then, swiftly, came the Plague and the rush of the
barbarians in its wake, and all the juices of the orchard
went into cocktails.*

—BERNARD DE VOTO, 1948

IN DECEMBER 1932, a stylish if somewhat adrift twenty-four-
year-old with a forehead made prominent by his receding hair-
line arrived in southern California, looking for something to
do. A native of New Orleans, his name was Ernest Raymond Beaumont Gantt. Curious by nature and something of a proto-beatnik by
choice, he had spent the previous months vagabonding on the cheap
through some of the globe's more humid locales: Jamaica, Australia,
Papua New Guinea, the Marquesas Islands, and Tahiti. By the time
he washed up in Los Angles, his money had run out.

Gantt made do in the Depression economy through his wits and
odd jobs—working in restaurants in Chinatown, parking cars at
commercial lots, and engaging in a little freelance bootlegging in the
months before Prohibition ended. Sociable and charming, he be-
friended such Hollywood personalities as David Niven and Marlene
Dietrich, and through them found occasional work as a technical ad-

viser on films set in the South Pacific. Directors were evidently as impressed by his knowledge of the region as by his collection of South Pacific artifacts, which could be borrowed for set props.

A year after he arrived in Los Angeles, Gantt happened upon a newly vacated tailor shop just off Hollywood Boulevard and connected to the McCadden Hotel. It was small—just thirteen feet by thirty—but Gantt liked the feel of it, and signed a five-year lease for $30 per month. He built a bar that would seat about two dozen customers, and scattered a few tables in the remaining space. He decorated the place with his South Pacific gewgaws, along with old nets and parts of wrecked boats he scavenged from the oceanfront. He called his watering hole "Don the Beachcomber."

He approached his drink menu the same way he approached his decor: with an eye toward frugality. Rum was the least expensive of the spirits, and Gantt had already sampled a variety in his travels. He devised an exotic menu of rum-based drinks that complemented the bar's South Pacific theme, and scratched them out on a board behind the bar.

The combination of Gantt's outgoing personality and the intrigue of his drinks proved irresistible to Los Angeles movers and shakers. Among those first drinks was one he named the Sumatra Kula, which cost a quarter. A well-dressed man named Neil Vanderbilt came in one day and ordered one, then another and another. He said it was the best drink he'd ever had. He was a freelance reporter for the *New York Times*, and he soon came back with friends, including Charlie Chaplin. Word of Don the Beachcomber began to spread through Hollywood and beyond. "If you can't get to paradise, I'll bring it to you," he told his customers. (It didn't work for everyone; in July 1936 a wealthy businessman struck and killed a pedestrian while driving home after a night at Don the Beachcomber. His name was Howard Hughes.) By 1937, the restaurant and bar had outgrown the small tailor's shop, and Gantt moved to a larger spot in Hollywood. He added more South Pacific flotsam and imbued the place with a tropical twi-light gloom. The joint became so much a part of his personality that he legally changed his name. Ernest Gantt was now Donn Beach.

And Donn Beach was the inventor of the tiki bar, a new kind of place that, over the next thirty years, would migrate from the cities to the suburbs and beyond.

Beach's reign in Los Angeles proved relatively short-lived. When World War II broke out, he enlisted in the military, and was in a con-voy en route to Morocco when his ship was struck by a German U-boat. Wounded, although not badly, Beach spent the remainder of his enlistment doing what he did best: serving up hospitality. The military put him in charge of overseeing dozens of hotels and restau-rants where airmen could rest and recuperate—on Capri, and in Venice, Lido, and the French Riviera.

Beach's ex-wife, Cora Irene "Sunny" Sund, was left to run the business back in California. She proved as able as her ex-husband. When Beach returned home, he found that Don the Beachcomber had blossomed into a small chain with a handful of restaurants na-tionwide. Beach had little to do but sit at the bar and cash his checks. (The chain would eventually grow to sixteen locations, and was for a time part of J. Paul Getty's corporate empire.) Beach signed on as a consultant and then packed his bags for Hawaii, where he opened his own unaffiliated "Don the Beachcomber" in an up-and-coming resort area called Waikiki Beach.

Hawaiian tourism boomed after the war, as passengers abandoned slow steamships for more efficient air travel. Fewer than 30,000 tourists came to Hawaii annually prior to World War II; that rose to 250,000 by 1959. (It's 7 million today.) The flood of tourists came to bask in the South Pacific sun and style, and a growing army of entre-preneurs arrived to deliver it. Tiki style went wholesale, and restau-rants, nightclubs, hotels and luau grounds that could serve pu-pu planters to hundreds at a seating met the demand.

Donn Beach was among those entrepreneurs. His restaurant became an instant landmark—more Hawaiian than most of Hawaii itself. Beach amplified the faux tropical theme with palms and thatch and a sweeping shingled roof, part space age, part ceremonial Polynesian meetinghouse. The noted Hawaiian arranger and composer Martin Denny played at the restaurant's Bora-Bora Lounge for nine months straight. Beach was often at the bar, a genial host wearing a gardenia lei, that, he was quick to note, was for sale at the restaurant's gift alcove. A myna bird presided over the premises, trained to blurt out, "Give me beer, stupid!" In the boozy intimacy of late evenings, a gentle rain would often begin to patter on the corrugated metal roof over the bar—thanks to a garden hose Beach had installed. (Always the businessman, he had observed that late-night drinkers tended to linger for another round if they thought it was raining outside.)

Donn Beach remained a fixture in Hawaii until he died in 1989 at the age of eighty-one. The *New York Times* ran a short obituary that painted him as a sort of Thomas Edison of the thatched-roof bar, the inventor of eighty-four bar drinks, including one immensely enduring libation called the mai tai.

This was not without controversy. "There has been a lot of conversation over the beginning of the Mai Tai, and I want to get the record straight," Victor Bergeron—better known as Trader Vic—once said. "I originated the Mai Tai. Anybody who says I didn't create this drink is a stinker."

VICTOR JULES BERGERON was born in San Francisco in 1902, the son of a French Canadian waiter and grocery store operator. Before he was even six, he had survived the great earthquake of 1906 and a ravaging bout of tuberculosis that claimed his left leg. In 1934, with $300 of his own and $800 borrowed from an aunt, he opened a small beer joint and luncheonette in Oakland. It was called Hinky Dinks, and he sold beer for a nickel and a meal for a quarter.

Hinky Dinks would likely have come and gone like so many other small and largely forgettable restaurants, but Bergeron, like Donn Beach, didn't set low expectations for himself. Prohibition had recently ended, and Bergeron's customers displayed an uncommon curiosity about cocktails—the more outlandish and inventive, the better. In 1937, Bergeron and his wife took a vacation to New Orleans, Trinidad, and Havana, and sampled some of the famous cocktails then in fashion. They drank hurricanes in New Orleans, rum punch in Trinidad, and daiquiris made by the legendary Constantino at El Floridita in Havana. Back in California, an idea began to germinate. He visited a tropical-themed restaurant called the South Seas that had recently opened in San Francisco, and journeyed to Los Angeles to try out a place that all the right people were talking about. It was Don the Beachcomber.

Bergeron headed back to Oakland and set about reinventing his restaurant and himself. He got rid of the name Hinky Dinks (which he concluded was "junky") and cast around for a new one. His wife pointed out that he was always involved in some deal or trade. Why not Trader Vic's?

Why not? He liked it, and the name stuck. Bergeron hastily spun a whole backstory to go with his new name. He now told his customers that he had lost his real leg in a shark attack—and then would grab an ice pick and ram it into his leg. Like Don the Beachcomber, he filled his newly christened restaurant with South Seas flotsam, lined the walls with dried grass mats, used palm tree trunks as columns, and hung fisherman's floats, masks, and spears—all things that brought to mind the mysterious South Seas islands, none of which he'd ever visited. Bergeron would take the idea launched by Ernest Raymond Beaumont Gantt and upon it build an empire.

TRADER VIC'S BOTH tapped into the zeitgeist and helped shape it. The Pacific theater in World War II drew America's attention to a region of the world they hadn't previously given much thought to.

When the war ended, returning servicemen carried home stories and snapshots of exotic Pacific lands and people they met in transit and on leave. The public's imagination was further captured by the tales spun by a talented and evidently underemployed naval reservist, who had spent much of his enlistment typing out stories in a tent in Vanuatu. His name was James Michener, and the book he published was called *Tales of the South Pacific.* It won a Pulitzer Prize in 1948, and made it to Broadway as a musical called *South Pacific,* with songs by Rodgers and Hammerstein. The musical became a movie sensation in 1958; a year later, Hawaii joined the union amid fireworks and hullabaloo, and two years after that Elvis added his own brand of fuel to the South Pacific mania with his movie *Blue Hawaii.* If it had thatch and tiki torches and little statues (which Donn Beach liked to call his "cannibal gods"), the public would come.

Tiki began in the cities, but it was too powerful to remain confined there. It moved into the suburbs and beyond. Apartment buildings, bowling alleys, trailer parks, laundromats, and corner restaurants were dressed up with tiki heads and masks, rattan walls, dried blowfish, and electric tiki torches. Plans were even made for a tiki-themed fast-food chain, to be called Tonga Pup, although this regrettably failed to graduate from drawing board to street corner.

The tiki movement was in large part a reaction to the times. It was the era of the Organization Man, the Man in the Grey Flannel Suit, the vodka drinker. Ornament had been buried by a generation of architects and interior designers. Streets were lined with lean glass buildings, and the suburbs sprouted ranch houses with floor-to-ceiling sliders and sleek, tubular steel furniture. It was all frightfully austere. The tiki restaurant, in contrast, was nothing but ornament; without it, a tiki bar would collapse. Those coming of age after the end of the war were eager to make up for lost time and happy to be entertained. Disneyland opened in 1955, and among its first rides was an ersatz Jungle Cruise, in which boats drifted through a sort of tiki-inspired, animatronic wonderland. At tiki restaurants, you could enter an exotic world and engage in curious rituals amid hula girls and seductively unfamiliar music. Tiki historian Sven Kirsten calls those who succumbed the "modern primitives." The tiki bar offered escape for those who didn't want to drop out of society and play bongo drums all day, but weren't content with a circumscribed life. *"Warning,"* wrote the authors of the 1957 *Esquire* cocktail guide in offering advice to aspiring hosts. "Do not make up chicken salad, tuna fish salad, mixed-cream-cheese-olive-sawdust-combination salad, spread on bread, cut off the crust, and then slice them into little ob-longs or triangles. Your guests will hate you forever, and quite rightly."

Grand tiki temples cropped up throughout the country to meet the demands of the modern primitives—the Mai-Kai in Florida, the Kahiki in Ohio, the Kowloon in Massachusetts, the Tiki Ti and the Tonga Room in California, and a dozen or more places competing with Don the Beachcomber in Honolulu. Customers typically en-tered the tiki realm by passing over a low bridge or through a damp grotto, which offered a gentle transition from the harsh and unfortu-nate reality outside the door. It took a few moments for one's eyes to adjust, as the restaurants were invariably windowless. Who wanted to see the harsh sun, the parking lot, and the road outside? The tiki restaurant existed in a sort of perpetual twilight, lit by propane torches, the fiery eyes of tiki statues, and golden flames licking off the pineapple-and-brown-sugar entrées delivered by a hula girl. There was always the possibility that one might witness an elaborate cult rit-ual involving cannibalism or sex or both.

IF THERE WAS a cult at the tiki palaces, it was that of the tiki drink.

Few came to the restaurants solely because of the food. (Noting the flaming entrées, the *Columbus Dispatch* once noted of the Kahiki that it "is one of the few restaurants in Columbus in which food can injure you.") The lure was the drinks. Restaurants raced to outhustle one another in concocting the most outrageous cocktails, giving them fanciful names like "Pele's Bucket of Fire," "Sidewinder's Fang," "Molucca Fireball," "Tonga Surfrider," and the "Aku-Aku Lapu." (Not all bars showed imagination; many saw fit to name their specialty simply "the Mystery Drink.") These South Seas–styled cocktails, first concocted in the 1930s, were a cultural phenomenon that lasted well into the 1970s—"an unprecedented life span for a drink fad," writes tiki drink expert Jeff Berry.

Tiki bars marshaled whole stockrooms of custom-made ceramic skulls, pineapples, barrels, Easter Island heads, and statues in which to serve their potions. Specific drinks were reserved for specific vessels—the "Deep Six," for instance, was always to be consumed "from the horn of a water buffalo" (or a ceramic facsimile thereof), which was often available in the gift shop for a small consideration.

Tiki bars encouraged the shared consumption of drink, which enhanced the effect of ritual. "The Kava Bowl" was a specialty of Trader Vic's in the 1940s; it consisted of vast amounts of various rums and other mixings, and was limited to three per party of four. "The Volcano" at Don the Beachcomber had a central cone filled with flaming overproof rum. Communal drinks came to the table wrapped in ceremony, offering fleeting celebrity to those bold enough to order them. At the Kahiki, an exotic "mystery girl" would bring out a flaming drink for four amid the reverberation of gongs. ("This ritual symbolizes an ancient sacrifice, which reportedly stopped volcanoes from erupting," the menu claimed.)

The competition for the most elaborate drinks led to CIA-level secrecy, chiefly out of fear that a bartender might leave and take prized recipes with him. A 1948 *Saturday Evening Post* story noted that the bottles at Don the Beachcomber lacked the original labels and had been replaced by new ones with cryptic letters and numbers. Bartenders used coded recipes to mix these anonymous ingredients. "Infinite pains are taken to see to it that the service bar help cannot memorize Don's various occult ingredients and proportions," the *Post* reported.

Tropical juices and rums had intermingled long before the rise of the tiki bar, of course. Pineapple-flavored rum—made by infusing sliced pineapple in a puncheon of rum—was not an uncommon drink in the eighteenth and nineteenth centuries. Early sailors enjoying shore leave would smuggle rum back aboard by drilling a hole in a coconut, draining the milk, then filling it with rum and sealing it back up. Surreptitiously sipping from the shell was called "sucking the monkey."

During Prohibition, the corner soda fountains had assumed some of the social role of saloons and trafficked in nonalcoholic exotica. Drinks available legally in the late 1920s included the Hawaiian Special and the Mandalay Delight. When Repeal was passed, bartenders were quick to add alcohol to the fruity potions. A bartender at New York's Hotel Biltmore took top prize at the 1934 International Beer, Wine and Liquor exposition with his Fresco Cocktail: lime, pineapple, sugar, and Bacardi, shaken and strained into a cocktail glass. Parched soldiers in the Pacific during World War II were singularly inventive when it came to drink. A GI would turn brewer by punching in the three eyes at the end of a coconut, then adding sugar and raisins; a week later one of the plugs would pop, signaling that it was ready to consume. Servicemen in search of the harder stuff rigged up stills made of fuel drums and scavenged copper coils, distilling spirits from whatever they could swipe from the mess hall. It was "considered aged by the time it had cooled," wrote one soldier, Malcolm Anderson, in 1945, and "made you feel as if the top of your head had been jerked up by several inches, or even yards." Tropical juices would make it slide down easier.

The haute tiki cocktail bar took these coarse combinations, tinkered with them, and dressed them up. The juices at the better establishments were always freshly squeezed. "For the life of me I can't see why any bar uses anything but pure fresh lemon or orange juice," wrote Trader Vic in 1948. David Embury, whose drink-making bible was published the same year, was even more emphatic: "It should scarcely be necessary to caution you never, *never,* NEVER to use unsweetened canned juices," he wrote, and warned of the "exceptionally vile concoctions of the prohibition era" that involved the same. "The first commandment with respect to fruit juices," Embury said, "is to use nothing but fresh fruit, freshly squeezed."

The drinks weren't just fruit juice, of course. They were mostly alcohol. Some special drinks contained as much as twelve ounces of rum, although eight ounces was the more common amount in even the stiffer drinks. Perhaps the most legendary was the zombie, which can trace its lineage, as can so much tiki culture, back to Donn Beach. Popular lore says that Donn himself mixed up several rums and a few other ingredients to help revive a badly hungover customer on his way to a crucial business meeting. When asked later how it went, the man replied he felt like "the living dead." A name was born.

What went into the original zombie has been lost in the bleary-eyed mists of time. Beach's widow later published a recipe that involved five rums, including one thirty-two-year-old Jamaican—plus lime juice, bitters, maraschino liqueur, and absinthe. Numerous efforts to re-create it have also been published, including a recipe published in *Here's How Mixed Drinks* (1941) that likewise featured five varieties of rum, along with apricot brandy, brown sugar, lime juice, and pineapple juice. (The recipe's author suggests, "Perhaps it would be wise to locate the coroner before serving this.")

The zombie was accorded full-fledged celebrity at the 1964 New York World's Fair, where it was a bestseller at the Hurricane Bar at Flushing Meadows. Lucius Beebe wrote that it cost a dollar at the bar and was limited to one per customer, "by a management at once thrifty and mindful of municipal ordinances." Beebe noted that the zombie craze led to a run on 151 proof rum, which was typically floated on the top of the cocktail, and heretofore had been consumed only by lumberjacks, Grand Banks fishermen, and others who valued the rapid warming qualities of high-proof spirits.

Like any celebrity, the zombie made a high-profile target for spoilsports and other critics. "This is undoubtedly the most over-advertised, overemphasized, overexalted and foolishly feared drink whose claims to glory ever assaulted the eyes and ears of the gullible American public," wrote Embury. He allowed that he was "allergic to secret formulas," since "all this mystery, of course, is calculated to inspire curiosity and thus advertise the drink."

Other critics dismissed such tiki drinks as concoctions appealing only to uneducated palates—to those who preferred sweet to dry, who hadn't traveled Europe and understood that an aperitif was meant to titillate one's appetite, not to sate it with sugar and fruit. Sugar in drinks was for unmanly men and those from the lower ranks of society. "Sweet alcoholic drinks are favored by the young and callow of all classes," wrote Paul Fussell in his study of American social structure, "a taste doubtless representing a transitional stage in the passage from the soda fountain to maturity."

Critics overlooked one essential fact: Many tiki drinks were actually very good, even sophisticated. They were drinks taken quite seriously at the better places—like Don the Beachcomber and Trader Vic's—where rum was accorded the honor it deserved.

DONN BEACH WAS the Alice Waters of rum. He showed Americans that the spirit didn't have to be the tasteless, bland commodity of the sort exported in tankers from Puerto Rico. Done right, rum had local variations and nuance. Rum had history, and aged rum especially had an intriguing richness and depth. Beach had a rare nose for the subtle differences among the better rums, and made a point of traveling through rum-producing regions to study the techniques and processes of rum making. On his buying trips, he'd lay in a two-year supply at a time, and he stocked some 138 different types of rum. He was particularly drawn to the more robust Jamaican rums, and established lasting friendships with the makers of both Wray & Nephew and Myers's.

Back home in Hawaii, Beach would blend and test to find the perfect balance and combination of rums, and then layer in additions like lime juice or Pernod or vermouth or pineapple and coax it into the perfect drink. "Donn would sit there all day with his cronies mixing drinks," recalled restaurant supervisor Nash Aranas, quoted in Sven Kirsten's glorious history of the tiki movement. "He would test, test, test like a mad scientist." Even Trader Vic doffed his cap: "I salute Donn the Beachcomber as the outstanding rum connoisseur of our country," he said, and printed this accolade on his menus.

Many of the original drink recipes called for a wide range of rums: white, medium-bodied, and aged rums of the sort that you can't find today—and if you could, you'd sip them slowly, as if they were fine cognacs, rather than mixing them with pineapple juice. Beach called for rums from Jamaica, Guyana, and Puerto Rico to mingle in his Plantation Punch recipe (along with triple sec and falernum), and his navy grog likewise called for three rums, all heavy and dark. It's true that dumping five rums into the zombie was more for show than taste, but two or three rums from different regions complement one another exceptionally well, and made for a far more complex drink than one made with a single rum.

Beach was abetted in his mission to spread the gospel of rum by an unlikely ally: food guru James Beard. In the late 1950s and the 1960s, Beard penned a series of columns for *Better Homes and Gardens* that dwelled on the delicious rums he had discovered and the cocktails that highlighted them best. Beard took global cuisines seriously in an age when ham, brown sugar, and pineapple were deemed exotic and tropical. He brought to the attention of his readers serious wok techniques and authentic South American ingredients well ahead of the trends. And Beard approached rum with the same seriousness.

Beard suspected much of the public was embracing rum because of its novelty in fanciful drinks, like those touted by the tiki palaces. He encouraged his readers to look deeper. "Today rum is returning to its rightful place as a general favorite," he wrote in 1960. "We are rediscovering what the colonial knew—that, of all the liquors, rum is the most versatile. . . . You can drink rum straight, on the rocks, in a highball, in a rum old-fashioned, or a rum sour.

"Each rum has its own special flavor and quality," Beard continued. "Indeed, one of the assets of rum as a drink is the wide choice of types and their versatility." Beard was a pioneer in explaining how rums varied by island and by heritage. This was not news to rum aficionados—Embury had outlined the regional differences in his bar book in 1948—but for those who believed a bottle of Bacardi Silver was the final word in rum, it came as an overdue education.

Cuban rum, distilled at a higher potency, stripped out more of the flavors, and was filtered to refine it further still. Beard noted that Jamaican rums had a different flavor profile than these lighter, more processed rums. Barbadian rums like Mount Gay occupied terrain between Cuban and Jamaican rums—not quite as full as the latter, but more robust than the former. The Virgin Island rums were finding a niche in the middle, like Barbados rums, and the *New York Times* reported that they possessed "their own peculiar molasses flavor and are at their best when served in mixed drinks of the heavy type, such as swizzles, punches, and coolers."

Demerara rum had the powerful aromatics of Jamaican rum but an additional flavor of something slightly burned, and was at times flavored with bark. Martinique rums, while less common in the United States (even though the island had thirty-two rum distilleries and a long tradition of rum making), were strikingly different, more aromatic, made as they were from sugarcane syrup rather than molasses. Thanks to Beach, Bergeron, and Beard, a nation that knew how to speak whiskey learned how to speak rum.

And rum began to find its market. In one nonscientific study in 1962, an enterprising reporter tallied the jigger count at a bar near Grand Central Station over the course of a twelve-hour bartending day. The result: straight whiskey remained dominant with 185 jiggers, followed by Scotch (125) and gin (120). But rum was closing in at 90 jiggers, and was still outpacing vodka. Indeed, that year rum sales grew 16 percent. Rum now accounted for 2.5 percent of the liquor market.

ONE OF THE remaining landmarks of Waikiki Beach's first tourism boom is a Moorish-style confection the color of cotton candy that rises among palm trees midway down the beach. The Royal Hawaiian Hotel, which opened in 1927, was built by a steamship company to promote Hawaii as a destination. It's now surrounded by charmless high-rises that cast it alternately in shadow and glare, but on the hotel grounds you can still find evidence of the lost era at the outdoor bar just steps off the beach. Here, exceptionally elaborate drinks are served amid tiki torches as you listen to both crashing waves and a crooner with a wireless mike working the tables looking for guests to sing along. ("Remember that one? It's by a guy named Neil Sedaka.")

This is the Mai Tai Bar, and the namesake drink is a vision to behold. It's served in a glass big enough to house Japanese fighting fish, and is richly but discretely colored, like a hazy sunset. A wedge of pineapple perches on the rim, lording over a shrub-sized sprig of mint, a bright cherry, a purple floating orchid, and a small, colorful parasol. The whole tableau is as lush and tidy as a Victorian conservatory.

The mai tai remains the quintessential tiki drink. It's also a survivor, persisting when so many other concoctions of the era have perished. There's a good reason for its longevity—it's an exceptionally fine drink when made well. (A mai tai was the first thing asked for by Patty Hearst, the Symbionese Liberation Army kidnapee turned co-conspirator, upon her release on bail in 1976.) The problem is that it's much easier to make one poorly than properly. A mai tai can easily become unbalanced—too sweet, too tart, too alcoholic—and it's the rare bartender who can craft a worthy mai tai consistently. It's no wonder that mai tai premixes have come to be so popular, and why the mai tai has suffered such a quick descent into mediocrity. A traveler treads into dangerous terrain when ordering a mai tai at an unfamiliar bar—or strip-mall Chinese restaurant.

A classic version starts with the same building blocks of all outstanding rum drinks—lime and sugar (in this case, in the form of grenadine)—which is mixed with at least two rums, a light and a dark, and a touch of curaçao (an orange-flavored liqueur). The secret ingredient, if there is one, is orgeat (pronounced *or-ZHAY*), an almond-flavored syrup now often found as a flavoring in trendy coffee shops.

Like any good rum drink, a mai tai enhances and brings out the quality of the rum. In other words, better rums always make a better mai tai. This isn't true of another tropical drink, the piña colada, which I would classify as among the worst examples of the tiki cocktail. The piña colada was invented in 1954 by a bartender at the Caribe Hilton in Puerto Rico. It was an instant hit—and why not? Pineapple and coconut are the linebackers of the taste world, and can flatten the harshest of rums. It's no great surprise that it was invented in Puerto Rico, where so much rum was meant to be hidden rather than heralded.

The Royal Hawaiian is probably the best-known place to order up a mai tai at Waikiki Beach, but it's by no means the only place. The mai tai is actually inescapable—as unavoidable as the mojito in Havana or the hurricane in New Orleans. The Halekulani Hotel's surfside bar serves a mai tai nicely garnished with a splint of sugarcane. The Kaimana Beach Hotel serves its drinks under gnarled and ancient hau trees, where the whole of the Hawaiian experience has been condensed in a single glass. That the drink was invented in California hardly matters.

THE MAI TAI has more fathers than one can reasonably hope to count. There's a good explanation behind the volume of claims. The Los Alamos–like secrecy that prevailed in many tiki bars meant that no standard recipe rose to the top. Trader Vic Bergeron published two cocktail recipe books at the height of his fame, yet neither included the mai tai. So anyone with access to a few bottles of liquor could throw together anything and call it a mai tai. And they did. Inexplicably, many involved pineapple juice—which Trader Vic's original assuredly did not.

Bergeron spent a fair amount of energy in his later years defending his paternity. That others claimed to be the mai tai's inventor, he said, "aggravates my ulcer completely." The mai tai arose as many fine cocktails do, he said, as the result of an impromptu mingling of ingredients. It was 1944. "I was at the service bar in my Oakland restaurant," he recalled in 1970. "I took down a bottle of seventeen-year-old rum. It was J. Wray Nephew from Jamaica; surprisingly golden in color, medium bodied, but with the rich pungent flavor particular to the Jamaican blends. The flavor of this great rum wasn't meant to be overpowered with heavy additions of fruit juices and flavorings. I took a fresh lime, added some orange Curacao from Holland, a dash of Rock Candy Syrup, and a dollop of French Orgeat, for its subtle almond flavor. A generous amount of shaved ice and vigorous shaking by hand produced the marriage I was after. Half the lime shell went in for color [and] I stuck in a branch of fresh mint . . ."

He said he first served the drink to friends, a couple visiting from Tahiti named Ham and Carrie Gould. Carrie smiled and said, "Mai tai roa ae"—which means "the best" in Tahitian. Bergeron christened the drink on the spot. It later made the leap from Oakland to his San Francisco and Seattle restaurants. And in 1953, according to Trader Vic, the mai tai was exported to Hawaii when he was hired by the Matson Steamship Lines to create a drink menu at the Royal Hawaiian Hotel.

The chief countervailing genesis tale comes, not surprisingly, from Donn Beach, who claimed he invented the mai tai at his bar around 1933. The Beachcomber's version started with heavy Jamaican rum and light Cuban rum, then added lime, bitters, Pernod, grapefruit juice, falernum, and Cointreau. A newspaperman who claimed to have been drinking with both Beach and Bergeron in the early 1970s says that Bergeron admitted that Beach was the mai tai's inventor.

Maybe, maybe not. Donn Beach may very well have been the first to apply the name *mai tai* to a drink. But the one served at Trader Vic's is the source of today's classic mai tai, and is far and away the better drink. It deserves to prevail.

BY THE LATE 1970s, tiki was tacky. The thatched roofs were ratty, the hula girls passé, and the drinks too potent and elaborate for the emerging era of white wine spritzers. The actor Yul Brynner came down with trichinosis after eating at Trader Vic's at the Plaza Hotel in New York. (He settled out of court for $3 million.) A decade later, Trader Vic's was closed by then-owner Donald Trump, who announced that the restaurant had "gotten tacky." (In 1994, a haute Polynesian restaurant called Gauguin briefly opened in the space once occupied by Trader Vic's.) Bergeron eventually turned over control of the chain to his children and retired to pursue a quiet career as a painter and jeweler. According to the *New York Times*, he liked to paint "ice-skating nuns and perky otters."

Perhaps the most startling death knell for tiki rang out in 2000, when the glorious Kahiki restaurant in Columbus, Ohio, built in 1961 and featuring a forty-foot-high tiki with a fireplace in its mouth, was demolished to make way for a Walgreen's drugstore.

A tiki revival flourished in the late 1990s, prodded by hipsters who took the so-called loungecore movement in a more ironic direction. Tiki mugs that languished in Salvation Army shops were snapped up and traded on eBay, and tiki aficionados gathered at events and went on road trips to see the remaining icons of the era. A surfeit of tiki cocktail guides made their way into print. At the trendy clothing and gewgaw chain Urban Outfitters, shoppers could buy plastic coconut drink mugs and dashboard hula girls. Wink, wink.

The revival is all about kitsch: the faux-primitive statues, the blow-fish lamps, the netting, the thatch over the home tiki bar, the Martin Denny albums. But few seem to have embraced the demanding craft of the tiki cocktail. (The author Jeff Berry is the most rigorous tiki cock-tail archaeologist practicing today, and his two tiki cocktail guides—*Beachbum Berry's Grog Log* and *Beachbum Berry's Intoxica!*—offer a small ray of hope.) Getting the drinks right takes a measure of pa-tience and time, not to mention cash to invest in the best rums.

THE COLLAPSE OF the original tiki culture is nowhere as shocking and complete as at Waikiki Beach. Don the Beachcomber's old place has been demolished, and Trader Vic's is gone. All the other tiki palaces have likewise disappeared. The Tahitian Lanai, a tiki hotel and restaurant with individual grass dining huts off a lagoon, was bulldozed for holiday condominiums. (Lost with it was the "Lovely Lovely," a potion of high-proof rum, brown sugar, lemon and lime juices, and curaçao.) Even the tiki rooms at the larger, more estab-lished hotels have vanished. The Mai Tai Bar at the Royal Hawaiian, which was never very tiki, could serve as a backdrop for a Jimmy Buf-fett album.

I had heard about a surviving tiki bar that hadn't yet succumbed to the times a few miles from Waikiki Beach, and I set out to find it. La Mariana Sailing Club turned out to be north of the city in a grim in-dustrial area of blank concrete walls and dusty roadside debris. It was a low building in a compact, overgrown waterside oasis of palms next to a manufacturing plant that processes crushed aggregates.

I walked inside. It took a few moments for my eyes to adapt to the gloaming. But when they did, I felt like Hiram Bingham at Machu Picchu, stumbling into a lost culture. There was a waterfall behind the tables in the main room, and colored lights twinkled throughout. Corky, an unsocial African gray parrot, performed pitch-perfect ren-ditions of car alarms and digital telephone rings.

As Honolulu's other tiki bars had shut down, owner Annette Nahinu, now eighty-eight, had gathered up bits of the past and installed them in her place. The tables were from Don the Beachcomber; the blowfish lamps from Trader Vic's. The huge clamshells next to the waterfall came from the Hyatt's Tiki Room, and the tiki support posts from the Sheraton's Kon-Tiki. When the Tahitian Lanai shut down, La Mariana acquired not only the woven lauhala walls from the Waikikian, but also Ron Miyashiro, the bar's former pianist. He plays on Friday and Saturday nights, and the place fills up, often with regulars who migrated with him.

I pulled up a stool at the bar and ordered a mai tai. They didn't get many tourists tracking them down, said Tito Calace, the bartender that night. But the locals still came religiously. "They like the aloha," he said. And then he made up a classic mai tai, redolent of the sun and the tropics.

Sitting out of the mainstream, far from the high camp and layered irony of the modern tiki revival, I had found what I was looking for: the perfect tiki moment.

[MOJITO]

Place 4 *to 6 freshly washed* MINT LEAVES in tall glass. Add *two teaspoons* BAR SUGAR or simple syrup and *three-quarters-ounce* fresh LIME JUICE. *Muddle* vigorously with MUDDLER. Add *two ounces* of good aged RUM. *Fill* glass with ICE and SODA WATER. Garnish with mint.

Chapter 10

[MOJITO]

Rum is an American term applied to an American invention.

—*PROHIBITIONIST'S TEXTBOOK*, NATIONAL
TEMPERANCE SOCIETY AND
PUBLICATION HOUSE, 1877

RUMORS ABOUT A MAN named Stephen Remsberg surfaced early on when I began researching this history of rum. This Remsberg fellow, I had been led to believe, was an attorney who lived in New Orleans and liked rum. He liked rum *a lot.* He had also amassed what knowledgeable people told me was the largest private collection of rum in the world. Naturally, I was intrigued. So when I went to New Orleans (not long before Hurricane Katrina rearranged the city's culture and geography), I tracked Remsberg down and called him up. Yes, he said, he was the Stephen Remsberg who collected rum, and yes, he would be happy to meet with me. He invited me to stop by his law offices not far off Canal Street.

Remsberg is fifty-eight years old and has a slight paunch and an expression that suggests he's often undecided whether he means to express surprise or disdain. He speaks slowly and with some deliberation. His office is clean and tidy, as one might expect of a lawyer who

specializes in commercial contracts, and the space is otherwise unremarkable save for the views toward the Mississippi River. A few minor
rum graphics are hung here and there, but little else to suggest an un-
healthy obsession.

Nor was there anything to suggest that he had arrived at his abiding interest in rum through a long and profound love of tiki drinks.
His first sip of a Polynesian-style drink, which he recounted dreamily,
occurred in London in the 1960s. He had gone to visit his older
brother, and the two set off for Trader Vic's at the London Hilton. He
ordered a vodka drink made with pineapple and coconut—"sort of a
beginner's drink" is how he describes it. But his experience at Trader
Vic's was not unlike that of an agnostic who visits the Vatican and
comes away devoutly Catholic.

While at law school in Washington, D.C., Remsberg spent his
weekends unwinding at the local Hilton's Trader Vic's. Later, living
in Chicago, Remsberg had the good fortune of residing just around
the corner from a Don the Beachcomber restaurant. "I discovered
Don's early on," he said, "and then I found paradise." Remsberg is
perhaps one of a handful of people who not only recognizes that tiki
drinks can vary widely in style, but can discourse knowingly about
them. "I prefer the Don the Beachcomber's bartending style," he told
me. "Trader Vic's drinks are very good, and I think his mai tai is fab-
ulous. But his drinks are certainly sweeter."

Remsberg in time became a serious tiki cocktail detective, and
devoted hours to cracking codes and re-creating drinks of the era.
One major discovery occurred when he was visiting Don the Beachcomber's flagship restaurant in Los Angeles some years ago (it's since
closed) and he noticed that the bartender finished his cocktail litur-
gies at the bar, eschewing the usual custom of slipping into the back
and doing it in the sacristy. Remsberg noted he added a few dashes
from a pair of unmarked cruets. So he casually inquired what they
contained. Pernod and Angostura bitters, he was told. For years,
Remsberg had been trying to figure out the "secret ingredients" in the

Beachcomber's tiki drinks, and here it was, laid out before him, much simpler than he ever thought. It was as if he was Howard Carter and here was the door to Tutankhamen's tomb.

Remsberg's interest migrated from specific drink recipes into rums in general; one of his early epiphanies was that outstanding tiki drinks required outstanding rums. What's more, many drink recipes he uncovered employed identical juices and sweeteners, and varied only in the types of rums that were used.

So rums became a small hobby of his. Then they became a large hobby. He acquired bottles when he traveled to the Caribbean, and before he knew it he had a growing collection of hard-to-find rums. Friends and relatives started to seek out obscure rums for him on their travels. He started prowling old bars for historic bottles of rum and, more recently, has delighted in what one can turn up on eBay. ("What do you search for?" I asked. "I type in 'rum,' " he said.) As will happen when one embarks on such an endeavor, the collection became somewhat unwieldy. At the time of our meeting, he said he had in excess of seven hundred different rums, although he hadn't taken inventory in some time. And that didn't include the little airline-sized bottles, of which he had maybe twice as many.

We swapped notes about some rums we enjoyed, and speculated on what had happened to once-popular brands. But my time was winding down. I rose to leave. He looked up at me from behind his desk, and I was uncertain if he was regarding me with surprise or disdain. "What are you doing tomorrow?" he then asked. "Do you want to stop by the house?"

STEPHEN REMSBERG'S HOUSE might be regarded as the Louvre of rum, that is, if the Louvre were built around a small kitchen, and then spilled into a small adjoining room with a thatched-roof tiki bar. It was smaller than I expected, but he had fit much into the space, mostly by attaching to the walls many linear feet of narrow but tall shelves about the height width of, say, a rum bottle.

What's striking about the collection is not the sheer acreage of liquor—which is actually quite impressive—but that it's an active tasting collection. "I don't collect empties," he said. "I collect rum, not bottles. And I'll open any bottle that I have two of." As such, Remsberg's house is more than a mortuary of defunct brands. It's a museum of tastes, some of which have been wholly lost.

Strolling around the collection with my knowledgeable tour guide, we visit with some old friends of mine. "This is my one sample of the old heavy rum from Puerto Rico that was especially made for planter's punch. That would have disappeared around 1950." He points. "And these are three old Barbados rums, and this"—a bottle of Finest Old Jamaican Rum, dating to about 1910—"is one of the first two or three rums I believe to be sold as a brand in the bottle." (Rums before that were invariably sold in bulk from the barrel, he explained.)

Remsberg clears a spot on his kitchen counter, sets out some short glasses, and we work our way through history, an inch at a time. We sample the dense Jamaican Wedderburn- and Plummer-style rums, named after nineteenth-century plantations. Both were popular in England, Remsberg said, and neither very popular in North America or even Jamaica. We sample London Dock rums, shipped from Jamaica or Guyana to be aged in the barrel in the cool, damp environs of the London docks, which gave it a rich, mellow taste that was in much demand. We take a brief detour to sip an Egyptian rum, which was curiously floral and not very pharaonic.

"And these are my six remaining New England rums," Remsberg says. His Boston rums date from the last gasp of the Boston rum era, with samples from the early to the mid-twentieth century. They include Caldwell's, Pilgrim, Old Medford, Chapin, Il Toro, and one privately bottled rum that likely was collected by a butler right from the barrel at a distillery. We sample Caldwell's, and it is just as I hoped it would be—

dense and cloying and filled with the rich, yeasty taste of molasses. "By 1900 they were making a serious rum in New England," Remsberg says.

He returns to his shelf and pulls down a bottle of white rum—a rarity here, since he generally prefers dark. "This doesn't look like much," he says. He's right; it doesn't. It's a bottle of white Bacardi dating from 1925, straight out of the crypt of Prohibition. I wrinkle my nose slightly—I find most white Bacardi harsh and industrial tasting, and I drink it only when nothing else is available.

Remsberg notices and smiles. "You should really taste this," he says to me. "This would have been the old Bacardi White Label they used to make the first daiquiris in Havana. This would have been aged four years, then they would have stripped the color out of it by filtering it through charcoal. I don't have limes or I would make you Constantino's El Floridita daiquiri. But you can say this is what started the daiquiri—this rum."

He pours out a bit more than a thimbleful into a glass, and I bring it under my nose. It's not in the least medicinal, but complex and inviting. I sip. My word. It's like tasting in Technicolor—it's full, complex, and not too flowery, but also lacking any trace of unpleasant heaviness. It's unlike any other white rum I've tasted.

Remsberg was grinning at my inability to hide my shock. "So you can see why Prohibition-starved Americans flooding El Floridita would have said, 'This is good!' There was something about those early Cuban cocktail rums. They were just better rums than the world had seen. Nobody is producing a white rum today as pleasing as this."

TODAY, VIRTUALLY ALL traces of Bacardi have been erased from Havana, like a Stalin-era apparatchik airbrushed out of a Soviet politburo photograph. When Bacardi left the island in 1961, fleeing before it was nationalized by the Castro regime, the company abandoned millions of dollars worth of distilling equipment, a century of local contacts, and that whimsical tower designed by Maxfield Parrish. But the Bacardi family took what was most important: its trademark. It would rebuild its production and markets abroad, but neither forget nor forgive Castro and his "bearded ones."

Today, old Havana is looking less dowdy and more refreshed than it has since Prohibition days. The Bacardi tower was recently spruced up by the Cuban government as part of its ongoing restoration of the historic downtown. Tourism revenues are replacing sugar subsidies from the old Soviet Union, with investors and travelers coming from Canada, England, Spain, and Latin America. Old Havana is bustling with stone masons perched on wooden scaffolding of questionable safety. Men approach travelers on the street and in halting English offer cigars, women, and rum.

As was the case in the 1920s, a number of bars today exist to serve the tourist, and many of the old cocktail recipes have been resurrected. Old Havana can feel like an alfresco museum of forgotten drinks. Tall men in short-waisted scarlet jackets bustle about outdoor cafes off Obisbo Street, taking orders for daiquiris and Mary Pickfords and MacArthurs and mojitos.

Especially mojitos. If you walk into any Old Havana bar—except for Hemingway's El Floridita, where daiquiri pilgrims make their obeisance—and hold up two fingers without comment, the odds are favorable you'll get two mojitos in return.

Bodeguita del Medio is Havana's mojito mecca. It's a ten-minute walk from El Floridita on a quiet street around the corner from the Plaza de Armas, and you could easily pass by the robin-egg's-blue storefront without giving it a second look. It was first opened in 1942 by Angel Martínez, who called it the Pleasant Storage Room and sold rice, beans, and other staples. He expanded into serving lunch, changed the name to Martínez House, then in 1950 changed it again to Bodeguita del Medio. He served drinks—including very good mojitos, it turns out—and the place became a hipster haven in the 1950s, attracting visiting celebrities like Nat King Cole, Errol Flynn, Pablo Neruda, and an unknown university student named Fidel Castro.

The bar survived Fidel's revolution; a black-and-white photo on one wall shows Che Guevara in jungle fatigues sitting comfortably with others, the multiple condensation rings on the table suggesting this wasn't merely a photo opportunity.

Today, drinkers arrive by the busload, ushered through by tour guides who announce that their charges have fifteen minutes to sample one of the famed mojitos before heading to the next attraction. The front room is no more than twenty feet wide, with an L-shaped bar that seats fewer than a dozen (everyone else crowds in or spills out into the street), a compact dining room in the back, and a small upper galleria with some artifacts and photos. A three-man band clusters in a corner and plays songs from the *Buena Vista Social Club* sound track. Where El Floridita strives for elegance, La Bodeguita specializes in a scruffy informality, and drinkers for years have left their mark by scrawling their names on the walls—Che Guevara's signature is said to be somewhere. (Customers today pen one name over another using increasingly thick markers.) The bar also features the Hemingway stamp of authenticity: a framed inscription evidently written and signed by the man's own big hand reads, "My mojitos in La Bodeguita. My daiquiris in El Floridita."

The Cuban government, which today owns virtually all the restaurants in Cuba, understands the allure of the bar's name among capitalist marketers, and has licensed other Bodeguita del Medios—in Dubai, Oman, Paris, and Milan. There are also samizdat variations in Miami and Palo Alto, the latter of which has a cardboard cutout of a grinning Ernest Hemingway propped outside to lure in customers to sample their "coastal cuisine with a Cuban influence." The Palo Alto version serves many rums, although none from Cuba.

Mojitos at La Bodeguita in Havana are made by unflappable bartenders in unfathomable quantities. They line up a battery of tall glasses along the bar during lulls, and preload them with mint, lime juice, and guarapo. When the mojito orders flood in with the arrival of each tour group, a bartender adds a splash of club soda and then pulverizes the whole mess with a wooden muddler the size and shape of a souvenir baseball bat. The process results in a small, frothy geyser, which sprays the bartender and a few patrons. No one seems to notice. Then comes ice. Then rum is lavished on top freehand.

The mojito is a simple drink—it's basically a rum collins with the addition of mint. The drink most likely started as a rural farmworker's favorite in the nineteenth century—the mint, sugar, and lime could divert a drinker's attention from the singular nastiness of cheap rum— and migrated to the blue-collar beaches of Havana. From here, it was a short hop to the more trendy Havana nightclubs that flourished under U.S. Prohibition, when the ice and bubbly water were introduced. The second volume of Charles Baker's *The Gentleman's Companion, Being an Exotic Drinking Book, or Around the World with Jigger, Beaker, and Flask,* first published in 1939, talked of the "greatly improved rum collins" served at Sloppy Joe's bar in Havana, made all the more delectable with a spiral of lime peel wrapped around the ice and garnished with "a bunch of fresh mint."

Like the daiquiri before it, the mojito set across the Straits of Florida and spread north after Repeal. It cropped up in the teeming post-Prohibition bars: During the 1939 World's Fair in New York, a mojito was featured in a free cocktail guide for visitors to the Cuban pavilion. That same year Trader Vic was advertising mojitos in newspaper ads for his Oakland restaurant. The 1941 book, *Here's How Mixed Drinks,* featured a mojito recipe typical of the era, which called for a twist of lime and a garnish of mint leaves—although not muddled to bring out the richer flavor.

After an initial fling with celebrity, the mojito mysteriously fell out of fashion in America. Maybe it was the requirement of mint leaves, which had to be fresh. During the Spam and Wonder bread era, prepackaged drinks were ascendant—think of the instant daiquiri and mai tai mixes. Or maybe it just met the fate of so many excellent drinks that have slipped from the radar for no discernible cause. Whatever the reason, the mojito reverted to being a local Cuban drink without a broad following overseas.

This state of affairs persisted until the 1980s, when the mojito resurfaced stateside, first at Miami restaurants serving gentrified Cuban cuisine, then around the country, in many cases attached remora-like to the Nuevo Latino fare of chefs looking for the next big thing. Los Angeles became the mojito center of the West Coast (where the *Los Angeles Times* called the mojito, for inscrutable reasons, "a cosmo for the more adventurous,") and the cocktail raised its profile sufficiently to make cameos in such series as *Sex and the City*. In 2002, the mojito had its biggest scene in *Die Another Day*. Finding himself in Cuba, James Bond orders a mojito instead of his traditional martini. ("Mojito? You should try it," Pierce Brosnan says to Halle Berry, which admittedly lacks the flair of "shaken, not stirred.") Overnight, the mojito was everywhere: in Cleveland and Boston and Houston, and then on to the chain bars in the suburban strip malls. Where this all ends is uncertain, but it seems a safe bet the mojito will land safely outside the boundaries of passing fad and establish itself as an enduring classic cocktail.

For all this trendiness, there's a little secret behind the mojitos you get in Havana bars: They aren't very good. The mojitos I sampled at Bodeguita del Medio and a number of other Havana bars—and I sampled a scientifically valid number—were oddly disappointing, and in much the same way. It was as if they had been manufactured in a centralized tall-drink facility somewhere beneath the cobblestone streets of Old Havana, then distributed via a rusting pipeline. They were insipid, off-tasting, slightly metallic. There was an aftertaste of cleaning fluid. The mint wasn't minty, the lime wasn't limey, and the bubbly water wasn't bubbly. The guarapo may have been sour. I don't know. Some of my disappointment may be ascribed to my American-trained taste buds, which expect bigger, more robust flavors. But even so, I had to force myself to drink them after a day or two. I've had better mojitos at airport bars.

WHILE BACARDI is no longer the rum that defines Havana, the responsibility has been taken up with considerable zeal by Havana Club, a rum manufactured by the Cuban government. The simple, circular logo is splashed on bar signs, umbrellas, swizzle sticks, and cocktail glasses, and is every bit as omnipresent as Cinzano in Italy. The Havana Club Rum Tour is in a historic building at the edge of Old Havana, just across the road from the shipping port. No rum is actually made here, but artifacts of rum-making are on display, and on multilingual tours you cross a catwalk over a Disneyesque model of a sugar processing plant and distillery. The tours end—as is customary on such adventures—at the factory store, where you can buy bottles of rum or T-shirts or cocktail glasses while sampling some of Havana Club's aged rums. (The Havana Club headquarters during Prohibition was on Plaza de Cathedral, but the building is now a museum of colonial art—and, sadly, free rum drinks no longer flow for tourists seven days a week.)

Havana Club rum was for decades produced by the Arechabala family in Cuba. Owner José Arechabala proved not quite as nimble as the Bacardis when Castro came to power; Havana Club—both the name and the facilities—was expropriated by the Cuban government in October 1960. The Arechabalas moved to Spain and left the rum business.

In 1995, the Bacardis came to the Arechabalas and purchased the rights to the Havana Club name, then started producing a Havana Club rum out of the Bahamas. One problem: The Arechabalas technically no longer had any rights to sell. The Cubans had taken it over on the island, and in 1973 registered the trademark internationally after the Arechabalas—believing it no longer had any value—

stopped paying fees to maintain it. In 1994, Cubaexport entered into a joint agreement with Pernod Ricard, the French liquor giant, to distribute Havana Club globally. (This, of course, didn't include the United States, which has maintained an embargo on Cuban products since 1963.)

Bacardi's effort to wrest control of the name made perfect business sense. Havana Club's agreement with Pernod Ricard made it likely that the upstart could offer serious competition to the dominant Bacardi brand—the largest-selling single brand of any liquor of any sort today. Havana Club was selling briskly in Italy, Canada, and elsewhere. It didn't require any special powers to foresee that if the United States eventually dropped its Cuban embargo, then Havana Club would be in a good position to make a run at Bacardi's dominance.

And so Bacardi embarked on an elaborate multifront campaign to ensure that Havana Club would never cross the Straits of Florida to America. After claiming that it had legally acquired the name from the Arechabalas, it launched a Byzantine lobbying campaign in the U.S. Congress to block the sale in the United States of any good whose trademark had been expropriated. In 1998, Florida Senator Connie Mack introduced a tiny amendment to the huge four-thousand-page appropriations bill, effectively nullifying Cuban-owned U.S. trademark registrations without the consent of the original owners—an amendment narrowly tailored to the Bacardi–Havana Club dispute. (Bacardi had been generous donors to Mack's campaign.)

The Bacardis also became entangled with then-prominent Texan Republican Tom DeLay, donating $40,000 to political action committees he supported. Whether by coincidence or design, one of DeLay's Texan allies, Representative Lamar Smith, introduced legislation that would further ensure that Bacardi controlled the Havana Club trademark. (Since it was attached to a defense bill rather than a trade bill, the move sent up red flags and was ultimately killed.)

The war over the trademark moved to the courts. The U.S. courts have regularly upheld the legislation favoring Bacardi's ownership of the trademark; world courts have been mixed. Interestingly, some large U.S. corporations have opposed the Bacardi legislation, noting that it puts at risk long-standing international trademark agreements. (Castro has threatened to start producing a soft drink called "Coca-Cola" and exporting it worldwide.) The legal outcome is still unclear.

Nonetheless, the tussle has resulted in a fascinating spectacle: two foreign-owned companies battling in U.S. courts for the rights to a name for a product that has no connection with the United States.

And perhaps that's emblematic of what's become of rum. In the mid-eighteenth century, the fight over rum imports to the colonies was based on actual rum or the ingredients to make rum. Today, it's a far more ethereal battle over intellectual property rights, rather more like something in *The Matrix*. Rum disputes have become unmoored from the underlying product, which exists only as a symbol.

Much the same could be said of much of the rum that lines the shelves at liquor stores today. In the taxonomy of rum, two kingdoms exist: the party rums and the premium rums. As with vodka, the taste of the party rums, which dominate the market, is increasingly manufactured by the advertising. Party rums are generally stateless and islandless, despite their claims to carrying on the best traditions of Cuba or Puerto Rico or Jamaica. They have no geographic anchorage, but find temporary harbors with international conglomerates, which discard and pick up brands for their portfolios like cards in a poker game. The liquor industry went through its most sweeping consolidation in the 1990s, when regional firms were bought by national firms, and national firms by international. The ten largest producers worldwide now own some 70 percent of all liquor brands, and that concentration is certain to rise. Every widely known brand of rum sold in America today is owned by a major international player.

Captain Morgan—the number two rum worldwide—is owned by the world's largest seller of alcoholic beverages, Diageo, which controls nearly one in five of the top-selling premium spirit brands. This includes the number one vodka (Smirnoff), the top two Scotches

(Johnnie Walker and J&B), the leading stout (Guinness), the top tequila (Jose Cuervo), and the bestselling liqueur (Baileys Irish cream). Diageo was formed in 1997 by the merger of two European companies, Guinness and GrandMet. The new company was so huge it attracted the attention of antitrust regulators in the United States, which feared a near-monopolistic dominance in the rum market. Regulators required that Diageo divest itself of its Malibu brand.

So Malibu rum, produced on Barbados, was sold to Allied Domecq, the world's second-largest spirits company. (The company's other holdings include Maker's Mark bourbon, Canadian Club, Courvoisier, Beefeater, Tia Maria, and Kahlúa.) A few miles from Malibu's island distillery is the blending and aging facility of Mount Gay rum, now owned by the Rémy Cointreau Group, which was formed by a merger of two venerable French firms in 1991. Malibu's siblings include Cointreau liqueur, Piper-Heidsieck champagne, and Rémy Martin cognac.

The largest-selling rum brand worldwide remains Bacardi, the family-owned company that arguably started the party rum trend nearly a century and a half ago. Bacardi has not only acquired Bombay Gin and Grey Goose vodka, making it the fifth-largest spirit company in the world, but it has aggressively subdivided its rum category, focus-grouping rums to appeal to every style of drinker.

With rum, as with so many aspects in the life of an American consumer, it's unclear where freedom of choice ends and tyranny of choice begins. When Bacardi began producing rum in the mid-nineteenth century, only one rum was available; it was called Bacardi. By the early 1960s, Bacardi sold seven kinds of rum in the United States, ranging from the light two-year-old to a six-year-old extra dry introduced to compete with whiskey. With today's market fragmentation, it's hard to maintain a count: there's Bacardi 8, Bacardi Superior, Bacardi Gold, Bacardi Solera, Bacardi O, Bacardi Razz, Bacardi Limon, Bacardi Coco, Bacardi Vanila, Bacardi Anejo, Bacardi Black, Bacardi Light, and Bacardi Reserva. Niche marketing has turned a mass-market magazine age owned by *Time* and *Life* into a thicket of specialized magazines, a three-network television world into a tangle of cable stations, and a walk down the aisles of a liquor store into a confusing, overlapping swamp of rums.

Major rum manufacturers, with state-of-the-art column distillation facilities, are so efficient that they can now strip out virtually all the natural essences of rum, creating a product with the aroma and character of a well-managed medical clinic. The resulting spirit is so free of the natural cogeners that give rum its rich, evocative smell and flavor that something artificial often needs to be added back in to give it character.

And so we see the rise of flavored rums, the fastest-growing subcategory, which now account for about one in every three bottles sold in the United States. These rums come in many flavors, mostly tropical, which play off the spirit's Caribbean heritage. Malibu's coconut-flavored rum and Captain Morgan's spiced rum (a sort of cinnamon, cloves, and sugar blend) are among the best known, but most major spirits companies have joined the hunt for the younger drinker brought up on intense, Jolly Rancher–style flavors. Bacardi Limon, introduced in 1995, proved to be one of the most successful spirit launches in history, and now sells around a million cases a year. Bacardi later added citrus, coconut, raspberry, and vanilla rums to its stable. Cruzan Rum Distillery, which traces its roots back to 1760 and has been quietly exporting a palatable Virgin Island rum for decades, now aggressively markets no fewer than eight tropical flavored rums, including pineapple, mango, banana, and orange.

Infused rums have been traditional in the West Indies and beyond for centuries—and commercially flavored vodkas were offered as early as 1960. (These were pulled from the market because the flavors weren't stable and tended to go off.) The current crop of coconut rums, however, have about as much in common with a coconut as a Glade scented air freshener has with an alpine meadow. It matters little if they're flavored artificially or naturally—they're soft drinks for adults who like the concept of exotic drinks but may never have tasted an actual mango or papaya or fresh coconut. Malibu coconut rum in pineapple juice makes a sort of piña colada; Bacardi O with heavy cream and orange juice makes a drink called a creamsicle.

Where is it all headed? In April 2004, Mount Gay announced that it was teaming up with ScentAir Technologies, which produces promotional scent machines, to roll out a new in-store marketing campaign. ScentAir gives customers sample scents of products for sale, which apparently cause a person to drift into a dreamy reverie and then instantly reach for his or her wallet. ("Just as Muzak provides retail sound, ScentAir scent systems provide retail scent," says the marketing copy.) When you approach a Mount Gay display at select liquor stores, a motion detector signals a small machine to send a dry scent of either Mexican Mango or Madagascar Vanilla your way.

The scent machine is the perfect match for the modern flavored party rum. The aroma is wholly independent of the spirit itself, thrown on like a bright but ill-fitting housecoat. What we have now are bitter fights over brand names, and rums divorced from their island heritages and their natural flavors. It doesn't bode well for a happy future.

But good news can be found. Another powerful trend is making its way through the rum world. Some distillers are happily letting rum be rum—and coaxing the best from it. And serious cocktail drinkers, part of the new cocktail renaissance, are rediscovering how sophisticated rums make immensely sophisticated drinks. It's as if William Morris had appeared with a handcrafted cocktail shaker amid the cogs of industrial alcohol production.

A DRAM OF RUM sits before me. Nearly two dozen years ago, it came out of a still in the lowland tropics not far from Guatemala's Pacific Coast. It was clear as water when it was decanted into charred oak barrels, then it was trucked to the mountains and aged in warehouses at 7,650 feet. The makers employ the solera method used to make sherry, which means that rum lost to natural evaporation is replaced by rum from the following year's distillation. (For instance, rum in a cask aged ten years is topped off with rum from the nine-year cask.) Subtle chemical interactions between alcohol, oak, and oxygen take off the rough edges, the charred barrel gives the rum its pleasing hue, and the varying elevations give it . . . well, I'm not exactly sure. The mountain coolness slows evaporation from the casks, no doubt, but whatever else happens is a trade secret of the La Nacional, the company that has made Zacapa rum for decades and is said to have one of the largest reserves of well-aged rum in the world.

The casks were deemed ready for consumption when the average age of the rum was twenty-three years old, and then the rum began another journey. It was bottled, and the bottle was adorned with tightly woven dried royal palm leaves. The rum was boxed and put on pallets and shipped north, and eventually it appeared on the table where we sat, some twenty of us, in a ground-floor meeting room of a large and modern hotel on the Canadian island of Newfoundland. With pencils in hand and bland crackers before us, we readied ourselves to sip.

The 2003 International Rum Festival was part industry kaffee klatch, part public debauch (sampling booths were open to the public for two days out of the four), and part competition. An island that keeps close company with icebergs may seem an odd choice for a rum conclave—where are the palm trees?—but not if you know a little about the early history of the Atlantic trade. In the seventeenth and eighteenth centuries, salt cod was shipped to the West Indies to feed the slaves working the sugar plantations where rum was made. The cod was often purchased with rum, which was sent north and eagerly consumed by fishermen to keep warm as they hauled nets in the cold north Atlantic. Newfoundland shipped its cheapest, nastiest salt cod to the West Indies, since it was used mostly to feed slaves. Returning the favor, the West Indies planters shipped its cheapest, nastiest rum north. Newfoundlanders developed a fondness for rum in general, and bad rum in particular. One of those facts that suggests the persistent influence of the past is this: Rum accounts for about half of all spirits sold in Newfoundland today, compared to about 13 percent across Canada and 12 percent in the United States.

Newfoundland's affection for scarcely potable rum evolved into a lasting fling with a rum called Screech, which was made in the West Indies and bottled locally. (The transaction now involves cash rather than cod.) Newfoundland Screech was once famous for being all but undrinkable—strident and overproofed enough to cause a hasty imbiber to involuntarily emit the sound after which it was named. Visitors to bars along rowdy George Street in St. John's are today asked innocently if they've been "screeched in." If not, an impromptu ceremony is arranged. This involves repeating some nautical jargon, vouchsafing one's allegiance to the island, publicly kissing a taxidermied and well-worn codfish, then downing of a shot of Screech.

Screech is now a trademarked brand marketed by the provincial liquor authority, and it has been greatly tamed and gentrified in recent years. After tinkering with the blend and upgrading the product, the province sells Screech that is now surprisingly smooth and tasty. At the 2003 rum festival, Screech even won a gold medal, which is awarded to the top-scoring third of all rums in each category.

Preparing to judge the superpremium rums, I now lift the Zacapa rum to eye level in concert with the other judges and admire its rich amber color under the light. Zacapa is considered by many who can (and do) argue at length over such things to be the best commercially available rum today. I have seen bottles of Zacapa hidden on shelves in the offices of competing West Indies distillers, who have sheepishly admitted they were striving to reproduce it, as yet without success. Zacapa achieved a score of 98 points at the Beverage Testing Institute in 2001, and it remains the highest ranking rum ever rated. It won top honors at the festival's rum judging event five years running, and in 2003 the festival coordinators chose to retire it from competition.

They enshrined it in a newly established rum hall of fame with the democratic idea of allowing other competitors a shot at the top award. The Zacapa rum we're served this day is not in competition. It is our benchmark rum, allowing us to calibrate our palates for the blind tastings to follow.

I swirl it gently and bring it under my nose. It has a dense, sweet fragrance, an earthy bouquet, like roses grown in a compost of chocolate and cherries. I sip. I close my eyes. The first taste washes over me and brings to mind the scene in *The Wizard of Oz* in which the black-and-white world suddenly bursts into color. A dozen or more sly flavors dart around my mouth—pralines and roasted nuts and vanilla. A gentle warmth spreads from my lower spine slowly upward through my neck. I'm transported to a sunnier climate, far from the icebergs. This is, without doubt, an extraordinary rum.

The pourers circulate through the room with the first of the twenty-three rum samples we'll be judging in this session. Then we'll have a break, and go into the next session, and the next, with the event spread over four days. We'll judge a total of 166 rums, and the event will take us around the globe: a United Nations of sugarcane-based liquor, with representatives from—no surprise—much of the West Indies, but also Nepal, Mexico, Australia, Canada, and the United States. (Notable absentees include the Philippines and China, which produce vast amounts of rum, virtually all of which is consumed locally.)

Rum judging is a curiously quiet and solemn affair, especially given rum's raucous history. Every judge has his or her own tasting technique. Some put their hand over the top of the glass and gently swirl, to release and capture the subtle scents. Others cup the glass in both hands to allow a little warmth to bring out the liquor's more elusive qualities. Some noses go fully into the glass; some hover an inch above and sniff tentatively. A few judges slurp slightly to allow in some air; most sip silently, then hold the rum on their tongues for several long seconds. Only one judge spits out his samples after tasting; the rest of us swallow. For each rum, judges mark down a score of one to ten for each of three qualities: smoothness, taste, and "extras," which might include aroma or character. This is then totaled up, for a possible high score of thirty.

Judges were cautioned at the outset not to emit grunts of distaste or sighs of contentment that might influence their colleagues. (This etiquette is discarded when it comes to flavored rums. The judging is then punctuated by gasps, gurgled sounds, and other signs of small distress. The judges take rum seriously, and the invasion of the lollipop flavors cannot be brooked without registering some dissent.)

About two dozen judges, who include master blenders, rum collectors, and connoisseurs, have been recruited for scoring. The number of judges ebbs and flows throughout the four days, hitting a low point when the harsh overproof rums are graded. But nearly every seat is filled when the time comes to rate the best of the rums—the premium and superpremiums—which have been called the "cognacs of the Caribbean."

These rums mark a bright spot for the industry. Like the lighter party rums, the more densely flavored upmarket rums have also been in demand these days, although among a smaller group of drinkers who are willing to pay more for quality. For decades distillers have hectored U.S. consumers to appreciate the subtley of finer rums—as early as 1952, Bacardi was urging consumers to sip its aged rum after dinner in a brandy snifter. But rum had that shabby reputation to overcome, and only now does it seem to have shaken loose its sordid past and been allowed from the street into the manor house. More than one hundred varieties of rum sell for upwards of $25 a bottle, about double the number a decade ago. The U.S. Federal Trade Commission now pegs retail sales of premium rum at more than $1 billion per year, and the market has been showing double-digit growth of late. The supply of aged rum is straining to meet the demand; Jamaica's Appleton Estate has seen tremendous demand for its twenty-one-year-old rum and laments that it has only enough to produce about a thousand cases each year.

Rum has arrived. Again.

"WOULD YOU LIKE to sniff my bung?" asks Phil Prichard. He's a tall, gregarious sixty-four-year-old with a booming voice and thinning red hair, and he's holding out a wooden plug that was until very recently used to seal up a cask of Prichard's Fine Rum. This line is delivered with a wry smile; he uses it all day long when touting his rum, which he manufactures in a distillery in a shed attached to a disused schoolhouse in Kelso, Tennessee. His whole operation occupies a space about the size of a moderately serious woodshop. State or local laws typically prohibit Prichard from offering samples to passersby at liquor stores and meetings of package store associations, where he spends the bulk of his waking hours signing bottles and talking up rum. But there's no law against sampling the aroma. "People are always interested in history," Prichard says. "When you weave the quality of this rum with its historical aspect, I sell more with sniffs than with tastes."

Prichard is a representative of another welcome trend: the return of the American rum distiller. They no longer number in the hundreds, but a handful have appeared in the continental United States in the past few years, producing spirits in the old tradition. In Delaware, Dogfish Head Spirits produces creditable aged and white rums. In New Orleans, Cane Louisiana Rum was distilling a foursome of fine rums, both aged and unaged, made of molasses and sugarcane juice. (Hurricane Katrina flooded the distillery and wiped out the aging stocks, as well as much of the distilling equipment; the distillery has said it hopes to produce rum again someday, but it's unclear if that will happen.) Small-batch rum is again being produced near the sugarcane fields of Hawaii.

Prichard's operation, just a short drive from the Jack Daniel's distillery, may be the most unlikely. After whiskey poached on rum's terrain and drove it out two centuries ago, rum now appears to be launching a rear-flank action on whiskey's turf.

At $30 a bottle, about three or four times the cost of a mass-market party rum, getting Prichard's off the store shelf and into the home liquor cabinet has taken some work. Building consumer demand for aromatic, quality rum is a gradual process—one bung sniff at a time. What's more, Prichard has to grapple with a larger, more metaphysical obstacle: He has to convince the consumer that rum isn't solely about sunny beaches and palm trees or swaggering pirates muttering, "Yarrr." Rum can be pure Early America, Prichard says, as American as white church steeples and New England village greens. When Prichard talks about rum, it's not reggae playing in his head, it's a fife and drum. In his brochures, Prichard even features a rendition of *The Spirit of 1776,* the famous 1891 painting of three bedraggled Revolutionary musicians marching beneath a tattered flag. "We lay no claim to being the only rum made in America," Prichard explains. "But we do stake our claim that we are producing an authentic American rum. I don't know anyone else who's doing that."

Prichard took an interest in rum in the mid-1990s, after a thirty-year career manufacturing dental implants and running a gift shop with his wife in Vermont. He got the notion of opening a microdistillery, and noticed that sales of premium rums were growing at an appealing rate compared to other liquors. His first thought was to distill a rum made from the sweet syrup of Tennessee-grown sorghum. Federal liquor regulators told him he was welcome to do that, but he just couldn't label it as rum. By definition, rum sold in America must come from sugarcane or its by-products.

So Prichard scouted around and ended up contracting for molasses from Louisiana. At first, he drove the molasses north himself in a thousand-gallon plastic tank strapped on the back of his truck. But after sliding out of control in a slick intersection one rainy day, he went professional and bought a four-thousand-gallon stainless steel tanker trailer and hired a trucker. Prichard buys a high-quality table-grade molasses, which he swears is not all different from the stuff American rum distillers imported from the islands in the eighteenth century. He ferments the molasses in three stainless steel fermenting tanks, then double distills the wash in a five-hundred-gallon copper pot still that he bought from a defunct New England distillery. He casks the distillate in fifteen-gallon new white oak barrels that have been charred on the inside. Smaller barrels (most distilleries use a fifty-two-gallon size) mean more barrel surface to each gallon of rum, so the aging process is quicker than in larger casks. As for the charred insides, Prichard says that colonial distillers would have done the same thing, trying to burn out the taste of salt fish or turpentine or whatever else merchants might have shipped before selling the used casks to the distillers. Prichard's rum, about a million dollar's worth at any given time, is aged in a pair of forty-foot steel cargo containers that sit in the distillery's yard surrounded by chain-link fence. Weeds sprout lavishly, stray dogs wander through, and you'd need an exceedingly fertile imagination to conjure up the Caribbean.

Prichard isn't beholden to colonial distillation methods. For instance, he doesn't use the lead pipes that caused the dry gripes, and he pays closer attention to his yeast than his eighteenth-century counterparts would have. (No dung in the fermenting vats.) Before bottling, his rum passes through a series of filters of the sort found in the plumbing aisles of Home Depot. But he stands by his product as the genuine article. "We spend almost every waking hour attempting to define the American rum, versus what we refer to as the tropical types of rum." And it does taste different from most of today's West Indian rums—more austere and less sweet, perhaps bringing to mind the better sipping bourbons made just north in Kentucky.

Prichard has a warm chuckle that's a shorthand way of saying, "Get a load of this." He seems to take a special delight in beating the system and making rum without all the overpriced equipment to which the larger distillers are addicted. His shipping-container warehouses cost just $2,000 apiece delivered, and he bought the still and doubler at a distress sale for less than half of what it would have cost to buy a smaller one new. He designed the gravity-fed bottling line himself, and often fills bottles on Sunday, when he's not traveling the liquor store circuit. His wife sits beside him, gluing individual yellow ribbons over the top of each bottle.

"You know what that is?" Prichard says, pointing to the top of a small Rube Goldbergesque apparatus in a dim corner next to the fermenting tanks. "That's a salad bowl." Indeed, a restaurant-sized stainless steel salad bowl is inverted atop a restaurant-sized stockpot, held in place with C-clamps. A copper condensing tube extends upward from the bowl's apex nearly to the ceiling, then curves downward through a copper sleeve connected by a green garden hose to a sink faucet. This crude device was Prichard's first experimental still, and he still uses it when brewing up test batches. Prichard's operation has an engaging bootstrap inventiveness that's extremely American, even if the product is more refined than what you would have guzzled in Boston or Philadelphia three centuries ago.

Of course, striving to perfect the rum of eras past would be wholly missing the point. The story of rum is one of change, evolution, and adaptation. Rum resurfaces with each era. It's the true American spirit. Rum has been with Americans since our inception, and like us, rum has learned to work with whatever history gives it.

Rum doesn't like endings. And for a good reason: Rum is nothing but a series of fresh beginnings.

[*A Thumbnail Guide to Rum*]

Hundreds of rums are available around the world, and their flavor profiles vary so widely that you'll often swear you're sipping different spirits. And that's part of the adventure of rum sampling. While more regulated spirits like bourbon also differ from brand to brand, sipping your way through them is the equivalent of touring from Louisville to Lexington—the view doesn't change all that much. Sampling rums, on the other hand, is like going from Martinique to Maui by way of Medford—you just never know what surprises the next sip will bring. In part, this is because rum is produced in so many places, but also because there is no international oversight board; if it's made from sugarcane or its by-products, it can be called rum. The result is a vast and untidy marketplace of rum products.

When shopping for rum, a few key distinctions should be kept in mind.

Unaged or aged? In theory, white rum is unaged and dark rum is aged. And, in theory, the change in color comes from the inside of the charred barrels.

The reality is different. Some white rums are aged in oak barrels and then filtered to remove the color. And some lightly aged rums are colored with caramel to make them appear darker. (Black rums like Caldwell's or Myers's are rendered black as molasses with additional agents.) Aging also mellows rum, and an older rum tends to have fewer burrs to catch your throat on the way down. A general rule of thumb is that an older rum is a more complex rum (often fit for sipping), and unaged or lightly aged rums have less intrigue and usually can sing just one note (and are often fit for Coca-Cola). The fun comes in finding exceptions to the rule.

Sugarcane juice or molasses-based? The French islands tend to make rum from fresh sugarcane juice, with Martinique the sole supplier of what's called *rhum agricole*. (*Rum industriel* is the French term for rum made from molasses, which is used in the production of most rum worldwide.) *Rhum agricole* has been increasingly making its way into American markets.

Unaged sugarcane rum has a sharply distinctive flavor—you can really taste and smell the sugarcane base. That's largely because sugarcane liquor comes out of the still at a lower proof than molasses-based rum, allowing more of the distinctive qualities to come through. (Fermented molasses is typically distilled at a higher proof to strip out unpleasant aromas that can carry over at lower temperatures.) Aged sugarcane rums, which mellow and take on the flavors of the barrel, veer closer in taste to that of their aged molasses-based counterparts.

Pot still or column still? Most rums are made in efficient column stills, which allow continuous production and economies of scale. Some boutique rums are still made in pot stills (such as Prichard's), and many rums, such as a number from Jamaica and Barbados, blend a measure of pot-still rum with column-still rum as a flavor enhancer. For the most part, though, improvements in distillation technology and barrel-aging techniques have evened out many of the differences between the two distilling methods, so which still is used today is typically of small consequence. For instance, Ron Zacapa from Guatemala—among the most heavily-bodied of rums—is made in a column still. However, a boutique pot-stilled rum has a distinct if subtle flavor profile prized by many rum connoisseurs.

Listed alphabetically on the pages that follow are some of the rums that impressed me during the course of research ... clined toward the heavier rums and prefer those ... so these suggestions probably skew in that directi...

I haven't included rare rums, nor those mythica... only on certain days on certain West Indian island... can be found somewhere in a U.S. liquor store. Selection varies widely by state; some stores are still overseen by a feudal, government-run distribution system, and some are free market. But even among the free-market states, you won't find all the smaller labels, since few distillers have the budget to roll into all national markets at once. The inconsistency can be aggravating, but it also adds a welcome element of suspense when traveling across the United States. My rule of thumb: Never visit a new state without stopping by a liquor store to see what's in stock.

You may notice that I don't include any flavored rums on this list. Some of these may be perfectly fine in some mixed drinks, but I assume that you're interested in rum, not candy.

Appleton [Jamaica]

The Appleton VX is a rich, full-bodied, slightly peppery rum that goes superbly in a mai tai. It's a blend of rums five to ten years old, which benefit from a shorter secondary barrel aging afterward. It has many of the characteristics of a traditionally robust Jamaican rum but is tempered for a more sophisticated palate.

Rhum Barbancourt [Haiti]

Barbancourt is made from fresh sugarcane on an island with a strong French heritage, but it's technically not a *rhum agricole* (that name is reserved for rums from Martinique). Barbancourt is a sublimely dry rum, wonderfully austere and oaken. (It's aged in French oak, not American bourbon barrels.) Note the stars on the label—three stars mean it's aged four years and five stars for eight years, while the

e du Domaine is aged fifteen years. The three-star makes an
.tstanding mojito.

Ron del Barrilito [Puerto Rico]

The tasty rums produced by Barrilito in Puerto Rico are a good example of crossover rums. Puerto Rico has long been famous for its
light, almost vodka-clear rums, and a half-century ago such a full-
bodied rum wouldn't be commonly available on the island. But tastes
and markets change, and Barrilito has responded well. Aged in used
wine casks from Spain, both the two-star and three-star rums have
distinct qualities. The two-star is lighter and makes a wonderful mixing rum; the three-star (aged six to ten years) has a slight smokiness to
it and is good for sipping as well as for mixing in drinks that call for
bringing more of the rum flavor forward.

Rhum Clément [Martinique]

The range of tastes found in Clément rums is impressive. The white
rum has a robust and pleasing sugarcane taste. The aged rums, such
as the VSOP (aged at least four years), lend themselves to sipping
neat. Clément also makes an orange-flavored liqueur called Créole
Shrubb, which is traditionally served on holidays. An El Presidente
cocktail made with the VSOP and Créole Shrubb is among my
favorites—sophisticated without taking itself too seriously. Also look
for Rhum J.M, produced at a separate distillery but also owned by
Clément. The aged J.M rums are supple and intricate; the ten-year
rums are bottled at cask-strength and are worth searching out. J.M arrived in select U.S. markets at the beginning of 2007.

Cruzan [Virgin Islands]

This high-volume producer of mass-market rums really knows its
product—the two-year-old white and amber rums are a great choice

for simple mixed drinks when you're more on a budget than in the mood for something special. Priced comparably to Bacardi, Cruzan is my much preferred everyday rum, with more of a rum taste and less of an industrial aftertaste. When you're ready to upgrade, the Estate Diamond Rum (an amber blend aged for five to ten years) will lend your cocktails an extra dimension without breaking the bank. The Single Barrel is better still, with the blend recasked for more aging and to farther mellow and mature. The result is a delightfully creamy and silken rum.

El Dorado [Guyana]

Guyana was the original source of the dense, heavy Demerara rums, the favored tipple among sailors, fishermen, and other disreputable sorts. El Dorado carries on the robust tradition, with a rich molasses flavor, but with an unexpected class that seems to call for a snifter, smoking jacket, and a faithful dog at one's feet. This pot-still rum is produced in five, twelve, fifteen, twenty-one, and twenty-five-year variations and is sold in most major markets and some smaller ones. I'm a fan of the fifteen-year—it has the gentle scent of a freshly unwrapped caramel but with enough rum essence to anchor it solidly in the past. The twenty-one year variation recently arrived in the U.S. market.

Mount Gay [Barbados]

Mount Gay Eclipse has long been my benchmark rum—and I'm not a sailor. It's highly pleasing straight up, but also not so rare or expensive as to be wasted in mixed drinks. Mount Gay and ginger ale with a lime is hard to beat on a sultry summer day when you're not up to mounting a more formidable attack on the home cocktail bar. Mount Gay Extra Old is the premium product from this Barbados distillery, which has been making rum continuously longer than anyone else in the world. The distillery runs both column and pot stills—a small amount of the more aromatic pot-still rum is blended with the more flavorless column-still rum before being barreled and aged. The Extra Old is silky and perfect over ice, with perhaps just a squeeze of lime.

Niesson [Martinique]

When you order a ti' punch in Martinique, the odds are high that the waiter will plunk down some lime pieces, some sugar, and a squarish bottle of Niesson *rhum agricole,* which you then use to build the punch to your own liking. This is a common rum with not much common about it. It has a strong sugarcane aroma and taste to it, which renders it hazardous to use in most cocktails—the taste is just overpowering—but it's ideal in a ti' punch. The older *rhum vieux* is uncommonly smooth. This rum comes from one of the few remaining family-owned small distilleries on the island and the only distillery that uses a slow fermentation method on their sugarcane juice.

One Barrel [Belize]

This is a light gold, molasses-based rum with a highly distinctive taste—is that a hint of coffee? Purists might object that it's got more aromatics than a pure rum should (a touch of peach? a touch of toffee?), but I know others who consider this their guilty pleasure. One Barrel is available in many western states and a few in the east, and it is nicely priced.

Prichard's [United States]

This is a pot-still rum made in small batches by Phil Prichard in Tennessee (see Chapter 10). Prichard's Crystal Rum is delightful and distinctive—a classic unaged molasses white rum that's distilled five times, yet retains an unusual butterscotch taste. Prichard's Fine Rum is aged nearly three years in new fifteen-gallon, charred, white oak barrels, and to my taste it shares the dry and oaken qualities of a great bourbon.

Pampero Anniversario [Venezuela]

Pampero Anniversario is a dense, slightly sweet rum filled with unexpected surprises, like a hint of orange on the first sniff and a touch of vanilla on the first taste. It's a blend of four- to six-year-old rums and is friendly and approachable while full of the tastes of a classic heavy rum. This is an ideal starter rum for those looking to appreciate the joys of sipping, and it will still bring joy to those who have years of rum experience.

Pyrat XO [Anguilla]

Like Ron Zacapa (below), Pyrat XO is a sipping rum—smooth, slightly sweet, and full of flavor. There are chewy caramel notes, but also a curious hint of orange, which allows it to fraternize nicely with a twist of lemon, lime, or orange. It's not produced on Anguilla, but blended there from various Caribbean rums that average about fifteen years in the barrel. The brand is owned by the same folks who make Patron tequila.

Santa Teresa 1796 Ron Antiguo de Solera [Venezuela]

Relatively new to the U.S. market, this high-end sipping rum is crafted at a Venezuela hacienda that dates to 1796 (hence the name) and where rum has been produced since 1857. This region has long been noted for producing a full-bodied rum, and Santa Teresa begins there, adding an intriguing complexity (the rum is aged fifteen years in French Limousin oak), with notes of cherry and apricot. This rum should be enjoyed straight.

Ron Zacapa Centenario [Guatemala]

Ron Zacapa, aged twenty-three years in the cool highlands of Guatemala, is to my mind the quintessential sipping rum. It's perfect to take the chill off a cool and damp evening; I wouldn't even taint it with an ice cube, never mind some fizzy mixer (although I'll sometimes spare a teaspoon for a float on a mai tai). Some find it overly syrupy and sweet—tiki drink expert Jeff Berry says he "can't imagine drinking it in anything other than a sno-cone"—but it's consistently won almost every reputable rum-tasting competition. The same folks also market a fine fifteen-year-old rum (called Zaya), which has slightly less depth and richness, but is still delicious. Inexplicably, Zaya is usually priced the same as the older Zacapa.

[*When It's Cocktail Time*]

R ECIPES FOR the main rum drinks addressed in this book are featured at the beginning of each chapter. Life would be extravagantly uninteresting if we were limited to just those cocktails. What follows is a wholly subjective selection of rum drinks that I like. I tend to prefer drinks tart or astringent to sweet, so those who like their libations somewhat sweeter might want to adjust sugar and liqueurs accordingly. These are listed in a rough chronological order, based on when they most likely first appeared.

Some items worth stocking that you might not have at hand:

> *Bitters (both Angostura and Regan's No. 6 Orange*
> *Bitters)*
> *Maraschino liqueur*
> *Simple syrup (boil one cup sugar with one cup water;*
> *let cool and refrigerate)*
> *Bar sugar (sold as "quick-dissolving sugar" or*
> *"superfine" at many supermarkets; never use*
> *confectioners' sugar)*
> *Muddler (something like a miniature baseball bat used*
> *to mash mint and fruit to extract essential oils)*

FISH HOUSE PUNCH

Perhaps the most famous "secret" rum drink recipe, made since the eighteenth century at an august Philadelphia fishing club.

>*2 ounces rum*
>*1 ounce cognac*
>*1 ounce lemon juice*
>*2 teaspoons sugar*
>*1/2 teaspoon peach brandy*
>*sliced peaches, for garnish*
>*water or club soda*

Mix the ingredients together in a glass with ice. Top up with water or club soda and garnish with freshly sliced ripe peaches.

ADMIRAL HOMOTO

A neocolonial maritime drink enjoyed at sea when nothing else is at hand, as recorded by tippling sailor John Carroll.

>*2 ounces rum (Mount Gay works best)*
>*2 ounces black tea*

Pour the ingredients together in a glass or mug and serve at room temperature without ice.

HOT BUTTERED RUM

This recipe is intended to be prepared at first frost and kept in the freezer, providing the base for delicious hot rum drinks throughout the winter.

1 pound butter
1 pound brown sugar
1 pound granulated sugar
1 tablespoon ground cinnamon
1 teaspoon ground cloves
1 teaspoon nutmeg
1 quart vanilla ice cream

Bring the butter to room temperature and mix all the ingredients except the ice cream. Add slightly softened ice cream and mix well. Store mixture in freezer. To make drinks by the mug, add 1 $^{1}/_{2}$ ounce rum, 1 tablespoon of ice cream mix, then fill mug with boiling water.

MEDFORD RUM PUNCH

A punch recipe as it appears in the 1887 edition of *Jerry Thomas's How to Mix Drinks, or the Bon-Vivant's Companion,* the first bartender's manual. Thomas calls specifically for "Medford rum," suggesting the persistence of this Boston-area rum. Substitute any full-bodied rum.

1 ounce Medford rum
1 ounce medium-bodied rum
1 teaspoon lemon juice
1 orange slice, cut into quarters
Seasonal berries and a lime slice, for garnish

Shake the ingredients and pour with ice into a tumbler. Garnish with seasonal berries and a slice of lime, and serve with a straw.

TI' PUNCH

Short for "petit punch," this popular drink is served throughout much of the French-speaking West Indies. It's also extolled loudly by Ed "Minister of Rum" Hamilton. The proper ingredients can be hard to come by but are essential. (Rhum agricole, distilled at a lower proof, has a more fragrant character; it also tends not to have happy results in any cocktail other than ti' punch.)

> *wedge of lime*
> *2 ounces rhum agricole blanc (sugarcane rum, preferably*
> *from Martinique)*
> *¹/₂ teaspoon sugarcane syrup* (sirop de canne)

Squeeze the lime wedge into a short glass and add the rum, the syrup, and the ice. Stir briefly, then allow the drink to sit several minutes to chill and blend before drinking.

RUM TODDY

From the *Stork Club Bar Book* (1946). Another guide (by Charles Baker, 1939) also recommends the addition of clove: "The result is quite aromatically happy."

> *1¹/₂ ounces Jamaica rum*
> *1 teaspoon sugar*
> *2 cloves*

slice of lemon
pinch of cinnamon
boiling water

Put the ingredients in an old-fashioned glass; add the boiling water.

RUM OLD-FASHIONED

The bourbon or rye old-fashioned is a nineteenth-century classic. The rum old-fashioned I find even smoother and more agreeable. A medium-bodied rum like Mount Gay or Appleton works best.

orange peel
1¹/₂ ounces rum
¹/₄ ounce simple syrup or bar sugar
2 dashes Regan's Orange Bitters
orange slice and maraschino cherry, for garnish

Lightly muddle the orange peel with the rum and the simple syrup. Remove the peel. Add the bitters and the ice and stir until chilled. Pour over fresh ice in an old-fashioned glass with the orange slice garnish and a cherry. (Regan's Orange Bitters makes a simple rum seem even more regal, but if you don't have it at hand, Angostura bitters is a perfectly fine substitute.)

BACARDI COCKTAIL

Use Bacardi rum lest the lawyers hound you.

> *2 ounces white Bacardi rum*
> *1 tablespoon lime juice*
> *1 teaspoon simple syrup or bar sugar*
> *$^{1}/_{2}$ teaspoon grenadine*
> *lime slice, for garnish*

Shake the ingredients with ice and strain into a cocktail glass. Garnish with a slice of lime.

PIRATE'S COCKTAIL

A simple, elegant rum Manhattan from the *Esquire Drink Book*.

> *3 ounces dark rum*
> *1 ounce sweet vermouth*
> *1 dash Angostura bitters*

Stir the ingredients with ice and strain into a short glass.

PLANTER'S PUNCH

David Embury's recipe from 1948.

> *3 ounces Jamaica rum*
> *1 ounce sugar syrup*
> *2 ounces lemon juice*

2 or 3 dashes Angostura bitters
soda water
fruit, for garnish

Shake the ingredients vigorously with crushed ice and pour, without straining, into a tall glass. Pack the glass to the top with more crushed ice, fill to within one-half inch with soda water, then churn with a bar spoon until the glass starts to frost. Decorate with fruit.

RUM BRONX

The original Bronx—once almost as famous as the Manhattan—was made with gin. This rum variant is sometimes called a Third Rail.

2 ounces medium-bodied rum
$^{1}/_{2}$ ounce orange juice
$^{1}/_{4}$ ounce sweet vermouth
$^{1}/_{4}$ ounce dry vermouth
orange peel, for garnish

Shake the ingredients with ice and strain into a cocktail glass; garnish with an orange peel.

RUM COLLINS

1^1/$_2$ ounces white rum
juice of ^{1}/$_2$ lemon
1 teaspoon bar sugar
club soda
orange slice and maraschino cherry

Shake the rum, the lemon, and the sugar in a cocktail shaker; strain into a tall glass of ice. Top off with club soda. Garnish with an orange slice and a cherry.

CUBA LIBRE

The liberal use of lime juice separates this from its more pedestrian cousin, the rum and Coke.

juice of ^{1}/$_2$ lime
2 ounces rum (Cuban if you can get it)
Coca-Cola
lime wedge, for garnish

Squeeze juice from half a lime into a tall glass. Add rum. Fill with ice and Coca-Cola. Garnish with a lime wedge. (Optional: add a dash of Angostura bitters.)

MYRTLE BANK PUNCH

Trader Vic's interpretation (1948) of a famous punch served to Prohibition-era tourists on the porch of one of the best hotels in Kingston, Jamaica.

1½ ounces dark Jamaican rum
¾ ounce fresh lime juice
1 teaspoon bar sugar
½ ounce grenadine
club soda
½ ounce maraschino liqueur

Shake the rum, the lime juice, the sugar, and the grenadine in a cocktail shaker with ice. Strain into a tall glass filled with fresh crushed ice, fill with club soda, and top with float of maraschino liqueur.

MACARTHUR COCKTAIL

In 1946, Lucius Beebe considered this one of the top rum cocktails.

1½ ounces light rum
½ teaspoon dark rum
¾ ounces triple sec
dash of egg white

Shake the ingredients with ice and strain into a cocktail glass.

HEMINGWAY DAIQUIRI

Said to be created for Ernest Hemingway by Constantino Ribalaigua Vert at El Floridita in Havana.

1½ ounces rum (lighter rum is better)
¼ ounce maraschino liqueur

³/₄ ounce simple syrup
¹/₂ ounce grapefruit juice
³/₄ ounce lime juice

Shake the ingredients in an iced shaker until good and frosty, then strain into a chilled cocktail glass.

EL FLORIDITA DAIQUIRI

From the 1934 *Bar La Florida Cocktails* guide.

2 ounces rum
juice of ¹/₂ lime
1 teaspoon bar sugar or sugar syrup
1 teaspoon maraschino liqueur

Shake the ingredients (or blend in blender) with crushed ice and pour into a cocktail glass.

MARY PICKFORD

Popular in Cuba during Prohibition, and better than it sounds.

1¹/₂ ounces white rum
1 ounce pineapple juice
¹/₄ teaspoon grenadine
¹/₄ teaspoon maraschino liqueur

Shake the ingredients vigorously with ice and strain into a cocktail glass.

EL PRESIDENTE

Another Havana drink from the Prohibition, named after Cuban President Mario García Menocal.

> *1¹/₂ ounces white or amber rum*
> *³/₄ ounce orange curaçao*
> *³/₄ ounce dry vermouth*
> *¹/₂ teaspoon grenadine*

Stir the ingredients with ice until chilled; strain into a cocktail glass. (Curaçao may be omitted.)

DARK AND STORMY

The classic Bermuda highball.

> *2 ounces dark rum (Goslings, if available)*
> *ginger beer*
> *lime slice, for garnish*

Mix the ingredients in a tall glass with ice and garnish with a slice of lime.

HURRICANE

This was invented during World War II at Pat O'Brien's in New Orleans and has likely contributed to more foggy memories of the French Quarter than any other drink. Most hurricanes today are made of mixes and artificial ingredients, but this is a fresher variation.

> *2 ounces light rum*
> *2 ounces dark rum*
> *2 ounces passion fruit juice*
> *1 ounce orange juice*
> *¹/₂ ounce fresh lime juice*
> *1 tablespoon sugar or simple syrup*
> *1 tablespoon grenadine*
> *maraschino cherry and orange slice, for garnish*

Shake all the ingredients in a cocktail shaker with ice and strain into a hurricane glass. Garnish with a cherry and an orange slice.

DON THE BEACHCOMBER'S MAI TAI

Either "the original" or "the alternative," depending on your reading of the tiki scriptures.

> *1¹/₂ ounces dark rum (such as Myers's)*
> *1 ounce medium-bodied rum (like Appleton or*
>   *Barbancourt)*
> *³/₄ ounce lime juice*
> *1 ounce grapefruit juice*
> *¹/₄ ounce falernum*
> *¹/₂ ounce triple sec*
> *2 dashes Angostura bitters*
> *1 dash Pernod*
> *mint leaves and pineapple slice, for garnish*

Shake the ingredients in a cocktail shaker with cracked ice and pour without straining into a double old-fashioned glass. Garnish with mint leaves and a pineapple slice.

ZOMBIE

David Embury notes (1948), "Twenty different bars serving this drink will probably put out eighteen to twenty versions of it." He adds, "This is undoubtedly the most overadvertised, overemphasized, overexalted, and foolishly feared drink whose claims to glory ever assaulted the eyes and ears of the gullible American public." Jeff Berry defends the original drink as unfairly excoriated. The original Don the Beachcomber recipe that Berry unearthed is similar to this, although it substitutes passion fruit syrup for the apricot liqueur.

> *1 ounce white rum*
> *2 ounces amber rum*
> *1 ounce dark rum*
> *1 teaspoon simple syrup*
> *³⁄₄ ounce lime juice*
> *³⁄₄ ounce pineapple juice*
> *2 teaspoons apricot liqueur*
> *dash of Pernod*
> *dash of Angostura bitters*
> *fruit, mint leaves, and powdered sugar, for garnish*

Shake the ingredients with crushed ice and serve with ice. Garnish elaborately with fruit, the mint leaves, and a dusting of powdered sugar.

HAI KARATE

A tiki concoction invented by Jeff "Beachbum" Berry.

> *2 ounces amber Virgin Islands rum*
> *1 ounce lime juice*
> *1 ounce pineapple juice (unsweetened)*
> *1 ounce orange juice*
> *1 teaspoon maple syrup (grade A)*
> *1 dash Angostura bitters*
> *lime wedge, orange slice, and a maraschino cherry,*
> *   for garnish*

Shake the ingredients with ice and pour into a tall glass. Garnish with a lime wedge, an orange slice, and a cherry.

PIÑA COLADA

If you must. Like the so-called modern martini, the piña colada is well suited to creative adaptation—Robert Plotkin's *Caribe Rum* lists thirty variations. This is a fairly generic version.

> *1 1/2 ounces light rum (cheap is fine)*
> *1 ounce dark rum*
> *2 ounces Coco López or other coconut cream*
> *   (not coconut milk)*
> *4 ounces pineapple juice*
> *pineapple slice, orange slice, and a maraschino cherry,*
> *   for garnish*

Blend all the ingredients with three-quarters cup of crushed ice in a blender for 10 to 15 seconds. Garnish with the pineapple, the orange, and/or a cherry.

PARISIAN BLONDE

An orange-flavored after-dinner drink.

> *1 ounce rum*
> *1 ounce triple sec*
> *1 ounce cream*
> *drop of vanilla extract (optional)*

Shake and strain. Dale DeGroff suggests garnishing with a drop or two of vanilla extract for added flavor.

MEXICAN BLONDE

The Parisian Blonde meets the White Russian, by Dale "King Cocktail" DeGroff.

> *$1^1/_2$ ounces light rum*
> *$^1/_2$ ounce coffee liqueur*
> *$^1/_2$ ounce curaçao*
> *1 ounce cream*

Shake all the ingredients in a cocktail shaker with ice and strain into a cocktail glass.

CAIPIRINHA

Made with cachaça, a rough-edged Brazilian sugarcane liquor that's inexplicably coming into vogue in the United States.

½ lime, cut into quarters
¾ ounce brown sugar syrup
2 ounces cachaça

Muddle the lime and syrup in an old-fashioned glass, then mix in the cachaça and ice.

GINGER MOJITO

One of my favorite variations of the refreshing Cuban tall drink.

4 to 6 mint leaves
1 teaspoon bar sugar
¾ ounce lime juice
2 ounces white or medium-bodied rum
ginger ale
mint sprig, for garnish

Muddle the first three ingredients in a collins glass. Add ice and the rum, then top off with ginger ale. Garnish with a mint sprig.

THE LYTTON FIZZ

Created for a rum competition in 2005 by bartender and cocktail sleuth John Myers. It's a great mix of classic and modern tastes.

4 fresh mint leaves
3 Thai basil leaves
$1/2$ ounce falernum
$1/4$ ounce lime juice
2 dashes Angostura bitters
$1/2$ ounce dark rum (Cruzan Black Strap recommended)
ginger ale

Muddle the first five ingredients in a collins glass. Add ice and the rum, top off with ginger ale, and stir.

Acknowledgments

THE SEARCH FOR rum's frequent if unheralded appearances through four centuries of North American history often felt like trolling in a very large sea containing very few fish. I'm thankful to those who happened upon information and passed it along to me, including Howard Mansfield, Kate Pocock, Will Foshag, and John Myers. Many took the time to share their love and knowledge of rum history, rum production, and cocktail culture with me, including Michael Delevante, Keith Laurie, Dennis Tosten, Luis and Margaret Ayala, Pat Davidson, Tim Forsythe, Stephen Remsberg, Edward Hamilton, Jeff Berry, Robert Hess, and Ted "Dr. Cocktail" Haigh. All errors, omissions, and misinterpretations of what actually occurred are, naturally, my own.

My thanks to the patient folks at various research institutions and libraries, including but not limited to the Bowdoin College Library, the New York Public Library, the New York Historical Society, the Barbados Museum, and the University of the West Indies. Barbara Cook was a great help at the Johnson and Wales University's Culinary Archives, as were Priscilla Webster and all the others at the Peaks Island branch of the Portland Public Library, which is all-too accommodating in fielding interlibrary loan requests.

Several authors and historians have, unbeknownst to them, served as guideposts directing me down paths I might not otherwise have noticed. I'd like to especially thank David W. Conroy for his work on taverns in the eighteenth century, John J. McCusker for his excruciating research on rum's importance in the American revolution, Sidney Mintz for his pioneering work on the rise of the sugar industry, Andrew Jackson O'Shaughnessy for his explication of the relationship between the mainland colonies and the West Indies before and during the American Revolution, and James Pack for his detailed chronicle of rum in the Royal Navy of England.

Thanks also to Jennifer Gates of Zachary Shuster Harmsworth for finding this idea a home, and to Rachel Klayman at Crown for helping me say what I wanted to say, only better. Finally, thanks to my wife, Louise, for being so indulgent, and for sampling all those cocktails that weren't quite yet ready for public debut.

For reasons too obvious to explain, I may have forgotten to mention others who have aided in this project. I apologize, and I owe you a drink.

Bibliography

ACRELIUS, ISRAEL. *A History of New Sweden; or, The Settlements on the River Delaware.* Translated from Swedish and notes by William M. Reynolds. Philadelphia: Publication Fund of the Historical Society of Pennsylvania, 1874.

ADE, GEORGE. *The Old Time Saloon: The Not Wet–Not Dry Just History.* New York: Ray Long & Richard R. Smith, 1931.

ANDREWS, KENNETH R., ed. *English Privateering Voyages to the West Indies, 1588–1595.* Cambridge, U.K.: published for the Hakluyt Society at the University Press, 1959.

BAKER, CARLOS. *Ernest Hemingway: A Life Story.* New York: Charles Scriber's Sons, 1969.

BAKER, CHARLES. *The Gentleman's Companion, Being an Exotic Drinking Book, or Around the World with Jigger, Beaker, and Flask.* New York: Crown, 1946 (reprint).

BARON, STANLEY. *Brewed in America: A History of Beer and Ale in the United States.* Boston: Little, Brown, 1962.

BARR, ANDREW. *Drink: A Social History of America.* New York: Carrol & Graf, 1999.

BARROW, THOMAS C. *Trade and Empire: The British Customs Service in Colonial America, 1660–1775.* Cambridge, Mass.: Harvard University Press, 1967.

BARTY-KING, HUGH, AND ANTON MASSEL. *Rum: Yesterday and Today.* London: Heinemann, 1983.

BEACHEY, R. W. *The British West Indies Sugar Industry in the Late 19th Century.* Oxford: Basil Blackwell, 1957.

BEEBE, LUCIUS. *The Stork Club Bar Book.* New York: Rinehart, 1946.

BENNETT, J. HARRY, JR. *Bondsmen and Bishops: Slavery and Apprenticeship on the Codrington Plantations of Barbados, 1710–1838.* Berkeley: University of California Press, 1958.

BENSON, ADOLPH, ed. and trans. *Peter Kalm's Travel in North America: The English Version of 1770.* New York: Dover, 1964.

BERGERON, VIC. *Bartender's Guide . . . by Trader Vic.* Garden City, N.Y.: Halcyon House, 1948.

———. *Frankly Speaking: Trader Vic's Own Story.* Garden City, N.Y.: Doubleday, 1973.

———. *Trader Vic's Book of Food and Drink,* Garden City, N.Y.: Doubleday, 1946.

BERRY, JEFF. *Beachbum Berry's Intoxica!* San Jose, Calif.: SLG Publishing, 2002.

BERRY, JEFF, AND ANNENE KAYE. *Beachbum Berry's Grog Log.* San Jose, Calif.: SLG Publishing, 1998.

BITNER, ARNOLD, AND PHOEBE BEACH. *Hawai'i: Tropical Rum Drinks & Cuisine, by Don the Beachcomber.* Honolulu: Mutual Publishing, 2001.

BOGGS, BENJAMIN RANDOLPH, AND MARY EMMA BOGGS. "Old Philadelphia" and "Inns and Taverns of the City." Unpublished clippings, photos, and typescripts at Philadelphia Historical Society, 1917.

BRIDENBAUGH, CARL. *Cities in Revolt: Urban Life in America, 1743–1776,* New York: Alfred A. Knopf, 1955.

BRIDENBAUGH, CARL, ed. *Gentleman's Progress: The Itinerarium of Dr. Alexander Hamilton 1744,* Chapel Hill: University of North Carolina Press for the Institute of Early American History and Culture, 1948.

BROWN, JOHN HULL. *Early American Beverages,* Rutland, Vt.: Charles E. Tuttle, 1966.

BURNS, ERIC. *The Spirits of America: A Social History of Alcohol.* Philadelphia: Temple University Press, 2004.

CARSON, GERALD. *The Social History of Bourbon.* New York: Dodd, Mead, 1963.

CARTER, HENDERSON DELISLE. "A History of the Rum Enterprise in Barbados, 1640–1815." Unpublished master's thesis, University of West Indies, 1992.

CHERRINGTON, ERNEST. *The Evolution of Prohibition in the United States of America.* Westerville, Ohio: American Issue Press, 1920.

CLARK, NORMAN, H. *Deliver Us from Evil: An Interpretation of American Prohibition.* New York: W. W. Norton, 1976.

CLARK, SYDNEY. *All the Best in Cuba.* New York: Dodd, Mead, 1949.

CONROY, DAVID W. *The Public Houses: Drink and Revolution of Authority in Colonial Massachusetts.* Chapel Hill: University of North Carolina Press, 1995.

CORDINGLY, DAVID. *Under the Black Flag: The Romance and Reality of Life Among the Pirates.* New York: Random House, 1995.

CRADDOCK, HARRY. *The Savoy Cocktail Book.* London: Constable and Company, 1930.

CRESSWELL, NICHOLAS. *The Journal of Nicholas Cresswell, 1774–1777.* New York: Dial Press, 1924.

CROWGEY, HENRY G. *Kentucky Bourbon: The Early Years of Whiskeymaking.* Lexington: University Press of Kentucky, 1971.

CULLEN, L. M. *The Brandy Trade under the Ancien Régime.* Cambridge: Cambridge University Press, 1998.

DEERR, NOEL. *The History of Sugar.* London: Chapman and Hall, 1949–1950.

DEVOTO, BERNARD. *The Hour.* Cambridge, Mass.: Riverside Press, 1948.

DOW, GEORGE FRANCIS, AND JOHN HENRY EDMONDS. *The Pirates of the New England Coast, 1630–1730.* Salem, Mass.: Marine Research Society, 1923.

DUNN, RICHARD S. *Sugar and Slaves: The Rise of the Planter Class in the English West Indies, 1624–1713.* Chapel Hill: University of North Carolina Press, 1972.

EARLE, ALICE MORSE. *Stage-Coach and Tavern Days.* New York: Macmillan, 1901.

EDWARDS, GRIFFITH. *Alcohol: The World's Favorite Drug.* New York: St. Martin's Press, 2002.

ELLMS, CHARLES. *A Pirate's Own Book; or, Authentic Narratives of the Lives, Exploits, and Executions of the Most Celebrated Sea Robbers.* Salem, Mass.: Marine Research Society, 1924.

EMBURY, DAVID A. *The Fine Art of Mixing Drinks.* Garden City, N.Y.: Doubleday, 1948.

EXQUEMELIN, ALEXANDER OLIVIER. *The Buccaneers of America.* London: George Routledge, 1924.

FIELD, EDWARD. *The Colonial Tavern: A Glimpse of New England Town Life in the Seventeenth and Eighteenth Centuries.* Providence, R.I.: Preston & Rounds, 1897.

FISCHER, DAVID HACKETT. *Paul Revere's Ride.* New York: Oxford University Press, 1994.

FORBES, R. J. *Short History of the Art of Distillation, from the Beginnings up to the Death of Cellier Blumenthal.* Leiden: E. J. Brill, 1948.

FOSTER, PETER. *Family Spirits: The Bacardi Saga.* Toronto: Macfarlane Walter & Ross, 1990.

FURNAS, J. C. *The Life and Times of the Late Deman Rum.* New York: Capricorn Books, 1973.

GALENSON, DAVID. *Traders, Planters, and Slaves.* Cambridge, U.K.: Cambridge University Press, 1986.

GAMES, ALISON. *Migration and the Origins of the English Atlantic World.* Cambridge, Mass.: Harvard University Press, 1999.

GRIMES, WILLIAM. *Straight Up or on the Rocks: The Story of the American Cocktail.* New York: North Point Press, 2001.

GUSTAFSON, AXEL. *The Foundation of Death: A Study of the Drink-Question.* Boston, New York, and Chicago: Ginn, Heath, 1884.

HANDLER, JEROME S. *A Guide to Source Materials for the Study of Barbados History, 1627–1834.* Carbondale: Southern Illinois University Press, 1971.

HANDLER, JEROME S., AND FREDERICK W. LANGE. *Plantation Slavery in Barbados: An Archeological and Historical Investigation.* Cambridge, Mass.: Harvard University Press, 1978.

HEDGES, JAMES B. *The Browns of Providence Plantations: The Colonial Years,* Cambridge, Mass.: Harvard University Press, 1952.

———. *The Browns of Providence Plantations: The Nineteenth Century.* Providence, R.I.: Brown University Press, 1968.

HEWETT, EDWARD, AND W. F. AXTON. *Convivial Dickens: The Drinks of Dickens and His Times.* Athens: Ohio University Press, 1983.

HIGGINS, BRYAN. *Observations and Advices for the Improvement of the Manufacture of Muscovado Sugar and Rum.* St. Jago de la Vega, Cuba: A. Aiken, 1797 and 1800.

HOOKER, RICHARD J. *Food and Drink in America: A History.* Indianapolis: Bobbs-Merrill, 1981.

HOYOS, F. A. *Barbados: A History from the Amerindians to Independence.* London: Macmillan Caribbean, 1978.

HUGHES, GRIFFITH. *A Natural History of Barbados,* London: n.p., 1750.

KIRSTEN, SVEN A. *The Book of Tiki.* Köln: Taschen, 2003.

LAW, ROBIN. *The Slave Coast of West Africa, 1550–1750: The Impact of the Atlantic Slave Trade on an African Society.* Oxford, U.K.: Clarendon Press, 1991.

LEE, ROBERT E. *Blackbeard the Pirate: A Reappraisal of His Life and Times.* Winston-Salem, N.C.: John F. Blair, 1974.

LENDER, MARK EDWARD, AND JAMES KIRBY MARTIN. *Drinking in America: A History.* New York: Free Press, 1982.

LIGON, RICHARD. *A True and Exact History of the Island of Barbadoes.* London: Frank Cass, 1970.

LINDSAY, PHILIP. *The Great Buccaneer.* New York: Wilfred Funk, 1951.

LUCIA, SALVATORE P., ed. *Alcohol and Civilization.* New York: McGraw-Hill, 1963.

MANCALL, PETER C. *Deadly Medicine: Indians and Alcohol in Early America.* Ithaca, N.Y.: Cornell University Press, 1995.

MARRISON, L. W. *Wines and Spirits.* London: Penguin, 1957.

MARTIN, SAMUEL. *An Essay Upon Plantership.* 4th ed. Antigua: Samuel Clapham, 1765.

MARX, JENIFER. *Pirates and Privateers of the Caribbean.* Malabar, Fla.: Krieger, 1992.

MARX, ROBERT F. *Port Royal Rediscovered.* New York: Doubleday, 1973.

McCUSKER, JOHN J. *Rum and the American Revolution: The Rum Trade and the Balance of Payments of the Thirteen Continental Colonies.* New York: Garland, 1989.

McCUSKER, JOHN J., AND RUSSELL R. MENARD. *The Economy of British America, 1607–1789.* Chapel Hill: University of North Carolina Press for the Institute of Early American History and Culture, 1985.

MINTZ, SIDNEY W. *Sweetness and Power: The Place of Sugar in Modern History.* New York: Viking Penguin, 1985.

———. *Tasting Food, Tasting Freedom: Excursions in Eating, Culture, and the Past.* Boston: Beacon Press, 1996.

MOREWOOD, SAMUEL. *An Essay on . . . Inebriating Liquors, with an Historical View of the Extent and Practice of Distillation, Both as it Relates to Commerce and as a Source of National Income: Comprising Much Curious Information Respecting the Application and Properties of Several Parts of the Vegetable Kingdom.* London: Longman, Hurst, Rees, Orme, Brown, and Green, 1824.

NASH, GARY B. *Red, White and Black: The Peoples of Early North America.* Upper Saddle River, N.J.: Prentice Hall, 2000.

NEWMAN, SIMON. *Parades and the Politics of the Street: Festive Culture in the Early American Republic.* Philadelphia: University of Pennsylvania Press, 1997.

NORTHRUP, DAVID, ed. *The Atlantic Slave Trade,* Lexington, Mas & Toronto: D. C. Heath, 1994.

O'SHAUGHNESSY, ANDREW JACKSON. *An Empire Divided: The American Revolution and the British Caribbean.* Philadelphia: University of Pennsylvania Press, 2000.

PACK, JAMES. *Nelson's Blood: The Story of Naval Rum.* Gloucestershire, U.K.: Sutton Publishing/Royal Naval Museum, 1995.

PAQUETTE, ROBERT L., AND STANLEY L. ENGERMAN, eds. *The Lesser Antilles in the Age of European Expansion.* Gainesville: University Press of Florida, 1996.

PARES, RICHARD. *Merchants and Planters,* Cambridge, U.K.: Published for the Economic History Review at the University Press, 1960.

———. *A West India Fortune.* Hamden, Conn.: Archon Books, 1968.

———. *Yankees and Creoles: The Trade between North America and the West Indies Before the American Revolution.* Hamden, Conn.: Archon Books, 1968.

PARRY, J. H. AND P. M. SHERLOCK. *A Short History of the West Indies.* New York: St. Martin's Press, 1968.

PEEKE, HEWSON, L. *Americana Ebrietatis; The Favorite Tipple of Our*

Forefathers and the Laws and Customs Relating Thereto. New York: privately printed, 1917.

PEGRAM, THOMAS R. *Battling Demon Rum: The Struggle for a Dry America, 1800–1933.* Chicago: Ivan R. Dee, 1998.

PERKINS, EDWIN J. *The Economy of Colonial America.* New York: Columbia University Press, 1980.

PITMAN, FRANK WESLEY. *The Development of the British West Indies, 1700–1763.* New Haven, Conn.: Yale University Press, 1907.

POWERS, MADELON. *Faces Along the Bar: Lore and Order in the Workingman's Saloon, 1870–1920.* Chicago: University of Chicago Press, 1998.

The Prohibitionists' Textbook. New York: National Temperance Society and Publication House, 1877.

PULEO, STEPHEN. *Dark Tide: The Great Boston Molassses Flood of 1919.* Boston: Beacon Press, 2003.

RAGATZ, LOWELL J. *Fall of the Planter Class in the British Caribbean 1763–1833.* New York: Octagon Books, 1963.

RAWLEY, JAMES A. *The Transatlantic Slave Trade: A History.* New York & London: W. W. Norton, 1981.

REDIKER, MARCUS. *Between the Devil and the Deep Blue Sea: Merchant Seamen, Pirates, and the Anglo-American Maritime World, 1700–1750.* Cambridge, U.K.: Cambridge University Press, 1987.

RICHARDSON, TIM. *Sweets: A History of Candy.* New York: Bloomsbury, 2002.

ROBERTS, W. ADOLPHE. *The French in the West Indies.* Indianapolis: Bobbs-Merrill., 1942.

RORABAUGH, W. J. *The Alcoholic Republic: An American Tradition.* Oxford, U.K.: Oxford University Press, 1979.

SALINGER, SHARON V. *Taverns and Drinking in Early America.* Baltimore: Johns Hopkins University Press, 2002.

SCHLESINGER, ARTHUR M. *The Colonial Merchants and the American Revolution, 1763–1776.* New York: Frederick Ungar, 1957.

SCHWARTZ, ROSALIE. *Pleasure Island: Tourism and Temptation in Cuba.* Lincoln: University of Nebraska Press, 1997.

SFORZA, JOHN. *Swing It!: The Andrews Sisters Story.* Lexington: University Press of Kentucky, 1999.

SHERIDAN, RICHARD B. *Sugar and Slavery: An Economic History of the British West Indies 1623–1775.* Baltimore: Johns Hopkins University Press, 1974.

SMITH, GEORGE. *The Nature of Fermentation Explained . . . Exemplified by the Process of Preparing Rum, as 'tis Managed in the West Indies.* London: n.p., 1729.

STEVENSON, ROBERT LOUIS. *Treasure Island,* New York: Pocket Books, 1939.

TAUSSIG, CHARLES WILLIAM. *Rum, Romance & Rebellion,* London: Jarrolds Publishers, 1928.

TERRINGTON, WILLIAM. *Cooling Cups and Dainty Drinks,* London: George Routledge, 1869.

THOME, JAS. A., AND J. HORACE KIMBALL. *Emancipation in the West Indies; A Six Month's Tour in Antigua, Barbados, and Jamaica in the Year 1837.* New York: American Anti-Slavery Society, 1838.

THOMPSON, PETER. *Rum Punch and Revolution: Taverngoing and Public Life in Eighteenth-Century Philadelphia.* Philadelphia: University of Pennsylvania Press, 1999.

TURLEY, HANS. *Rum, Sodomy, and the Lash: Piracy, Sexuality, and Masculine Identity.* New York: New York University Press, 1999.

WARD, EDWARD. *Five Travel Scripts, Commonly Attributed to Edward Ward.* New York: Facsimile Text Society by Columbia University Press, 1933.

——. *The Wooden World Dissected in the Character of a Ship of War.* London: printed for M. Cooper at the Globe, 1744.

WARNER, JESSICA. *Craze: Gin and Debauchery in an Age of Reason.* New York: Four Walls Eight Windows, 2002.

WATERS, HAROLD, AND AUBREY WISBERG. *Patrol Boat 999.* New York: Chilton, 1959.

WAUGH, ALEC. *A Family of Islands: A History of the West Indies from 1492 to 1898.* Garden City, N.Y.: Doubleday, 1964.

WILLKIE, H. F. *Beverage Spirts in America: A Brief History.* New York: Newcomen Society of New England, American Branch, 1947.

WOON, BASIL. *When It's Cocktail Time in Cuba.* New York: Horace Liveright, 1928.

ZACKS, RICHARD. *The Pirate Hunter: The True Story of Captain Kidd.* New York: Theia, 2002.

Index

About the Author

Wayne Curtis is a contributing editor to *Preservation* magazine, and his stories on travel, architecture, and history have appeared in the *New York Times*, *The Atlantic Monthly*, *The American Scholar*, and *American Heritage*. In 2002 Curtis was named Lowell Thomas Travel Journalist of the Year by the Society of American Travel Writers. He lives in Maine.